PATTERNS OF COMMUNITY STRUCTURE IN COLOMBO, SRI LANKA

An Investigation of Contemporary Urban Life in South Asia

Neville S. Arachchige-Don
International Research Foundation for Development
Cambridge Community College Campus of Anoka-Ramsey

UNIVERSITY PRESS OF AMERICA

Lanham • New York • London

University Press of America,® Inc.
4720 Boston Way
Lanham, Maryland 20706

3 Henrietta Street
London WC2E 8LU England

Printed in the United States of America
British Cataloging in Publication Information Available

Library of Congress Cataloging-in-Publication Data

Arachchige-Don, Neville S.
Patterns of community structure in Colombo, Sri Lanka : an investigation of contemporary urban life in South Asia / Neville S. Arachchige-Don.
p. cm.
Includes bibliographical references and index.
1. City and town—Sri Lanka—Colombo. 2. Colombo (Sri Lanka)—Social conditions. I. Title.
HN670.8.C6N48 1994
307.76'095493—dc20 94–19875 CIP

ISBN 0–8191–9606–1 (cloth : alk. paper)

∞™ The paper used in this publication meets the minimum requirements of American National Standard for Information Sciences—Permanence of Paper for Printed Library Materials, ANSI Z39.48–1984.

This book is dedicated to
my mother,
Seneviratne Mudiyanselage Louise Dassanayaka,

and to

my brothers and sisters,
Gunaseeli, Pathmasiri, Vineetha,
Amarasena, and Piyathilaka.

CONTENTS

Chapter 3 Resource Structure of the Community

Chapter 4 Migration and Kinship

Chapter 5 The Neighborhood Relationship

Chapter 6 Political Behavior

Chapter 7 Community Conflicts and Politics

Chapter 8 Religion and Politics: Behavioral Manifestations

Chapter 9 Patterns of Mobility and Community Integration

Chapter 10 Conclusion

Appendixes

FIGURES

TABLES

ABBREVIATIONS

CGR	Ceylon Government Railway
CMC	Colombo Municipal Council
CP	Communist Party
CTB	Ceylon Transport Board
ESCAP	Economic and Social Commission for Asia and the Pacific
GCE	General Certificate of Education
GCSU	General Clerical Socialist Union
ILO	International Labor Organization
IRC	Island Reconvicted Criminals
LSSP	Lanka Sama Samaja Party (Lanka Equal Society Party)
MP	Member of Parliament
PRO	Public Relations Officer
Rs.	Rupees
SLFP	Sri Lanka Freedom Party
SSC	Senior School Certificate
TULF	Tamil United Liberated Federation
UDA	Urban Development Authority
UNCRD	United Nations Center for Regional Development
UNDP	United Nations Development Program
UNP	United National Party
YMBA	Young Men's Buddhist Association

FOREWORD

As Neville S. Arachchige Don tells us, his research had its origins in his puzzlement over the wide gap that exists between social science knowledge of and public policy towards urban communities in South Asia. While doing research work in urban communities in Colombo in the early 1970s, Sri Lanka, he quickly realized that the problem was more than simple difficulty of translating Western social science into successful administrative policies. Indeed, he came to feel that the models suggested by Western social science theory were insufficient for the purposes of analyzing and understanding the situation he was meeting on the job. So, Neville has directed his efforts to producing a fresh approach to our knowledge of urban social structures in South Asia.

The result is a highly unusual book derived from fieldwork that preceded his formal doctoral studies in the Urban Studies Program at the University of Wisconsin-Milwaukee. Through his graduate studies in urban sociology, as well as his experience studying and implementing social policies in Sri Lankan urban communities, Neville has come to see South Asian urban social communities as networks bound together through five disparate dimensions: politics, kinship, ethnicity and religion, neighborhood involvement, and mobility. Individuals and households within urban neighborhoods vary in several, if not all, of these five dimensions or, as Neville refers to the, "arenas." The activity within each dimension can take quite a variety of forms ranging from reciprocity to political factionalism and produce four distinct types of outcomes: strategic integration, polarization, fragmentation or individualization.

Moving far away from simplistic, binary modes of social analysis that contrast modern with traditional or Western with Third World societies, Neville asks us to see the complexities of urban life in Colombo, and by extension in other parts of South Asia, as taking place within distinct communities. These communities might best be classified as "neighborhoods" having boundaries—sometimes administrative, sometimes obviously territorial, but usually containing mixtures of ethnic and religious groups, a considerable range of social classes, and significant variance in the inhabitants' experience with urban life. He believes that his five "arenas" of activity are the significant elements for the functioning of urban communities and pays less attention to class and gender or to forms of activity such as work, exchange, entertainment, and leisure.

Neville's fieldwork comes from a community within Dematagoda, an eastern ward of Colombo. The neighborhood he studied is tellingly referred to by its inhabitants as "*Appe Gama*" (our village), and Neville carefully describes the patterns of life within this urban village of some 4,500 inhabitants. Again and again, his account reminds us not to leap to conclusions based on one dimension—say, ethnicity or religion—when the nature of that dimension is affected by patterns of migration, Sri Lankan politics or something as mundane as neighborhood involvement.

Neville ends his study with careful statements concerning his four patterns of community structure. These move from a type of integration and proceed onward on a scale of declining social cohesion to polarized communities, fragmented structures and individualized communities. He suggests the strengths and weaknesses of each of the forms, but I see his own preferences on the more integrated side of the scale, although he realizes that whatever pattern exists there are some undesirable outcomes. It is this willingness to see weaknesses and drawbacks in all possible patterns of community organization that marks Neville's judgement about the future of urban life in Sri Lanka as one of balanced hopefulness rather than either an impossible utopian vision of harmonious and prosperous urban life or a bleak portrait of great teeming cities torn apart by the violent and negative tendencies that can arise from each and every pattern of community organization.

Yet, as always with good social science work, the insights from this investigation—after all a study of only a small piece of the larger mosaic of urban life in Colombo—cannot produce answers to the complex problems facing urban communities in Sri Lanka. Yet Neville's carefully drawn study may help bring the understanding that always must proceed solutions to the social problems we face.

David D. Buck
Professor of History, University of Wisconsin-Milwaukee and
Editor, *The Journal of Asian Studies*

PREFACE

After receiving my baccalaureate degree, I chose to work at the urban studies division of the Marga Institute, Sri Lanka Center for Development Studies. Several research projects of the institute focused on urban behavior in different social contexts: organization, the informal sector economy, and the urban community. One of the intriguing questions revealed in all of these studies was "Why do people not behave the way they are expected?" It has been noted that urbanites' behavior exhibited many ramifications for urban policy making in South Asia. The visible chaotic portrait of urban society was well documented without giving a comprehensive explanation. The limited studies with conventional theoretical impositions convinced us (at least some of us) of the necessity of breaking new ground for urban studies in South Asia. Dr. S.P.F. Senaratna, then the director of urban studies, a leading social anthropologist, set the ground for this new journey under the umbrella of a project named Urban–Rural Relations and Development Planning in Asia sponsored by the United Nations Center for Regional Development. Despite this effort, we could not achieve our goal due to a variety of bureaucratic reasons. Nevertheless, the brief study that I undertook in Dematagoda, on the eastern border of Colombo City, and in Kakirawa, a regional town of the North Central Province, some eighteen years ago, inspired me and haunted my mind.

Three years after the completion of the UNCRD project, Arthur T. Row, a UNDP chief advisor to the Urban Development Authority in Sri Lanka, commissioned me to develop the social development component of the slum and shanty improvement program. To this effect I evaluated three urban community projects sponsored by the U.S. Save the Children Federation and the Norwegian Redd Barna. This piece of comparative research aroused my intellectual curiosity to unravel the dynamics of urban behavior. Some years later, the framework for my doctoral dissertation provided me the opportunity to reembark on this journey. This book is a modest outcome of my incomplete and inspirational journey.

The conceptual models presented in this study have their roots in all of my empirical research both in urban and rural settings. These studies together form embryos of comparative structures of communities. These embryos gradually grew into more crystallized and solid forms in the womb of my doctoral dissertation. A more refined version of conceptual models is presented in this book.

The present study examines the anatomy of an urban community of the city of Colombo, Sri Lanka, within which people adopt their behavior in five arenas of activity: politics, kinship, ethnicity and religion, neighborhood involvement, and mobility. These provide the keys for understanding urban life in South Asia. The network implications of this behavioral adaptation provide a sense of community integration. More specifically, this network reveals itself in terms of reciprocity, mutual solidarity, patronage politics, conflicts and political factionalism, and the permanent or transitory character of an individual or group residence.

Four types of urban community structures appear to emerge from this study: (1) strategic integration, (2) polarization, (3) fragmentation, and (4) individualization. Each community system reveals different mechanics at the conceptual level. The interplay between resource complexity, distribution of power, the network of relationships, and the system of ideology has different forms of operational systems in different types of communities. Thus, each community structure has its own vibrant flow. Hence, the social change is not necessarily progressive and evolutionary, but rather circular in its direction. Moreover, integration, polarization, fragmentation, and individualization are not diametrically opposed systems. These community structures have multilectical dramatization. Therefore, it is of vital importance to estimate the strengths and weaknesses, as they relate to demand and decisional patterns, in order to formulate policy options for these communities. Community structures have to be understood in the context of micro–macro reciprocity and tension arising out of a dynamic interaction of different groups in an urban context.

ACKNOWLEDGMENTS

This book is the product of my empirical work in Colombo, and it would not have been possible without the cooperation of the people of Dematagoda who facilitated the completion of my field work. Words alone cannot express my appreciation for information and hospitality. I am indebted to my brother, S.A.D. Amerasena, and a family friend, V. Upasena, for their active roles in fieldwork under my supervision. Also, I am grateful to several of my undergraduate students at Sri Jaywardenepura University of Sri Lanka for helping me in administering a survey questionnaire.

I am greatly indebted to my mentor, Dr. S.P.F. Senaratne not only for breaking new ground in social research in Sri Lanka, but also for immeasurable intellectual inspiration and numerous secondary levels of support extended to me throughout my professional life. I also thank my dissertation committee members Professors Ronald Edari, Scott Greer, Ann Lenerson Greer, Joan Moore, David Buck, and James Smith at the University of Wisconsin-Milwaukee. Their advice and guidance was indispensable for the completion of this task.

I owe special thanks to Professor David D. Buck, Department of History, University of Wisconsin-Milwaukee and the current editor of the *Journal of Asian Studies*, for his valuable comments and suggestions and for encouraging me to publish this book and writing the forward.

My deep sense of gratitude goes to Mary Ann David, faculty secretary at Cambridge Community College, not only for her meticulous and painstaking effort in typesetting but also her dedication, deep concern, valuable technical comments, and her pleasant and friendly attitude during this modest academic enterprise.

Mark Widdel, business instructor at Cambridge Community College, provided the necessary computer graphics assistance. I appreciate his valuable time and expertise.

Use of the Cambridge Community College facilities and computer equipment for the typesetting preparation has been invaluable.

I want to give a special thanks to Paul Reasner, Philosophy Professor at Bethel College, for his helpful editing. He not only corrected errors of syntax but also helped me to remove some obscurities from the text.

I extend my sincere thanks to my wife, Soma Ruberu and two children Aruni Piumika and Nishantha Nuwan who helped me in a multitude of ways to bring this work to completion. In addition to their emotional support, my daughter helped particularly in the preparation of formats, basic survey data, calculations, and initial drawings of diagrams.

This book is a modified form of my dissertation. During the final stage of revision my son Nishantha put in long hours with me helping in numerous ways. His computer skills, specifically formatting the tables and graphics, and his dedication, and stamina were invaluable for the completion of this book. Above all, his companionship during the process of revision was an integral memory of this academic endeavor.

I would like to thank JAI Press Inc. for granting me permission to reproduce a revised version of the article, "Religion and Politics: Behavioral Adaptations in an Urban Community of Sri Lanka," from *Research in the Social Scientific Study of Religion*.

Chapter 1

Introduction

Since independence, cities in most of the Asian countries have grown tremendously as a result of both a general population increase and a heavy migration from rural to urban areas. According to UN studies, Asian cities have doubled in size during the last 20 years; this growth is expected to continue unabated beyond the year 2000 (McNamara 1985, 9). However, the pattern of this population concentration is heterogeneous in terms of origin, economic livelihood, ethnicity, social power and aspirations of urban inhabitants. This diversity has brought complex dimensions to the social, political and cultural fabric of the urban landscape of South Asian cities.

Urban population growth causes a variety of socio-economic problems. High density and deteriorating urban services are common sights in most Asian cities. Massive migration from rural areas without a commensurate expansion of employment opportunities transfers rural poverty to urban areas. These urban characteristics provide a ground for social interaction for urban inhabitants. The behavioral choices that stem from this interaction and their implications are the major concerns of policy making.

Urban issues, today, in South Asian countries are addressed by various plans and projects. There are overall master plans as well as specific programs and projects for slum and shanty improvement, road construction, traffic rearrangement, construction of market complexes, community development and so on.

Experts from western countries are also to be found in these cities, advising on the above programs. Moreover, Asian countries are not terribly deficient in trained urban managers and researchers. However, effective policies are yet to be found. Today, the urban crisis in Asian cities is the gap between the existing level and the desired level of results from these extensive development efforts.

Overwhelming evidence has proved that urban development programs face many obstructions and difficulties. Many studies express the view that the *urbanites* (involved either as actors or as beneficiaries) do not act in the manner expected of them. For example, those who are elected or appointed to community welfare organizations sometimes exhibit attitudes which are detrimental to their successful operation. Moreover, it is noted that "urban planning is frequently obstructed by powerful landowners; there is rampant corruption in relation to urban land questions and urban planning" (Evers 1975, 118).

Urban institutions often do not function with the effectiveness that is expected. For example, institutions which are responsible for housing do not operate in an efficient manner. Hence, landlords fail to meet the maintenance requirements for rented houses while many tenants fail to pay the rent regularly. Individuals build shelters which violate the zoning regulations and housing standards. "Administrative reforms are carried out but bureaucratic inertia and corruption continue to increase" (Qadeer 1983, 4). These are some of the behavioral problems common to those who seek change oriented development in these Asian societies. These issues continually pose dilemmas to policy makers and the main actors contributing to the development process (Gunatilleke and Tiruchelvam 1983).

Individuals at various levels not only lack the dedication to "civic consciousness" which is expected of them but may also openly violate the rules which govern their work. The violation of rules and lack of civic consciousness constitute a "state of chaos" from the viewpoint of observers.

> There is order and regularity; an order that may exact heavy social costs, yet order it is. The paradox of invisible order and visible chaos has not been acknowledged in the literature on Third World urbanism.... The first task for a researcher of a Third World city is to uncover the indigenous order and to outline its evolving form. Only by knowing the structure of a local social order can one begin to predict and direct the change. (Qadeer 1983, 5)

In order to grasp the "structure of a local social order," the pattern of behavior must be discovered. It is, therefore, important to understand urban community structure in terms of behavior so as to unravel the policy implications for these Asian countries.

URBAN BEHAVIOR AND THE STATUS OF SOCIAL SCIENCE KNOWLEDGE

RESEARCH–POLICY GAP

Existing social science knowledge is inadequate to uncover the structure of a local social order and the patterns of behavior. It is apparent that there is a gap between research and policy in social sciences in Asia. Despite the fact that the social sciences are increasingly gaining ground in Asia, many policies are devised without reference to research (Ratnam 1980). This is largely due to reservations by policy makers as to the utility of the social sciences in Asia. Specifically, (1) social scientists' explanations, predictions, and prescriptions on various policy issues have not been sufficiently adapted to the socio-economic and political context in Asia; (2) social science, by way of compartmentalization and sophistication of methods, usually focuses on parts rather than on the total process (Sharan 1986); (3) the discipline of economics dominates in policy making in Asia; (4) social anthropological studies are done in an isolated fashion, not in relationship to policy making; (5) contemporary rural–urban studies within the discipline of sociology have tended to descend into arid quantification with limited theoretical and fundamental usefulness in comprehending social forces, so their "explanations" have reference to symptoms and not to basic conditions (Neville 1982); and (6) linkage between macro and micro phenomena at the explanatory level is absent (UN 1981).

An effort has been made in Asian countries to overcome these limitations by an interdisciplinary approach at the policy making level. However, this effort still lacks theoretical integrity and therefore has had little impact on policy making. In Asia, the problem of making the social sciences respond more positively to the needs of society has been aggravated by the contextual inappropriateness of such a large proportion of current social science knowledge and information.

> Not only is the bulk of social science literature Western in origin and content but even when the subject matter has been Asian, the perceptions, theories, and methodologies underlying the analysis have been heavily influenced by the intellectual traditions of the West and, in many ways, were responsible for nurturing what has come to be recognized as contemporary social science. (Ratnam 1980, 1)

Although sociologists have shown increasing awareness of the need to develop an indigenous tradition of theory and methodology, they have not yet developed any alternative models. The uncritical replication of the empirical methodology of the Western writers is apparent in these countries. In the case of Pakistan, authors did not go beyond a re-exposition of certain propositions derived from the structural–functional and symbolic interaction theories well established in the European and North American tradition. Furthermore, it has been identified that the heavy emphasis on statistical survey methodology has distracted attention from the need to develop a more relevant conceptual foundation (Hassan 1971, 132-141).

Western models for the collection and analysis of data might have applicability beyond the Western world; but thoughtless application of Western models provides the most effective way whereby a barrier separates the researcher from his data (Gutkind 1974, 44). Both inapplicability and thoughtless application of Western models suggest the necessity of indigenous theory to understand the Southeast Asian cities (O'Connor 1983).

Three criticisms, along the same lines, have been put forward by indigenous scholars from developing countries. They are: (1) Western concepts, models and paradigms not only grossly distort realities but also impose a developmental framework in which everything Western is by definition "modern," "developed," "secular/rational," and therefore, presumptively superior; (2) the concepts and paradigms imported are inherently value laden and ideologically biased toward conservatism; and (3) Western theories, concepts and paradigms are inherently and demonstrably culture-bound and Western countries' claims about the universality of Western social science are chimerical, if not arrogant (Stifel, Davidson, and Colman 1982: x).

The gap between research and policy in the social sciences in South Asia is even more apparent in urban studies. Of the South Asian countries, India has conducted the most research in urban studies. Such research in Pakistan, Nepal, Bangladesh and Sri Lanka is at an extremely rudimentary level. The dynamic structural process in these countries remains untouched.

MACRO THEORIES: ECOLOGY AND POLITICAL ECONOMY

Most theorists have dealt with the question of urban change only at a macro level. Replicating the Western model was one of such explanatory devices in which Third World cities are seen as instruments of growth and centers of modernization. The inappropriateness of this model has been recognized on several grounds (Frank 1967; McGee 1971). Most important, social change in terms of the "urban way of life" is not occurring in a manner similar to the West (McGee 1967, 98).

Ecological theorists view urban behavior within the neo-classical economic models. The assumption is that the behavior is governed by the market forces, and the market process is the outcome of a series of uncoordinated individual decisions. This model fails to include the factors that are specific to Asian society.

A group of theorists have applied modified versions of ecological theory to the analysis of Asian cities (Gist 1974; Prakasa 1983; Mukerjee 1940). They have come up with various modifications of ecology in terms of Asian historical, social, economic and political contexts. By recognizing the basic differences between Asian cities and Western cities, this group of theorists have accepted the universal position of ecological theory. Based on empirical evidence from Bangalore, Gist argues that despite many differences between Asian cities and cities in the United States, ecological segregation in one form or another appears to be almost universal, but the particular form is highly variable. Changes in segregative patterns are affected by broad ideological, political, economic and technological changes (Gist 1968, 177-178).

According to the findings of this group, the "polynuclear principle" is somewhat appropriate for Asian cities (Gist 1968, 149-150; Thomlinson 1969, 170). Other than economic factors, this group emphasizes cultural values, sentimental associations and symbolism as important determinants of community spatial structure (Mukehrjee in Thomlinson 1969, 170). However, this group fails to analyze the dynamic interaction of social, economic, and political factors at the micro level and does not address the changing behavioral patterns in community context.

The dependency model, derived from a neo-Marxist radical perspective, advocates a political economic approach to cities in South Asia. But this model fails to address internal micro dynamics of urban centers. Dependency theory focuses on the dialectic relationship between capitalism and underdevelopment. In this framework, cities are seen as parasitic and exploitative of the hinterland, and the view of social structure is centered on the international economy. As a result, the dependency model fails to take account of autonomous internal forces and their potential role in the processes of social change (Alejandro Portes in Abu-Lughod 1977, 124-125).

The radical perspective assumes that specific urban behavior and social problems represent the inevitable consequences of the structure of capitalist institutions. In spite of its strong emphasis on the structure of the society, this approach reduces the analysis to abstract economic class categories. The absence of a comprehensive methodological device originating from its conceptual framework and its conceptual penetration into the reality inhibit the understanding of complexities in the social process. The class conflict analysis ignores the dynamic character of the distribution of power at the micro level. In other words, the radical approach deals largely with the class foundation of power rather than the operation of power. In this analysis, the operational aspect is confined only to a few institutions that are associated with the class foundation. Also, the continuous flux of power distribution of different operational groups (those groups may not necessarily be synonymous with ethnicity, income, religion, education, and "class," but may be coincidentally formed) are not considered in the radical analysis. In a given set of circumstances, why some categories of people enjoy more power than others is not approached in a comprehensive manner. The radical approach deals only with the structural influence on individuals through a few selected institutions, and they ignore the impact of individual variations on the structure.

DUALISTIC PERSPECTIVE AND URBAN COMMUNITY

Both at the behavioral and conceptual levels, urban change is often seen as social differentiation within a dualistic perspective. The rationalization of this perspective is always associated with Western urbanization, the growth of a market economy and the "modern man." This doctrine theoretically originated from grand theories of social science in which social change is seen as "great transformations" from one stage to another.

Emile Durkheim's "mechanical solidarity" and "organic solidarity," Ferdinand Tonnies' "community" and "society," and Robert Redfield's "folk–urban continuum" are perhaps the best examples of the classic theories. The contemporary distinction between "tradition" and "modernity" is the counterpart theme of this classical thought. However, the envisaged direction of change which is embedded in this analysis of Asian social change is Westernization (Qadeer 1974; Moore 1963; Eisenstadt 1964).

Theories of social differentiation are grounded on the dominant perspective of evolution. This perspective is based on several assumptions: (1) a wide assortment of bipolar theories which compress the many former evolutionary stages into ideal–typical extremes, (2) the notion of "social differentiation" as a continuous and largely irreversible process, and (3) "evolutionary universals" (Abu-Lughod 1977, 113).

These assumptions have very little empirical validity, particularly in the Asian context. It is invalid to assume that the urban life is necessarily unilinear and the bipolar categories are by no means mutually exclusive. The degree of combination may vary in time and space depending on the changing nature of underlying societal mechanisms.

The concept of urban dualism, which refers to the "coexistence of two parallel economies, modes of production, and even cultures in a society" (Brookfield 1975, 34) developed by Boeke, poses a serious methodological problem in that it focuses on the end-point manifestation rather than the process of urban economy. This failure also reflects its origin in the grand classical theories of Western sociology.

This dualistic view of urban economy in the Third World has been postulated as firm sector vs. bazaar sector (Geertz 1963) and formal vs. informal (ILO 1972). These two sectors are characterized by a vast array of bipolar characteristics of social and economic organizations. Some of the assumptions of this perspective are: (1) the myth of homogeneity and independence, (2) the parochial view of the informal sector perceived only as an urban phenomenon, (3) the formal–informal dichotomy implying a pessimistic approach (subordination view), (4) the "target group" view which assumes that this sector can be improved through elimination of negative governmental attitudes, and (5) the assumption that the informal sector and the poor are synonymous.

These assumptions are invalid due to inaccurate conceptualizations of the urban economy as it focuses on end-point manifestations. Those who believe in this dualistic perspective are already faced with the problem of definition: formal and informal economy (Qadeer 1983, 20). The end-point manifestation of economic activities in Third World countries is not dual but is stratified and subjected to continuous changes according to the internal and external economic, social, and political structural changes of a given country. Under these structural conditions, the end-point manifestations of economic activities are composed of a set of flexible strategies of entrepreneurs to exploit market opportunities (Marga Institute 1978, 40-48).

Most of the informal sector studies have not adequately explored the processes by which economic activities operate in Third World cities. One serious deficiency is in the understanding of community structures in which economic activities operate. The geographical distribution of these economic activities gives some insights into the widely differentiated clientele which come from different strata of urban society. Goods and services are provided for the community in a variety of ways: exclusively by one strata of the distribution end, by a few stratas, or by all the units of the distribution end. Therefore, in order to understand the activities of the urban economy it is necessary to shift the focus from end-points to processes (Senaratne 1975). In such an exercise, it is necessary to demonstrate the relationships that are generated through the exploitation of available opportunities and how these relations form the basis of groups which have not merely economic but also social, cultural, and political characteristics. In short, economic activities in Asian cities should be understood in their total context, since they are closely intertwined with community structures.

THEORY OF INDIGENOUS URBANISM

Richard O'Connor's theory of indigenous urbanism is a form of response to the dualistic perspective. He has claimed that theory must be indigenous in order to create a realistic model for Southeast Asian cities. According to O'Connor, studies of Southeast Asian cities which are based on Western theories "begin and end with alien constructs ... while urban life is embedded in indigenous meanings, urban studies have been embedded in Western meanings" (O'Connor 1983, 1-2). O'Connor is quite critical about the explanations given in modern social theories, such as central place theory and the theory of urban ecology. O'Connor argues that the city is not the simple sum of individual cost efficiency decisions. According to modern social theories, it is only by market forces that the traditional ties of kin and community are broken down.

In O'Connor's theory of indigenous urbanism, community and status hierarchy are the main themes. These are the important symbolic complexes which tend to create the reality. Community and hierarchy have their own idiom—a coherent way of symbolizing what people think, say, and do. In short, community and hierarchy shape the city's meaning and give meaning to urban life.

O'Connor tries to set the meaning of community within his social theory. He delineates his own way of treating the community from Tonnies' concept of Gemeinschaft. The differences, as O'Connor identifies them, are as follows: Tonnies fuses culture and society while O'Connor focuses on the culture or symbols of community. For Tonnies, it is critical whether a group is really a community or not. But O'Connor uses the word "idiom" precisely to avoid the difficult and secondary question of how communities are identified. In other words, Tonnies gives his priorities to boundaries while O'Connor gives his emphasis to the analysis within the idiom with which he is concerned. O'Connor states:

> Like Tonnies, I consider patron-client relations and patriarchal rule as well as the idiom's unseen consequences such as endemic factionalism and the importance of manpower. In sum, my subject overlaps Tonnies', but my approach follows from the priority of symbols. . . . Tonnies' concept of Gemeinschaft captures the Southeast Asian sense of community. (O'Connor 1983, 6)

O'Connor further emphasizes the persistence of community in the modern Southeast Asian city, which has been neglected by the Gesellschaft. The "indic idiom" which defines the social hierarchy in the old world has been replaced by the hierarchy of modernity. Modernity took over the old civil and military bureaucracies and created a new educational one. Today an idiom of modernity rules these core institutions that rule society (O'Connor 1983, 7).

O'Connor's theory of indigenous urbanism is of doubtful value because of its limited generalizability. This theory was generated from Thai urbanism. It is also important to note the following analytical deficiencies of this theory: (1) This provides, even for Thai society, a very static picture. The operational dynamics of status hierarchy within a local community are absent. (2) This theory is more descriptive than analytic because O'Connor is concerned with "what makes the city what it is." He has neglected the question, Why the city becomes what it is. (3) Community and status hierarchy are more conceptual reductions than explanatory schemes. This conceptual reductionism and its penetration into reality, inhibit the understanding of the complexities in the social process. In other words, this is an oversimplification of reality. The presentation of community and hierarchy as a symbolic idiom takes the form of static ideology leaving out the following important questions: Under what circumstances does a symbolic idiom flourish? What is the degree of persistence of community and what factors determine the particular degree of persistence? What is the changing form and degree of this symbolic idiom? Is it always the organizing principle of urban life?

Another limitation of O'Connor's theory is that it assumes that the modern status hierarchy is synonymous with the power structure of the society. This is not always true. It is important to understand the underlying mechanism of the coincidence of status hierarchy and power structure, or a gap between these two. There is an empirical possibility that status hierarchy is inactive while the non-status groups control the decision making process of urban life. Another possibility is the equal sharing of power by both status hierarchy and non-status groups. These variations of empirical reality have been neglected by O'Connor's theory due to the simplistic view of the distribution of power.

HISTORIOGRAPHICAL APPROACH: COLLECTIVE ACTION AND COMMUNITY

Some historians have used the concept of community as a fundamental mode of analysis in India. As opposed to the views presented by Tonnies, Sandria B. Freitag argues that the concept of "community" has survived beyond the temporal dividing line of pre-modern and modern. She focuses on the ideological construction and expression of community through collective actions in public arenas such as rituals, symbols, religious and civic events. The emergence of communalism in North India is defined as a "politicized community identity or the consciously-shared religious heritage which becomes the dominant form of identity" (Freitag 1989, 4-6). Her perspective is somewhat different from the conventional historiographical approaches. The previous approaches have placed their emphasis on organizations and make a distinction between popular—often violent—reactions to issues and the elite reactions of petitions and institutionalized protest (Freitag 1989, 12). Contrary to this conventional approach, Freitag shifts her focus to behavior as "text." She emphasizes the underlying connections, ideology, and popular participation. This connection is considered as the process by which participants constructed the respective "communities." Freitag states:

> In this process certain shared values and behaviors were self-consciously chosen for emphasis: participants simultaneously defined their own community and created an "other" encompassing these outside the boundaries they drew. The articulation of these constructions, in turn, calls to our attention the universe in which community came to be expressed. (Freitag 1989, 13)

Freitag claims new historical interpretation through collective activities. She analyzes the values and motivating forces of the crowd. The crowd behavior is placed within the context of historical changes. The events of history are seen as an outcome of the interplay between the collective acts of individuals and the larger economic and political forces of a world organized around an imperial order. However, she has identified some limitations in her study; there is no way to trace thoughts of individuals who make up a crowd. Only the ideas of the leader of the crowd can be traced through historical records. Individuals within the crowd may have had different motivations from one another and from the group as a whole (Freitag 1989, 13).

Historiographical approaches are inadequate to focus on individual behavior at various spatial levels such as family, neighborhood, groups, organizations, and community. The analysis of collective actions and group behavior in historical context undoubtedly provides some insights into the dynamics of community structure; but the changing aspects of individual expectations and the factors which govern individual behavior remain untouched. Also, the context where different sets of options are available to individuals has to be explored. Only then will the analysis illuminate the complex decision making processes of individuals, families, groups, etc. Therefore, in order to grapple with contemporary complex policy issues, the full spectrum of behavior has to be uncovered.

What is a community where behavior takes place? It is not my intention to trace the lengthy debate on the concept of community to answer this question. Nevertheless, it is worthwhile to present some conclusions which are based on the agreements of sociologists. There are three major elements in defining community: (1) A form of territorial base which represents an organizational pattern through which persons meet their daily needs in a local area. All the other institutions—families, churches, schools, etc.—exist in a territorial milieu. This territorial unit is potentially able to meet the full range of physiological, psychological, and social needs. (2) Community must be analyzed in terms of interaction, as a social group, or as a social system. (3) Community is a basic unit with which people identify and from which they gain a sense of security and belonging. (Poplin 1979, 23)

A New Perspective: Multiplex Modeling

Concept of Community

Considering all these theoretical discussions, in this study, I argue that an urban community is both an ideological and a territorial construction. In this sense, the concept of community has a broad interactional dimension which provides subjective meanings for human life. Territory is not merely an arbitrary administrative demarcation; it is rather symbolic and has a shared meaning. Common infrastructural facilities and institutional services provide a basis for this subjective meaning. These elements—interactions, territory and ideology—together produce a politicized community which reflects a wide range of behavioral patterns. In a heterogeneous community, we cannot expect a dominant symbolic ideology in terms of religion, ethnicity, and caste. Instead, a pluralistic symbiosis is superimposed. However, this pluralism cannot be expected to reach a level of democratic consciousness. Collective consciousness is very often reflected as civic consciousness. Although, the level of dedication to civic activities varies from one individual to another, the concept of civic consciousness is the center of focus in behavioral responses. The degree of participation and involvement, and the permanent and transitory character of behavioral responses, can be associated with the level of civic consciousness. The level of civic consciousness is an outcome of the process of interactions at various levels.

BEHAVIOR AS TEXT: COMMUNITY AS CONTEXT

The present study uncovers behavioral responses and the anatomy of urban change by examining the network of relationships in which people are involved at various levels, such as individual, family, neighborhood, community as a whole, and the community's outside connections. What are the different types of "urbanites" in this community? How do they behave towards each other in community context? What is the nature of individual decision making in community activities? How do they perceive and rationalize their behavior? How does their domestic setting help us to understand their perspective? What are the consequences of this perspective for their work and for their community? What is the degree of community sentiment or integration? What is the changing character of this integration? What common interests bind a community together to defend itself from outside forces?

This study examines the important consequences of the total network of community relationships. For example, what is the nature of the relationship between the extent of community integration and the volume of in/out migration? Could the migratory pattern be described as a regulatory one?

Some of the issues related to policy planning are also discussed. What are the practical implications of the existing level of community integration in providing urban services? How does it affect the municipal administration? How do the municipal administration and politics, in turn, affect the level of social integration? How do other social institutions such as kinship, religion, ethnicity, and locality operate in this setup? What is the role of these institutions in urban change? What are the urban socio-economic opportunities? What is the response to those opportunities? What is the nature of choices? Most simply, who does what economic and social activities through which connections?

PATTERNS OF URBAN COMMUNITIES

Individuals in urban setting are adopting different behavioral strategies under different circumstances. They are making decisions ranging from household matters to community matters. The central argument in this book is pivoted around five arenas of activity: politics, kinship, ethnicity, religion, and neighborhood involvement and mobility. These arenas in community activities provide the keys to understanding urban life. The underlying rationale of decisions pertaining to these activities is closely associated with individual and group expectations. Individual expectations and group expectations either reinforce or are contradictory to each other. However, the aspirational gap of each individual and the strategies of behavior are in a constant flux as a result of the interplay between economic and political factors within and outside of communities.

As a result of political and economic interplay and the dynamic nature of individual and group behavior, it is not possible to extract a fixed model to understand urban communities in South Asia. Also, an emerging model does not exclude ingredients and characteristics of alternative models. In other words, one model is not diametrically opposed to the other. Instead, the pattern of rotation and combination of ingredients which have bearing on individual strategic decisions, provide a complex set of community structures. Therefore, the findings of this study do not claim to reveal all these facets, but rather extract, at least, possible abstractions in order to bring to the surface the inner drama of the social fabric of an urban community.

This kind of behavioral analysis discards the notion of dualism at the individual level, group level, community level, organizational level, and geographical level. The behavioral orientation is not fixed. For instance, community oriented vs. non-community oriented, political activism vs. political apathy, religious vs. secular, traditional vs.

modern, formal vs. informal, etc. Instead of dualism, the behavior is reflected in a non-linear continuum. A particular point in the continuum in any behavioral arena is an individual choice and a strategy within the given context of a network of relationships. The aggregate points of all the behavioral continuums reflect the abstract form of the community structure at any temporal moment.

I argue, in this study, that people adopt one of four general approaches to their behavioral arenas in the community: strategic integration, polarized identification, fragmentary response, or individual response (fig. 1.1). The aggregate characterization, on the basis of the weight of each approach, provides insights into the structure and processes of the community. Furthermore, this identification and characterization of the community provide some sense of the permanent or transitory character of the individual or group residence. Each approach presents a range of community involvement and the impact of polarization and ad hoc association.

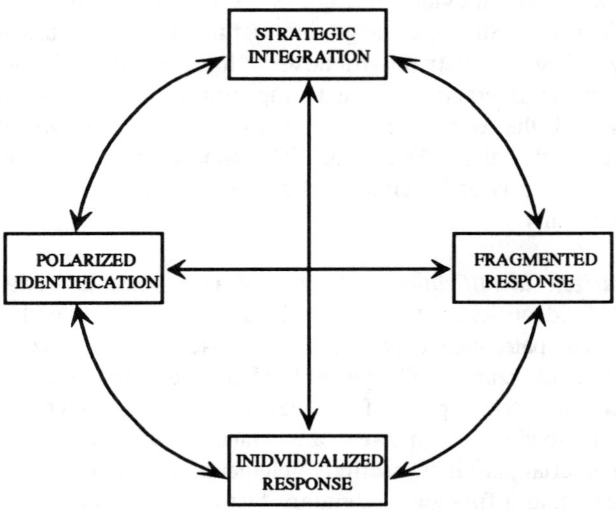

Fig. 1.1. Behavioral Approaches

Strategic integration. Strategic integration reflects ethnic and religious plurality and political power sharing. Community identity is constructed and expressed through plurality rather than ideological orthodoxy. The conventional, orthodox, and symbolic elements twist and shift to a new form of ideological ground which emphasizes the concept of plurality, interdependency, and coexistence.

"Strategic integration" is characterized by a system of patronage. Marginal groups (in terms of ethnicity, caste, and income) are absorbed into this system. Mutual solidarity and reciprocity in the arenas of politics and neighborhood are prevalent. Political alliances cause the reduction of tension between diverse social and economic groups and subdue the hierarchical arrangements. The majority of the residents show a permanent stake in the community. Even those who do not have mutual solidarity and reciprocity within the system of patronage, neighborhood, and in other public arenas, are provided by the community with a sense of identity and a symbolic meaning to their economic position and individuality. The only category which does not fit into this system is the transitory population and a group of people which has lost its power and social identity. This group is totally aloof from community activities and shows a significant aspirational gap in people's lives. Strategic integration is further characterized by high density of social network–friendship, local identity, kinship, and neighborhood interaction; a mediating political role between power centers and the community forms the *modus operandi* which is pragmatic rather than ideological. This modus operandi provides not only the solidarity and reciprocity but also the sense of identity within the community.

Polarized identification. There are two possible variations in polarized identification: (1) Political factionalism with a dual hierarchical patronage network, and (2) ascriptive polarization with political legitimization. The power holders, concentrated at the apex of the hierarchy, derive power from their respective resource base. The common sources of power are: land ownership, professions, entrepreneurial activities, ascriptive elements such as dominant castes, clans, regional affiliations, migratory history, numerical strength, and the role of political agents. Depending on the socio-economic and political circumstances of a country, either political factionalism or ascriptive elements prepare the groundwork for polarization with ideological support provided by the other element. For instance, when political factionalism is strong, it provides ground for polarization with ascriptive ideological legitimization and vice versa. The degree of polarization is determined and maintained by the numerical strength of marginal categories which needs economic and social support from the patronage network. The patrons' capacity for internal political mobilization and the quality of external linkages reinforce each other. Political or ascriptive polarization is maintained with the balance of power between dominant groups. The ascriptive elements of community structures and external political factionalism are magnets to each other.

Contrary to strategic integration, neighborhood relationship has wider collective meaning than individual reciprocity. External kinship connection is less important than neighborhood. The recruitment of rural immigrants to urban community is strongly monitored through a three dimensional framework: neighborhood, kinship, and politics. Unlike strategic integration, there is a limited scope for personal variations in polarized communities. For instance, neighborhood and kinship connections are encircled either with a political or ascriptive boundary.

Fragmentary response. Fragmentary response is a very common phenomenon in marginal settlements in South Asian cities. These communities are characterized by quasi-social groups emerging from different neighborhoods. Locality feelings and length of stay are the basis for this neighborhood consciousness. The intense rivalry between neighborhoods and temporary alliances is a frequent phenomenon in their social relations. The conflicts, alliances, and coexistence between these groups occur over the issues of common infrastructural facilities and access to external resources (governmental and non-governmental). The rivalry between these quasi-social groups is not strong enough to remove territorial consciousness from their minds. The reality of "geographical antiquity" makes for social distinctions from larger society. The lack of facilities, poor living conditions, and the stigma attached to them by external institutional authorities separate them from the mainstream life of the city. However, these communities are somewhat connected to the politics of the mainstream. The external political power-brokers usually approach these communities on an ad hoc basis. Temporary political factionalism emerges during the period of national or regional political campaigns. These temporary political affiliations do not channel ingredients for a system of patronage. Despite the external stigmatization, these communities, both at individual and group levels, show upward mobile aspiration. They are not completely isolated from mainstream thinking. Hence, these communities are potential breeding grounds for alternative forms of responses: strategic integration, polarized identification, and individual responses.

Individualized response. Individualized responses are not very common in urban communities in South Asia. Nevertheless, the anatomy of such structures is not totally absent. Such communities would be characterized by a broad-based equality of power. Residents of these communities are largely independent in terms of income and infrastructural facilities. Political factionalism is not significant in social interactions within their residential territory. The residential territory is a political entity combined with professional and entrepreneurial activities. The sense of community is symbolic in terms of status which has a Western outlook. However, modified versions of kinship, religious and cultural values are ingrained in their life styles.

An Approach to the Study

As this study is largely drawn from the domain of sociology and social anthropology, social network analysis has some theoretical relevance (Mitchell 1969; Burt 1977; Marsden 1982; Blau 1982). The network linkage, the actual flow of resources within the network, individuals' strength of access and control of resources and influence on one another, the way in which the brokerage and patronage behavior influence the distribution of power, the network structure and the development of an ideology are some of the prominent concepts in the network paradigm (Marsden 1982). However, the application of these concepts seems somewhat ad hoc in nature and lacks theoretical integrity. It is necessary to organize them into a coherent framework considering politico-economic and socio-cultural factors in different territories.

In spite of its conceptual significance, the present study does not replicate network analysis as presented elsewhere in studies of urban communities. This is a new approach developed in a rural context by a leading sociologist of Sri Lanka, S.P.F. Senaratne, and has been applied to the studies of South Asian rural society in a limited way. The present study is the first attempt to use this approach in an urban community. Since the rural–urban distinction in sociology and anthropology is unproductive in the South Asian context, it is legitimate to draw the relevant concepts, methods, and techniques from both sociology and social anthropology. More specifically, the participant observation method, social network, and the holistic perspectives are drawn from social anthropology, while from sociology emphasis is given to the need for organizing rigorous collections of data in terms of specific issues. However, the holistic perspective is adopted quite differently from those aspects of the community study method on which anthropologists normally concentrate. In contrast, the proposed study will utilize a dynamic approach which brings into consideration the external determinants (in a limited way) of the internal social structure.

CONCEPTUAL FRAMEWORK

This study involves research into the social system of an urban community within an integrated conceptual framework. This framework focuses on the interrelationships of four major concepts: (1) the network of relationships, (2) the complex nature of resources, (3) the distribution of power, and (4) the system of ideology (Senaratne 1977). In other words, the theoretical focus is on the power structure which reveals the network of the relationship of the interplay between power and resources, along with variations in ideological manifestations. Economy, kinship, neighborhood, religion, ethnicity, and politics constitute the social fabric texture of community life. The main assumption in this study is that these factors cannot be separated from the total social network.

In order to understand the social network, it is necessary to decode the pattern of behavior from the mass of everyday events. Explanation, not identification of behavior, is difficult. Investigations may reveal frequency of a particular behavior without illuminating the logic of that behavior. For example, it may be noted that a significant percentage of individuals in the category of landowners have obstructed the development programs while others keep silent or comply with the program. The rationale for such behavior cannot be identified easily. The explanations given by the landowners who have obstructed the program may not necessarily reveal the true reasons. Therefore, very often the analysis is reduced to the level of speculation. In order to understand the inner logic of behavior, it is an important task to examine the context from which the attitude springs.

An individual's behavior is not idiosyncratic. Urbanites in an organization, a community, neighborhood, or in a family unit in a given context, exhibit some regularities in their behavior. Through these regularities, it is possible to identify groups among individuals. However, even though the behavior is similar, individuals of one group do not behave identically given the same circumstances. Thus, there is both an individual element and a shared or common element in behavior. The crucial task is to disentangle the two elements. If an urban landowner who has obstructed the urban development program is completely unregulated (meaning the landowner is free to choose his/her own form of behavior in his community), then it would be possible by applying the right institutional force on the landowner to change his/her behavior. On the other hand, if an individual's behavior is completely ordered by regularities, it would be in conflict with his/her own experiences. The balance between these two elements must, therefore, be understood. It becomes necessary to understand the behavior of individuals, both in terms of the rules of relationships as well as their operations. In the operational context, it is necessary to shift the focus from individual behavior to sets of relationships.

Dimensions of relationship. The normative aspects of a relationship reveal the governing rules: what is right and what is wrong. These rules are justified through reference to a system of values that are ultimately grounded in a religious, political, or other system of belief. Associated with these rules are various types of sanctions which begin to operate if the rules are broken. The rules are expected to regulate an exchange which is the most important feature of a relationship. Exchange means that items move between the parties. Every relationship is distinctive in the nature of its exchange.

Relationships are connected with "resources." Some relationships between landowner and tenant, for example, are directly generated by control and use of resources, while other relationships are influenced by resources in varying degrees.

The quality of relationship has some elements of power. Office holders of a community organization may be stronger than the members of the organization or vice versa. The existing strength may have its origin in a total set of relationships of a person. The total set of relationships within the community provides the pattern of relationship.

Resources and their dimensions. The resources available to a community can be described as sources of income, factors which increase the value of this income, and factors reducing expenditure. The specific dimensions are: (1) Resources owned and handled by individuals both internally and externally (land, occupational skills, income, trading other wealth). (2) Public resources—common infrastructure, economic and social. (3) Accessibility of external economic functions. (4) Potential resources to which people are aspiring. (5) Changing nature of resources (some resources are contracting while others are expanding; for example, commercial functions may increase, some are eagerly welcomed while others are strongly rejected, and governmental resources may decrease rather permanently or temporarily). (6) Relative importance of each avenue of resources corresponding to the family's resource condition. (7) Degree of limitation in choices to restrict resources for individuals, groups, and the total community. (8) Through the choices available, a person develops relationships. The aspiration for resources is intense and may go beyond their absolute value. The new resources may induce changes in relationship in the community network.

Dimensions of power. In the context of choices, both resources and network, there are four important attributes of power that we will be considering it in this study: (1) Power is a function of the degree of interaction (through formal or informal channels) between an individual and his/her community. Such individual power may arise from the resources of occupation and wealth, political bases and ability to mobilize people. (2) Power is derived from the quality of an individual's relationship. Every individual has a set of relationships. If one has a large set and plays a superordinate role in the majority of them, he/she is more powerful. In this sense, it is important to examine power by looking at the operations of concrete relationships, rather than defining it. The number of alternative choices a person has in a desirable set of relationships is the determining factor of his/her power.

The identification of how power is distributed within a given territory is a somewhat complicated analysis which cannot be limited to listing the attributes of a few political/community leaders, landlords and businessmen. S.P.F. Senaratne has described the complicated nature of this power analysis in the following manner:

> It is necessary to identify the different bases from which power springs, and the strength of these bases. It is also necessary not to confuse the operation of power with its foundation. In the strict sense, power is undifferentiated. There is neither economic power, nor political power, but merely power which derives from either an economic base or a political base. The extent of the power of an individual is the nature of relationships and the superordinate role in the large majority of these relationships. (Senaratne 1981, 8)

Dimensions of ideology. In the dynamic operation of networks of relationships, ideology plays a vital role. Changes in relationships adjust and twist the norms and values deriving from political, economic, and/or religious ideologies. Therefore, ideology has several functions in the operation of power relations: (1) strengthening the existing relationship, (2) stressing certain norms and values, (3) manipulating conflict situations, and (4) influencing the acceptance or rejection of some of the resources. Ideology is the language of solidarity, as it is also the language of conflict and controversy. It is essential to recognize that ideology is not floating in the upper regions but is strongly connected to the resources, relationships, and power which are characteristic of the total network of relationships.

The above mentioned four concepts are central to understanding the behavior of individuals in a community. The interaction between these elements is not linear but is like a pattern of quadrant points on a circle. Each of the four elements is directly linked with every other.

METHODOLOGY

THE NATURE OF THE DATA

The required information, within the given theoretical framework, was on behavior and the network of relationships. Actual operation of relationships was the main variable. In this respect, many episodes of power relations in a particular time frame were focused. The factual data base has embraced major events, groups, and individual decisions, alternatives and options, perceptions and attitudes, and case studies on institutions (Appendix 1).

This study is aimed at identifying the behavior and extracting the underlying rationale of decisions pertaining to individual or group behavior. Therefore, the empirical focus of the study was on relationships. The collected data pertaining to relationships are as follows: (1) resources on which the relationships are based, (2) norms which regulate the relationships, and (3) episodes portraying the actual operations of these relationships.

In order to interpret this network of relationships and the structure of power, additional data on households and institutions was collected. Household data can be divided into three overlapping areas: (1) resources, (2) network (kinship, political, civic, economic, and leadership), and (3) options and choices. The changing nature of these elements was traced (Appendix 2).

The nature of the data is more qualitative than quantitative in character. The analysis of both types of data is embodied in this study. The quantitative data is supplementary to the qualitative interview data. The qualitative data will reveal the mechanics of the networks of relationships. The quantitative data shows the distribution of the characteristics of particular networks.

The explication of power relations through the analysis of qualitative data is the major task in data analysis. Categorization and the formation of a data matrix to depict the categorical relationships are essential tasks. Summaries of episodes of different categorical relationships provide illustrative examples for the analysis. This qualitative data analysis will explain the trends exhibited in the community. On that basis, the generation of conceptual structural models is also possible in this process.

FIELD WORK PROCEDURE

The study was undertaken in three major phases: the preliminary phase, the intensive phase, and the concluding phase.

The preliminary phase. During the preliminary period I used two basic methods to gather information: (1) A basic survey to collect general socio-economic and demographic data on each household and enumeration of economic activities of the location (Appendix 3). (2) Contacting several key informants to gather some descriptive information on key local institutions, history of the community, and to identify key social groupings of the community.

The intensive phase. Having identified principal factions, groupings, and characteristics on institutions, the in-depth interviews and selected observations on certain community activities gradually began. Sampling is largely based on stratified and random selection with purposive selection of some key members of the community. During this phase, the continuous contacts with key informants were continued. Eighty-five in-depth interviews were completed within five months (Appendix 4).

The concluding phase. This last phase was overlapped with part of the intensive phase. Halfway through the intensive phase, based on the knowledge acquired through in-depth interviews, a detailed questionnaire was formulated and then administered to 125 households on a random basis. The purpose of this survey was to capture the attributes of social networks in a larger sample to present a quantitative analysis. However, this particular data was not used for this study. In addition to the final survey, during this concluding phase the gaps of various sorts in the data were filled.

THE METHOD OF DATA ANALYSIS.

In the analysis period, immersion with the data yielded generalizations and abstractions on networks of relationships and the distribution of power. In this process of analysis, categorization of social relationships and formation of a data matrix to depict the categorical relationships were the major tasks. Summaries of episodes for different categorical relationships were prepared.

Among the techniques of qualitative data analysis, the use of McBee Cards was of vital importance to this study. After reading in-depth interviews, a comprehensive code system was developed (Appendix 5), and data was coded and stored on the McBee Card system. In addition to the McBee Cards, a master sheet was developed and the qualitative data was transformed into a quantitative form for the purpose of developing quantitative descriptive data (Appendix 6).

Chapter 2

Growth of the Capital City and the Socio-Economic Setting of the Community

According to the earliest records, Colombo city was known as a Moorish trading settlement as early as the eighth century. The harbor was frequented by ships from China, Persia, India and Arabia. During the period of the three main colonial rulers (Portuguese, Dutch, and British), this harbor was the principal port through which the produce of the colony was exported to the trading centers of the world. There were also improved ancillary activities such as storage for produce, banking and commercial facilities, and the growth of commercial activities concurrently with the increasing importance of Colombo as a port. During the British period Colombo grew in importance as the capital city, becoming the center of judicial, legislative, administrative, educational and commercial activity. The legislative council was established in 1833, and the head offices of the more important government departments began to emerge in Colombo. Several mercantile establishments, catering to the different needs of the plantation sector, also arose to add to the increasing complexity of the metropolis. The rapid growth of activity in Colombo and the improvement of the city's infrastructure resulted in a population increase.

The growth of the city of Colombo can be measured through an analysis of its demographic changes. Cities grow because they offer employment opportunities, attractive shopping and marketing facilities, cultural and recreational facilities, superior educational and health services, and convenient urban amenities. The growth of Colombo city, too, can be traced to these factors.

The percentage of increase in the city population had exceeded that of the national population in all of the censuses up to 1946, after which the rate of increase has steadily declined. From the last decade of the nineteenth century, city population outpaced that of the country (table 2.1). Migration swelled the city population. Information regarding the migrant influx into the city is furnished below.

Migration to Colombo City

Years	Migrants
1901-1911	62,770
1911-1921	44,602
1921-1931	36,725
1931-1946	16,585
1946-1953	10,212

Between 1953 and 1963, the city population increased by 86,758 migrants. During 1963 to 1971, the population increased by 50,776 and during 1971 to 1981 it increased by 23,356 migrants. Thus, a declining rate of migrants into the city can be observed. This indicates that the city could not absorb more migrants (De Mel 1982, 36-37).

The massive workforce required by the expansion of the functions of the city of Colombo could not all be accommodated within the city. During the early part of this century, port and railway workers were accommodated within the city in tenement gardens. Lack of adequate housing and buildable land within the city (because of marshes which even today amount to 10% of the total land area) served to increase rentals and land values. Thus during this period (during and after the Second World War), more and more workers sought shelter in the

Table 2.1

Population and Density of Colombo City, 1871-1981

Year	Area Sq. Miles	Population	Density Per Sq. Mile	Increase City Pop. (%)	Increase Net Pop. (%)
1871	9.5	95,843	10,142	—	—
1881	9.5	110,502	11,693	15.3	15.0
1891	9.5	126,825	13,350	14.8	9.0
1901	10.5	154,691	15,469	22.0	18.6
1911	11.9	211,274	17,698	36.6	15.2
1921	12.9	244,163	18,872	15.6	9.6
1931	13.0	284,155	21,858	16.4	18.0
1946	13.3	362,074	27,852	27.4	25.4
1953	13.8	425,881	30,694	17.6	21.6
1963	14.3	511,639	35,729	19.9	31.0
1971	14.4	562,420	39,056	9.9	20.0
1981	14.4	585,776	40,678	4.2	16.8

Source: Census Reports, Census and Statistics, Dept. Colombo (1911, 1953, 1971, 1981).

outlying areas of the city because these offered relatively cheap land, cheap rentals and because transportation was satisfactory and subsidized. With more migration into these areas, they became more and more subjugated to the economy and power of the city of Colombo.

MIGRATION AND ITS IMPACT ON COLOMBO

Some of the important characteristics of migration which have contributed to the Colombo socio-economic configuration should be noted. The United Nations ESCAP Population Division has presented a few generalizations, based on 1971 census data, concerning the impact of migration on Colombo (ESCAP 1980, 42-74).

Considering the total migration pattern of the high density, medium density, and low-density areas, Sri Lanka is still dominated by rural movements. The most important flow is within each region. It is interesting to note that in the pattern of migration of each region, the second most important flow is to greater Colombo. But when the case of intra-district movements is considered, the largest single flow is to the Colombo urban area (table 2.2 and fig. 2.1). There are no significant urban centers of attraction other than those around Colombo.

The migration pattern is clearly dominated by the flow of movement to Colombo district, largely from the densely populated wet zone districts of Kalutara, Galle, Matara, and Kandy. There is another significant long distance migration flow: Jaffna to Colombo. With the exception of Jaffna, wet zone districts with high outflow are mainly rural with the urban component varying from six percent in the district of Kulutara to 22 percent in Nuwara Eliya.

The two major migration flows are characterized by the following attributes: (1) Movement to a rural destination is taking place between villages for reasons of marriage and is significantly biased towards women. (2) The intra-district movement to Greater Colombo and Colombo's other urban areas is also dominated by women. However, the interregional movement to these urban destinations is strongly dominated by men. (3) There is no dominant age group among the migrants. Contrary to what is often suggested for developing countries, there is no suggestion of a disproportionate number of unemployed young men migrating to major urban centers in search of work. (4) The low country Sinhalese tend to be the largest group of migrants in most

Table 2.2

Net Migration Pattern by Districts, 1963-1971

Districts With Net Outmigration		Districts With Net Inmigration	
District	Total Net Outmigration (%)	District	Total Net Inmigration (%)
Kandy[a]	29.1	Colombo	54.6
Nuwara Eliya[a]	8.9	Matale	1.7
Galle[a]	11.8	Hambantota[c]	4.7
Matara[a]	17.4	Vavuniya[c]	5.7
Jaffna	10.5	Batticaloa[c]	3.4
Mannar[c]	5.3	Amparai[c]	0.2
Kurunegala[b]	1.3	Trincomalee[c]	3.9
Badulla[b]	3.5	Puttalam[b]	3.1
Kegalla[a]	12.2	Anuradhapura[c]	11.4
		Kalutara[c]	0.6
		Polonnaruwa[b]	5.5
		Moneragala[c]	3.2
		Ratnapura[b]	2.0
Sri Lanka	100.0	Sri Lanka	100.0

Source: Data from United Nations Economic and Social Commission for Asia and the Pacific (1980).

[a]High-density region.
[b]Medium-density region.
[c]Low-density region.

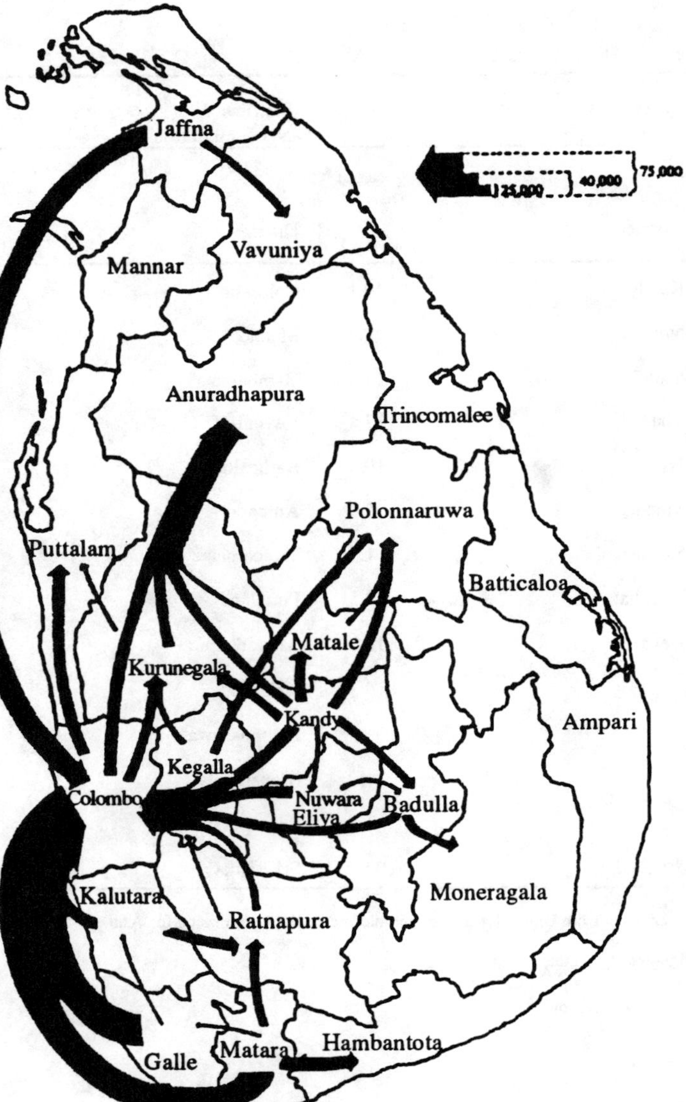

Fig. 2.1. Volume of Net Migration from district of birth to district of enumeration.
Source: ESCAP, Migration, Urbanization and Development in Sri Lanka, Fig. XV. United Nations, New York, 1980

urban areas. In Colombo, unlike other parts of the country, the influence of the low country Sinhalese migrants is lessened because of the greater proportions of Kandyan Sinhalese and Tamils which contributes to racial and ethnic tensions in the area. (5) With respect to the sex ratio, Tamil and Moor groups are highly male-dominated whereas the other major groups tend to be female-dominated. This is largely attributed to religious and socio-cultural factors. (6) In contrast to the other developing countries, there is no mass of uneducated people converging on the cities and there is no over-concentration of the more educated in one particular area. (7) The data clearly indicates that higher proportions of migrants in both age groups (15 to 24 and 25 to 64) and both sexes are employed. This is particularly the case with the younger age group, 15 to 24. There is a high student proportion in the never moved population for this age group. This suggests that migrants are entering the labor force earlier than non-migrants. This may be attributed to two reasons: (a) the never moved group can afford to delay their entrance into the labor force by staying on at school, and (b) they have the social and economic support to remain unemployed longer. (8) In the case of Greater Colombo and Colombo's other urban areas, there is no significant difference in the rates of unemployment between the longer established migrants and recently arrived migrants. (9) According to the 1971 census, the migrants did not make a direct major contribution to urban unemployment in Sri Lanka. (10) Among the male employed population, there are higher proportions of migrants in white collar employment than there are in the never moved population. There are higher proportions of employed male and female migrants in service activities than in the never moved population. Migrants, both males and females, may enter into domestic service but they also seem to be entering the so-called informal sector. (11) In summary, the data indicates, at least until 1971, migrants were being successfully integrated into the urban economy of Sri Lanka. They seemed neither to have disproportionately added to the unemployed nor to have entered lower paid employment. In fact, quite the reverse is true: migrants seem to perform the greater part of most productive tasks with proportionately higher activity rates than non-migrants.

Historical Profile

The Municipal Jurisdiction

Dematagoda Municipal Ward is demarcated by the Kolonnawa Canal as the eastern boundary, on the north are the Urban Council limits of Kolonnawa, on the west the Municipal Council Ward of Maligawatta, and on the south the Municipal Council Ward of Wanathamulla. This ward comes under the Borella State Assembly electorate. The area has an extent of 168.09 acres and the total population is 13,587. The density per acre is 80.83.

This is mainly a Sinhala dominated area with Tamils and Muslims coming second and third respectively. The Burgher community (descendants of Dutch citizens) is also fairly represented. The majority are Buddhists (table 2.3).

Dematagoda is situated three miles inland from *Pettah*, the city. This area also has connections to the surrounding rural areas such as Wellampitiya, Gothatuwa, Kirindiwella, and Angoda within the Colombo district. Many routes run through this ward connecting those areas as well as the High Level Road, Galle Road, Negombo Road, and Kandy Road. The Kolonnawa bridge is one of the important entrances to the low level road which leads to Kaduwela, Hanwella, Avisawella, Ratnapura, etc. The Kelani-Valley Railway Line passes through this ward (Baseline Road Station) and ends up at Opanaike. The Kandy Railway Line runs along the west boundary of the ward, i.e., Maligawatta Halt. The railway track from the Port to Kolonnawa Oil Installation is built on an elevated flood protection bank which checks the spread of the floods westward.

The Kolonnawa Canal had been cut by the Portuguese for the purpose of transportation of goods. This canal was formerly called *Diyawanna Oya*. During the British period, tea, copra, and desiccated coconut were transported by boats (*Oruparu*), and Dematagoda was used as a center port for unloading; from there, these goods were sent to the processing factories in the city for export. Firewood was transported by the same canal route for the use of Colombo residents. This canal transport system came to an end with the advent of the motor vehicle transport system.

Table 2.3

Ethnic and Religious Composition of the Ward

	N	Population (%)
Ethnic Composition		
Low Country Sinhala	7,323	53.9
Up Country Sinhala	739	5.4
Ceylon Tamils	2,381	17.5
Indian Tamils	1,005	7.4
Ceylon Moors	1,332	9.8
Indian Moors	188	1.4
Burghers	232	1.7
Malays	353	2.6
Others	35	0.3
Total (ethnic)	13,588	
Religious Composition		
Buddhists	8,008	59.0
Hindu	2,477	18.3
Muslim	1,828	13.5
Roman Catholic	1,008	7.4
Christians	241	1.8
Total (religious)	13,562	

Source: Sri Lanka Census of Population, Colombo District Report, Vol. 1, Ministry of Plan Implementation, Department of Census and Statistics (1971).
Note: Data on religious identification of 26 persons are not available.

During the Portuguese period, except for the few paddy lands that bordered along the canal bank, most of the area was covered with forest. There was cinnamon cultivation during the Dutch period in this area, and during the British period, coconut had been grown in this area and there was little paddy cultivation up to about 1910, especially along the canal back.

In the early days the study location belonged to the old Kolonnawa area. Before large-scale human settlements took place, this area had a thick vegetation of *Demata* trees. The derivation of the name of the area is probably due to its significance; but at a much later time the area was sarcastically referred to as *Demalagoda* by the Sinhalese due to the migrant Tamil population that settled down in this area.

Around 1850 this area (about 150 acres–the area under study is about 55 acres) was bought by one Abeysekere on which he built his *Walauwwa* (mansion). He was the *Maha Mudaliyar* (designated position under the British Administration) to Siyane Korale. At present, the Walauwwa has only about two acres because of land fragmentation due to several marriages. Gradually three generations of the *Walauwwa* (mansion) people sold their portions of land to outsiders. During the period of 1885 to 1900, there were a few families that migrated to the area and bought these lands. Five or six families bought the marginal area of the selected location. These families migrated from Kotahena, Kolonnawa, Kotte, Kaduwela, etc.

These families are considered as indigenous inhabitants in the area. From the turn of the century with the emergence of graphite processing industries and the harbor development, the graphite gardens became populated with workers. Around the 1920s, the graphite industry came to a gradual halt due to a drop of its export. During the latter part of 1920, the speculative entrepreneurs and land owners built up housing lines and shop buildings with little consideration for air, space, lighting, ventilation, drainage, etc. By 1930, there were four or five house owners and thirty to forty residents in the selected location. After 1930, particularly after the major floods, the population increased. Population increase accelerated after World War II. This area is considered as a residential area due to its proximity to the work places. Along with the population increase, Dematagoda has been commercially developed and today functions as an important economic center between the center of the city and the peripheral rural areas within Colombo District and the outside world. Today, this is an extensive bazaar and a thriving market center for peripheral rural areas for the purchase of commodities not substantially handled in the small local shops. The Dematagoda bazaar area provides every domestic requirement to the people of the area. As a result of the development, the land value has gone up.

STUDY LOCATION

This area was populated by different people from various parts of the country. Most of the migrants are from Western Province, Southern Province, Central Province, Sabaragamuwa Province and few in number from other provinces.

The latter part of the 1950s saw the establishment of a fiber industry in the locality. But the employment opportunities of this industry are exploited by outsiders who come from Kolonnawa, Wellampitiya, Gothatuwa, Kalutara, etc. At the initial stage of this industry, most of the employees had been recruited from the same locality. In the latter part of the 1960s a strike led to the dismissal of most employees. Subsequently the recruitment policy of the industry was changed which opened employment opportunities to rural areas such as Kalutara and even down South. Today, there are only about 30 persons from the same locality. The major economic opportunity to the area is outside employment. There are few industrial ventures which provide employment opportunities to the area within the ward. Such ventures include the Petroleum Corporation, CGR (Ceylon Government Railway) Running Shed, Government Factory and a few other companies within the ward. Most of the people are wage earners. To a small extent, social stratification can be seen in the area because of economic conditions, even among wage earners. There are also a few professionals and businessmen in the area and they are economically steady.

Business activities began to expand from 1930 onwards. At present the total business units in selected locations number nearly 200. Of these, 118 are in permanent or semi-permanent locations. The rest belong to the pavement business activities. Business activities of the area are largely handled by the Sinhalese, particularly by southerners.

Up to the 1950s most of the business premises were owned by the *Walauwwa* people. From 1930 to 1950 these business premises were rented out to outsiders. At that time there was no difficulty in obtaining these premises. Just after the 1956 general elections, these business premises were auctioned by the *Walauwwa* people, and investors from various parts of the country bought two or three business blocks each.

Some house owners also auctioned their houses, some of which were bought by the tenants themselves whilst the rest were bought by investors who subsequently rented them out. But no person bought more than three or four houses. During the latter part of 1960, one house owner tried to auction his houses. Since it was found to be in default for various reasons, his bare land (one and one half acres in extent) was vested in the State and a few flats put up on it. In 1970, these flats were given to the people of Maligawatta (four blocks of housing apartments with 200 housing units). In 1973, most of the private houses were vested in the National Housing Department. These house owners come under the Housing Ceiling Act. These changes of ownership led to the change in the relationship pattern of the area.

Land is a very scarce resource in the area. In the early 1960s there was some land owned by the *Walauwwa*. At that time a few rich people bought this land and put up houses for their own residence; land value was about Rs. 600 per perch (30 1/4 sq. yds.). These houses, put up by the rich people, showed a marked difference when compared to other houses of the area. There were mainly two types of housing which depicted the prevailing social and economic characteristics.

Government facilities extended to the area are not satisfactory. There is one Community Center under the control of the Colombo Municipal Council and two schools in the area—Anurudha Maha Vidyalaya has two sections, providing its services in terms of the major ethnic groups, Sinhalese and Tamils. Lack of school facilities and cooperative services (there are two cooperatives) create several problems for the inhabitants of the area. Sometimes these problems lead to communal quarrels between some families on a small scale. Lack of water facilities and drainage systems are major problems which have to be faced by the inhabitants. There are two main temples and one church rendering their services to the area. The major temple in the area, called Weluwanaramaya, was built by the mother of one of the Municipal Council members in 1930, with her own money on land she donated. The temple is built on the private land of the late *Nayake Thera* (incumbent) of the temple. At particular times, these two temples have been involved in politics.

The above mentioned essential facilities and services are the base of the total relationship patterns of the inhabitants of the area. The growth of resources and the nature of political activities are interconnected.

As far as the political and administrative set up of the area are concerned, the year 1876 is significant. The Municipal Council was established in this year and Colombo was divided into nine administrative areas in which Dematagoda comes under the Maradana Ward which prevailed up to 1935. After 1933 Dematagoda was separated, extending to the Kolonnawa Canal, for the purpose of administrative activities. In 1930, A. E. Goonesinghe, a prominent labor leader, took his politics to this area. S.W.R.D. Bandaranaike, one of the post independence prime ministers, was another person who engaged himself in the politics of the area prior to Independence. The Lanka Sama Samaja Party (Lanka Equal Society Party) had a great appeal to the people of the area for a considerable period of time. Since Independence, the LSSP was strong enough to retain its power in this area with the exception of one or two occasions. In the 1950s politically significant incidents had occurred. It was during this period that Kandasami, a blue collar worker, was killed when police opened fire on a demonstration. This is a landmark event for left politics in Colombo. The political history of this area has generated a specific political consciousness. There is a general impression among the people of the area, particularly middle aged and old people, that this area gives leadership in politics.

There are political organizations and youth organizations aligned with their political parties. There are many office-bearers of every major party within the selected locality. From 1971 to 1976 there was a *Janatha Committee* (People's Committee) which was dissolved in 1976. They handled some social activities such as organizing New Year festivals in the area up to the 1977 elections.

After the expulsion of the LSSP from the coalition government in 1975, a significant political change took place. During the mid 1970s, there was an emerging leadership of the Sri Lanka Freedom Party which put up a good challenge at the election in 1977. A former LSSP Municipal Council member has crossed over to the SLFP and has given his support to the new leadership. The SLFP candidate was the chairman of Salu Sala, one of the government textile manufacturing corporations. He had provided some drainage facilities to the area with his own money before the 1977 election. Despite these efforts, the SLFP candidate was defeated. The UNP (United National Party) candidate won the Parliamentary seat and is still continuing. After the introduction of proportional representation system, the MP's position was secured.

PHYSICAL STRUCTURE AND SOCIAL SETTING OF THE COMMUNITY

The selected location for this study is in Dematagoda, the eastern border of Colombo City (fig. 2.2). This area can be considered as a community which consists of a heterogeneous population. In fact, this as an identifiable entity defined by its physical boundaries and service institutions rather than by any traditional social cohesion. The clearcut physical separation is conducive to identifying this territory as one entity. This is demarcated by the Kollonnawa Road, Kollannawa Canal, Weluwana Road and by the commercial activities of the town (fig. 2.3). Nearly 30 households which are located in part of Thomas Lane were considered as part of this identifiable entity, even though these houses administratively belonged to the Wanathamulla Municipal Ward. These houses have more access to Palitha Place and Ganawimala Road which are interior roads of this location. Furthermore, the inhabitants of these houses have more social interactions with the people of this location than Wanathamulla.

In addition to these physical boundaries, the long standing inhabitants refer to this area as *Appe Gama* (our village) in the urban setting. The two Buddhist temples located in this area are considered to be a nuclear point of reference, in disregard of ethnic and religious diversity of the location. This symbolic reference point is an extension and variation to the concept of village in Sri Lanka. Nevertheless, this physical territory interlocks with the wider spatial entity, particularly in the sphere of politics, administration, services, and commerce.

The community, which appears as a unit from outside, reveals fairly clear physical divisions—neighborhood clusters—when examined from within. It divides itself into 30 more or less well defined physical segments. Most of these physical entities have become meaningful, not in terms of social divisions but in sharing common infrastructural

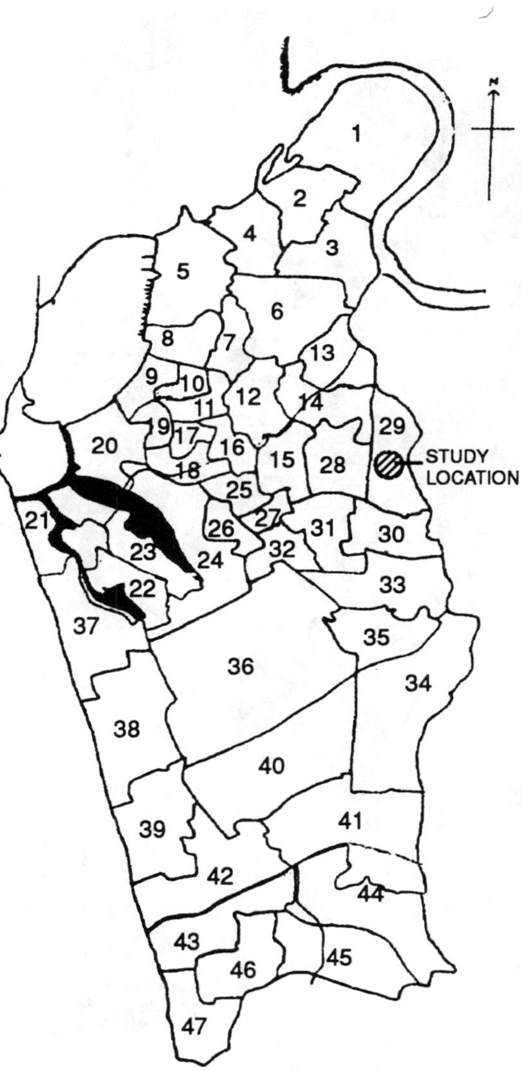

LIST OF WARDS

1. Mattakkuliya
2. Modera
3. Aluthmawatha
5. Lunupokuna
6. Bloemendhal
7. Kotahena East
8. Kotahena West
9. Kochchikade North
10. Ginthupitiya
11. Masangasvidiya
12. New Bazaar
13. Grandpass North
14. Grandpass South
15. Maligawatta West
16. Aluthkade East
17. Aluthkade West
18. Kehelwatta
19. Kochchikade
20. Fort
21. Kompannavidiya
22. Wekanda
23. Hunupitiya
24. Suduwella
25. Panchikawatta
26. Maradana
27. Maligakanda
28. Maligawatta East
29. Dematagoda
30. Wanathamulla
31. Kuppiyawatta East
32. Kuppiyawatta West
33. Borella north
34. Narahenpita
35. Borella south
36. Cinnaman Gardens
37. Kollupitiya
38. Bambalapitiya
39. Milagiriya
40. Thimbirigasaya
41. Kirula
42. Havelock Town
43. Wellawatta North
44. Kirullapane
45. Pamankada East
46. Pamandada West
47. Pamankada South

Fig. 2.2. City of Colombo

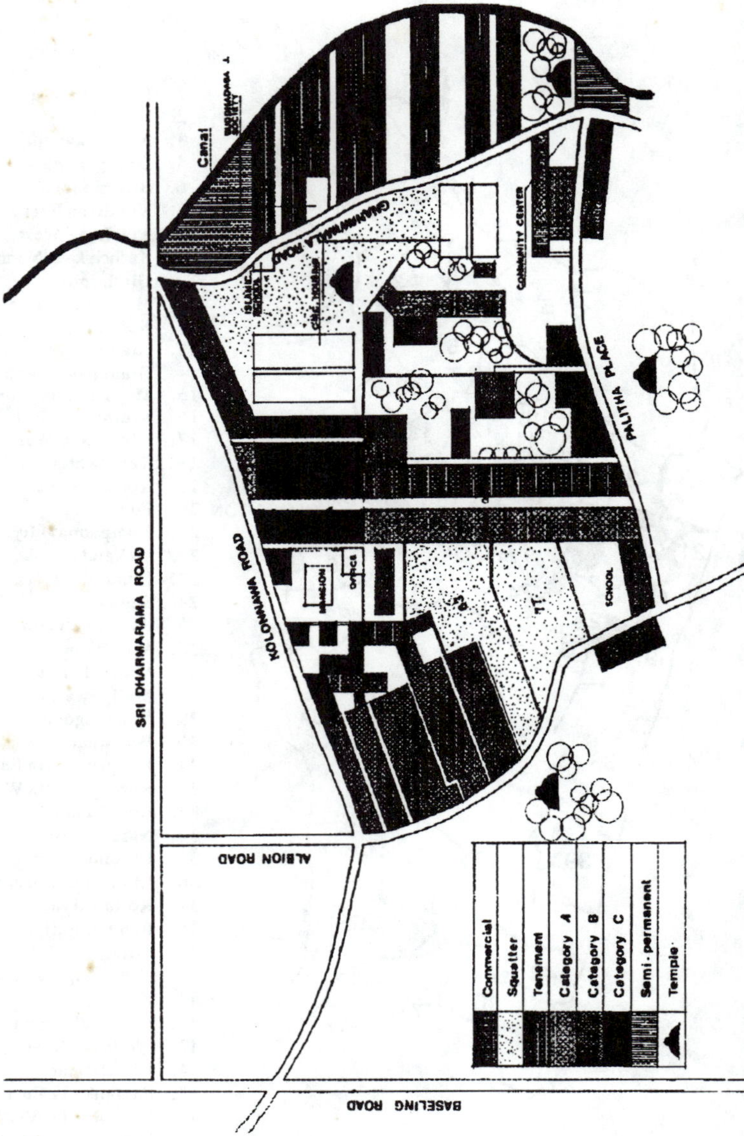

Fig. 2.3. Study Location

services and similar housing structures in which these urbanites live. Some physical segments are synonymous with social value attachments from the points of view of some inhabitants of each segment. Nevertheless, it seems that social distance in terms of these physical segments is an impossible task in this urban locale.

There are 724 households which include a population of 4,196 persons; 2,489 of these are Sinhalese, the majority. Muslims, including Malay (820 persons) and Tamils (737), form the second and third ethnic groups, respectively. One hundred fifty of the total population could be categorized as "other" which consists of Burghers and other ethnically mixed people. The population is almost equally divided by sex in all ethnic groups (table 2.4). As far as average family size is concerned the majority of the families of this community has six members or less than six, which is the national average. However, Muslims and Tamils have large families with an above average level compared to Sinhalese (table 2.5).

With respect to in-migration to the location, the large majority of household heads are from Western province (67%) while Southern province (14%) and Central province (7%) occupy second and third places respectively (table 2.6). In addition to Colombo District, Gampaha, and Kalutara Districts have sent more people to this location.

In the Southern province, Matara and Galle Districts are important in contributing to this inflow while Kandy, the capital of the Central province, is the significant contributor (table 2.7). The majority of the migrants are long standing residents of this community. Only 32% of the total have stayed less than five years in this community (table 2.8). The in-migration pattern of Dematagoda reflects the macro inflow stream of urban Colombo.

The inhabitants of this community, at a first glance, could be categorized into rudimentary social groups, considering many characteristics such as migrational history, land owning and occupational elements, ethnicity, and physical segregation (table 2.9). This classification is heavily based on common information presented by many informants.

Table 2.4

Population by Ethnicity and Sex

Ethnicity	*N*	Male (%)	Female (%)
Sinhala	2,489	50.0	50.0
Tamil	737	53.3	46.7
Muslim	820	49.6	50.4
Other	150	50.6	49.4
Total	4,196		

Table 2.5

Family Size By Ethnic Group

Ethnic Group	*N*	Above National Average (%)	Below National Average (%)	Equal to National Average (%)
Sinhala	445	28.6	55.0	16.4
Tamil	109	44.3	44.6	14.1
Muslim	124	51.3	36.1	12.6
Other	21	57.1	28.6	14.3
Total	699			

Note: National Average is six.

Table 2.6

Place of Origin by Provinces

Place of Origin	*N*	Household Head (%)
Western Province	476	67.2
Southern Province	101	14.3
Central Province	52	7.3
Sabaragamuma Province	25	3.5
North Central Province	1	0.1
Northern Province	0	—
Eastern Province	3	0.4
UWA Province	10	1.5
North Western Province	12	1.7
India	27	3.9
Other (China)	1	0.1
Total	708	

Table 2.7

Place of Origin by Districts

Districts	*N*	Household Head (%)
Anuradhapura	1	0.1
Ampara	1	0.1
Badulla	10	1.4
Kegalle	12	1.7
Kandy	36	5.1
Matale	6	0.8
Nuwara Eliya	10	1.4
Batticaloa	2	0.3
Puttalam	8	1.1
Kurunegala	4	0.6
Kalutara	14	2.0
Galle	35	4.9
Matara	68	9.6
Hambantota	2	0.3
Ratnapura	13	1.8
Gampaha	15	2.1
Colombo	447	62.8
India	27	3.8
Other (China)	1	0.1
Total	712	

Note: Districts of Polonnaruwa, Jaffna, Mannar, Monaragala, Mulathiw, Trincomalee, and Vavuniya reported zero.

Table 2.8

Duration of Stay of Migrants

Years Stayed	*N*	Migrants (%)
0 - 5	636	31.9
6 - 10	371	18.6
11 - 15	309	15.5
16 - 20	359	18.0
21 - 25	85	4.3
26 - 30	71	3.6
31 - 35	68	3.4
36 - 40	37	1.9
41 - 50	48	2.4
Over 50	8	0.4
Total	1,992	

Table 2.9

Predominant Characteristics of Social Categories

Social Categories	Income Sources	Ethnic/Locality	Migrational History and Land Ownership
1. Indigenous leading group	Both legal and illegal	Exclusively Sinhalese	3-4 generations; 20-40 perches
2. Indigenous professional group	Mainly from low level professional activities	Exclusively Sinhalese (majority from Colombo suburb)	In between 1880-1910; 8-40 perches
3. Leading business group	Mainly from retail (groceries) and textile trade	Predominantly Sinhalese (majority of Sinhalese are southern migrants)	After World War I: —residential land ownership; —partitioned or unpartitioned land in their native place; —majority from southern province
4. Sinhala residents	Mainly unskilled workers in the government (with a few low strata professionals)	Majority from Colombo Districts, significant percentage from South	Duration varies from 5-65 years. Some have unpartitioned land, significant percentage from southern
5. Indian Tamils	Bottom level, temporary economic activities of Colombo City	Tamils of South Indian origin (parents or grandparents were brought by British as plantation workers)	Migrated during last 50-60 years from the plantation sector

6. Muslims	Majority both unskilled workers and self-employed	Significant percentage from Central Province (remainder from Colombo)	Migrated during last 40 years from Central Province; some have unpartitioned ownership
7. Eurasians	Bottom level professional activities	Burgher Community	Eurasians-Descendants of Sinhala and European intermarriages
8. Residents in government flats (apartments)	Diverse economic activities (skilled, unskilled, self-employed small-scale business, etc.)	Mixed	Relocated from Colombo North after the establishment of Government Housing
9. Spillover group from government apartments (known as shanty dwellers)	Unskilled, unstable economic activities of Colombo City	Majority Sinhalese (with fair percentage of Muslims and Tamils)	Spillover from Government Housing; living in unauthorized structures; began in late 1970s
10. Recent migrants	Upper and middle-class professionals, company owners, shareholders	Predominantly Sinhalese and Muslims	Migrated during last 20 years; over 20-40 perches residential land; constructed their own residence

Indigenous leading group. This group is not confined to the selected community. Their functions and interactions cover a wider territory in Colombo. There are 15 households; three of those are in this community. Migrational history of this group goes back to three or four generations. The grandparents of the present generation started their life under harsh economic conditions. Most of them had involved themselves in thuggerism and made earnings largely from illegal activities. The present generation of this group do not possess inherited property. The land extent in which their residence has been put up is in the region of 20 to 40 perches (one perch is equal to 30 1/4 sq. yds.). In addition, they possess some extra houses, located within and outside the location which have been rented out to the migrants. Even today, a substantial portion of the earnings comes from illegal activities which include bucket shops, clubs, trade in liquor and narcotics, money lending, etc. Their legal business activities constitute the running of restaurants, selling fish, firewood, and renting houses. As an ethnic group all of them are Sinhalese.

Indigenous professional group. There are eleven households in this community. (The basic survey includes only eight households.) They have migrated during the period of 1880 to 1910. They possess inherited land in the range of eight perches to forty perches. Some members of this group have extended their land ownership, either buying adjacent land portions or buying some land in the periphery. Their economic dependence is largely on low level professional activities such as teaching and clerical work. However, today some members of these families earn their living through labor jobs. Two to three original families of this group have migrated from the southern part of the country and others from the hinterland of Colombo. This group also belongs to the Sinhala ethnic majority.

Leading business group. This group consists of 15 business units in the bazaar. Most of them are engaged in the retail and textile trade. This group largely consists of the people who have migrated from the southern part of the country. Everybody of the leading business group had inherited land and most of them were able to expand their ownership in their home areas. Very few original migrants of this group sold their inherited ownership after their parents died. All of this group reside in Dematagoda and in the periphery of Colombo. They have bought residential land and put up their houses. Some of them have bought extra properties in Colombo and in the suburbs after 1940.

Other Sinhalese migrants. (This category excludes the households in government apartments and spillover group.) This migrant population can be categorized into four types, in terms of place of origin. The distribution is given in table 2.10. Duration of residence of this group varies from five to sixty-five years. The majority of this group earn their living through labor jobs in government departments, corporations, and in private sector firms. A significant percentage (58%) of southern migrants claim that they have unpartitioned inherited land in their home areas. The data reveal the range of ownership from one-quarter to four acres. Migrants from other parts of the country own some unpartitioned land which does not exceed two acres. The people who are of Colombo origin have hardly any inherited ownership.

Tamils of South Indian origin. This group has 63 households. They have migrated during the last 50 to 55 years from other parts of Colombo, and very few have come from the hinterland of Colombo. Their parents or grandparents originally migrated as plantation workers from South India during the British period.

Other minority groups. This group consists of three ethnic categories: Muslim, Malay, and Burgher families. There are 53 households in this category. The majority of this group belong to the labor category and a few are engaged in bottom level professional activities and business activities. Their migrational history goes back 40 years. In this group, a very few Muslim migrants from the central province possess unpartitioned inherited land ownership.

Residents in government flats. This group is ethnically mixed. These government flats originally were given to the shanty dwellers in 1967 who resided in Maligawatta, Colombo North. Since then, a fairly high turnover rate has been noted. The original tenants tend to transfer these houses to newcomers. This transference has become a practice and socially acceptable even though it was not the original intention of the housing authorities. These residents have been categorically identified as *dwellers in government flats* by others. There are four flats

Table 2.10

Ethnic and Locality Composition of Groups

Ethnic/Locality Group	*N*	Group D (Other Sinhala Migrants) (%)	Group G (Government Apartments) (%)	Group H (Spillover Group) (%)
Southern Migrants (Sinhala)	90	20.0	12.0	6.0
Migrants from Other Districts (Sinhala)	78	16.0	10.0	10.0
Migrants from Colombo Hinterland (Sinhala)	69	16.0	7.0	6.0
Migrants from Other Parts of Colombo (Sinhala)	216	48.0	15.0	51.0
Tamils	50	—	22.0	15.0
Muslims	69	—	34.0	12.0
Total	572			

in this location which contain 50 housing units in each. Presently, there are 187 households (only 180 were surveyed). The locality and ethnic composition is given in table 2.10.

Spillover group from government flats. As a result of overcrowding, members of flat dwellings began to erect unauthorized structures in the latter part of the 1970s as dwelling units on the vacant land adjacent to the government flats. This land was considered as the playground and open space for the people of these flats. By the time of this study, the number of these unauthorized structures was about 70 (only 68 were surveyed). Ethnic breakdowns of this group are given in table 2.10.

Recent migrants. This group includes professionals, company owners, and shareholders. There are 15 households in this category and they reside in two separate physical segments. (The basic survey includes only six households.) There are about five company owners and the rest are professionals. Company owners are exclusively Muslims. They are mainly engaged in manufacturing, hardware, importing, and selling hardware. A few of them are engaged in exporting gems. The upper level professionals are lawyers, managers and directors in corporations, government departments, or in private sector companies. Their migrational history goes back 20 years. They bought 20 to 40 perches of residential plots from the Abeyasekare *Walauwwa* at the auction during the 1960s. There are a few families in this group who live in this area temporarily in rented houses.

Absentee house owners. There are about 15 to 20 absentee house owners. They reside in the rural hinterland of Colombo City. Most of them are Sinhalese.

Chapter 3

Resource Structure of the Community

The resource structure of Dematagoda provides insights into the social fabric of urban communities in Colombo. The main emphasis of this chapter is not mere enumeration of aggregate income and wealth, but to trace the combination of different sources, the ways in which inhabitants derive their income, the regularity and the stability, the pattern of income distribution, and the perception and evaluation of their own livelihood. All these attributes constitute the total package of the resource structure. This package dictates the life style and the pattern of relationships of urban inhabitants of this community. The total package also provides a symbolic meaning to their life and distinguishes social categories and status relationships of the community.

The social infrastructure lays the foundation for social dynamics of the community. Social dynamics in the context of resources can be understood in terms of regulation and control of income, wealth, ownership, and public infrastructure facilities. Therefore, the pattern of regulation and its changing characteristics have to be examined. The factors which govern these regulations are important aspects of social dynamics. These social dynamics have significant impact on the structure of relationships: landlord–tenant relationships, political and administrative relationships of the community, neighborhood relationships, patron–client relationships, and rural–urban connections. These patterns of relationships, in turn, shape the migratory flow, inward and outward, of the community.

Dematagoda is generally considered as a *working class* community. Residents derive their income largely from skilled or unskilled activities of the city of Colombo. However, the sources of employment and the pattern of income distribution indicate a marked variation that reflects on life style, living conditions, and social network of the community. Therefore, this chapter provides the resource contours in terms of social categories.

A Resource Profile

Level of Employment and Occupational Distribution

Although the active working age population (18 to 55 is considered as active working age, below 18 is underage, and above 55 is overage) is more than 50% in all ethnic groups (table 3.1), over 50% of them are unemployed. This is highest among the Muslims (63%) (table 3.2). Women are largely unemployed. It is interesting to note that a small percentage of the overage and underage population are also employed. Of the total employment, 5% to 7.3% in each ethnic group are either underage or overage (table 3.3). The dependency ratio of each ethnic group is a significant factor to note in this community. Although there is little difference among ethnic groups, the minorities have a higher dependency ratio than the majority (table 3.4).

More than 65% of employed people are in the working class category. This group consists of various sorts of activities in skilled, semi-skilled, and unskilled labor categories. Thirteen point one percent of the total employed are engaged in small scale, self-employed activities such as pavement hawking and mobile vendoring. The medium or large scale business category constitutes only 3.5% of the total employment. As a result of newly opened up employment opportunities in Middle East countries, 8.5% of this community presently earn their living from that source. However, this is largely constituted of unskilled labor categories, particularly job opportunities for women as housemaids. The clerical and allied category is 12.6%,

Table 3.1

Working Age Population by Ethnic Groups

Ethnic Groups	*N*	Working Age Population (%)
Sinhala	2489	56.5
Tamil	737	52.5
Muslim	820	57.3
Other	150	50.0
Total	4196	

Table 3.2

Unemployment by Ethnic Groups

Ethnic Groups	*N*	Unemployed (%)	Employed (%)
Sinhala	1406	55.8	44.2
Tamil	387	56.6	43.4
Muslim	470	63.4	36.6
Other	75	54.7	45.3
Total	2338		

Note: Percentage of unemployment is calculated on the basis of active working age population. Overage and underage employed numbers are excluded.

Table 3.3

Employment by Ethnic Groups

Ethnic Group	*N*	Employed Within Working Age (%)	Over/Under Age Employment (%)
Sinhala	670	92.7	7.3
Tamil	177	94.9	5.1
Muslim	186	92.5	7.5
Other	40	85.0	15.0
Total	1073		

Note: *N* includes over/under age employed.

Table 3.4

Dependency Ratio by Ethnic Group

Ethnic Group	*N*	Employed	Dependency Ratio (%)
Sinhala	2,489	670	3.7
Tamil	737	177	4.2
Muslim	820	186	4.4
Other	150	40	3.8
Total	4,196	1,073	

Note: Percentage of employment and dependency ratio is calculated on the basis of total population.

while the administrative and managerial category constitute 2% of the total employed in this community (table 3.5). Only 10.4% of Tamils, 12.6% of Muslims, and 2.2% of Eurasians employed are engaged in clerical or allied jobs. The Indian originated Tamils and Eurasians do not occupy any administrative jobs, while Muslims have only 19.0% of the administrative jobs (table 3.6).

The distribution of employed people by sector of employment is enumerated in table 3.7. The government sector employment constitutes only 26.6% of the total employment, though it holds the highest status among jobs in Sri Lanka. It is a striking feature to note that a significant percentage (33.6%) of the employed population among Sinhalese are employed in the government sector, while those similarly employed among minority categories constitute a much smaller percentage, 14.1% for Tamils and 12.9% for Muslims. The private sector employment is highest among Tamils (72.3%) while their representation in the Middle East employment category is lowest compared to other ethnic groups. The 11.3% of Muslims employed and 9.4% of Sinhalese are represented in the Middle East employment category.

INCOME DISTRIBUTION AND LIFE STYLE

As far as income distribution in terms of ethnic groups is concerned, Tamils are concentrated in the lower strata of income categories relative to the Sinhalese and Muslims. Income is more or less evenly distributed between the latter two categories. More than 50% of Tamils fall within the bottom two income categories while the majority of Sinhalese and Muslims are enjoying over Rs. 1000 in family income. Tamil representation in the top two income categories is below 2% while more than 10% of Sinhalese and Muslims fall within that category (table 3.8).

It is interesting to examine the profile of income more qualitatively in relation to the main sources of different social categories. Data on earnings and income which have been elicited by oral interviews of this study are generally subject to a bias of underestimates, particularly among people who are engaged in employment activities which are of a highly informal and illegal nature.

Table 3.5

Types of Employment

Type	*N*	Percent
Skilled Permanent	180	16.8
Unskilled Permanent	290	27.0
Unskilled Temporary	178	16.5
Self Employed	140	13.1
Business	38	3.5
Middle East	91	8.5
Clerical and Allied	135	12.6
Administrative and Managerial	21	2.0
Total	1,073	

Table 3.6

Types of Employment by Ethnic Groups

Type of Employment	*N*	Sinhala (%)	Tamil (%)	Muslim (%)	Other (%)
Skilled Permanent	180	72.2	11.7	8.9	7.2
Unskilled Permanent	290	61.0	19.7	16.9	2.4
Unskilled Temporary	178	40.4	34.3	22.5	2.8
Self-Employed	140	57.9	15.0	22.1	5.0
Business	38	76.3	2.6	21.1	—
Middle East Unskilled	91	69.2	2.2	23.1	5.5
Clerical/Allied	135	74.8	10.4	12.6	2.2
Administrative/ Managerial	21	81.0	—	19.0	—
Total	1,073				

Table 3.7

Sector of Employment by Ethnic Groups

Ethnic Group	*N*	Private Sector (%)	Govn't Sector (%)	Self-Employed (%)	Middle East (%)
Sinhala	670	40.6	33.6	16.4	9.4
Tamil	177	72.3	14.1	12.4	1.2
Muslim	186	54.8	12.9	21.0	11.3
Other	40	42.5	27.5	17.5	12.5
Total	1,073				

Table 3.8

Income Distribution by Ethnic Groups

Ethnic Groups	*N*	A 0-500	B 501-1000	C 1001-2000	D 2001-4000	E 4001-7500	F Over 7500
Sinhala	445	5.2	28.5	32.0	21.3	9.5	3.5
Tamil	109	12.3	43.0	31.7	11.4	0.8	0.8
Muslim	124	8.4	31.9	32.6	15.0	10.3	1.8
Other	21	—	28.5	19.1	28.6	23.8	—
Total	669						

Note: Total Number of households is 724. The data on income is available only for 699 households.

The indigenous professional group has a little over 52% in professional categories, 35% in the working class category, while 13% are in the business category. Even though this group has employed people in all these categories, the principal income earners belong to the professional category. The qualitative data shows that the majority of the indigenous land-owning group is engaged in professional activities while a fair proportion are engaged in working class occupations. Notable features of the occupational distribution among other Sinhala migrants are: (1) A fair proportion of the southerners and those who come from other areas of the country are engaged in professional activities. (2) Most of the medium and upper scale business activities belong to the southerners. (3) The bottom level business activities belong to the Colombo Sinhalese group. (4) The majority of the southerners and people from other parts of the country and other parts of Colombo are employed in the public sector. (5) Most of the people from the hinterland of Colombo work in private sector companies. (6) Tamils of estate or Indian origin largely work in the municipal council and slaughter house at Dematagoda.

As stated earlier, this community derives its income from various sources. But the pattern of the derivation of income is not the same in respect to each household or social group. There are households which derive their income solely from one source. Some other households obtain their income from many sources but one source is predominant, and there is another set of households deriving their income from two or three sources which are equally important.

The income of the indigenous leading group comes from activities such as bucketshops, clubs, trade in narcotics, moneylending, etc., and their legal business activities constitute the running of hotels, selling fish, firewood and renting houses. This group is the highest income earning group among all social groups except for the company owners and shareholders of companies. Most of the income avenues of this group have been inherited from their parents along with the clientele. Owing to their stable financial position they are able to enter into new areas of activity while expanding their existing activities. According to their perception, all family members should engage in income earning activities. Although the income of this group fluctuates, they are financially stable.

The second category of the indigenous land-owning group is comprised of those engaged in some other activities while the head of the household is employed in a private or a public sector institution. The major portion of income of these households is derived not from professional but from other activities such as running boarding houses, renting low cost houses, running small boutiques, moneylending, etc. There are no employed youth in this category; they are in the process of education.

Among the southerners, those who are engaged in medium scale business activities earn the highest income. The poorest among the southerners are those who are employed in working class occupations. In this group, unemployment is a significant factor.

There are a few southerners engaged in business activities within the area with temporary residences while their families reside in their home areas. Other family members are employed in home gardening, but the produce of home gardening is not enough even for the family consumption.

Those who have come from other parts of the country are largely engaged in working class occupations or in bottom-level professional activities. There are very marginal numbers engaged in even small scale business. Ten percent of employed persons in this category have some technical skills and are engaged in those activities on a regular or irregular basis. The residents who have come from the hinterland of Colombo derive their income mainly from working class occupations and from other non-skilled activities. In this category, few people are engaged in professional and medium scale business and no one is engaged in small scale business. A notable feature here is that the bulk of the unemployed persons is drawn from this category. The income capacity of each household in this group is relatively average, but this income is not enough for their consumption requirements owing to the fact that they have large families.

Those who have come from other parts of Colombo derive their income largely from working class employment. But a considerable proportion of this category earn their income in two to three ways. Apart from working class occupations, they are engaged in bottom-level professional activities. Small scale businesses, including brokering and some other technical and mechanical activities, are other income sources for them. Unemployment is marginal in this category.

Tamils of estate or Indian origin largely belong to the working class category but a large number work on a casual basis. There are a fair number of residents engaged in repairing umbrellas and padlocks as well as in cobbling activities. Some households engage in agricultural work in the city as coolie workers (unskilled labor). Most of the women in this category sell *green leaves* (vegetables). Some households in this category are engaged in sanitary services such as the drainage and scavenging activity in the Municipal Council. This group can be identified as the poorest group in the urban areas. In this group, there are no income disparities as in the other social groups in the community.

The lifestyle of the community was measured in terms of the nature of furniture that each household possessed and the internal household arrangement. Four types have been identified in this study and are described below. Note that these four types could be sub-classified generally into three categories on the basis of cleaning, maintenance, and organizing space within the house.

Type A: Houses constituted with separate living room, dining room, bedrooms and a kitchen. They possess furniture with the latest styles and modern appliances and electrical goods (refrigerators, fans, tape recorders). Houses are decorated with wall hangings; plaques and other ornaments are present.

Type B: As in the first type, they have enough space with specific functional rooms, but the space is not used for those specific purposes. They possess all the necessary furniture but not of the latest style and it is not well maintained. Electrical appliances are not predominantly used.

Type C: This type does not have adequate space, therefore the available space is used for a variety of purposes. Furniture is generally old or new but of cheap quality. The number of items varies from family to family but it is sufficient for their needs.

Type D: These houses with limited space possess only a couple of old or broken chairs, a low quality table, and a few mats for sleeping. In addition, they may have a trunk or two to hold clothing and a few kitchen utensils.

The majority of Sinhalese (52%) and Muslims (67%) belong to the Type C category, while the majority of Tamils occupy the Type D category (55%). A significant percentage of Sinhalese and Muslims enjoy Type B while only 5% of Tamils fall within that group. There are only 12% of Sinhalese and 2% of Muslims enjoying the Type A category while none of the Tamils enjoys the Type A category of lifestyle (table 3.9).

Table 3.9

Lifestyle Ranking by Ethnic Groups

Ethnic Group	*N*	A (%)	B (%)	C (%)	D (%)
Sinhala	445	12.6	19.3	52.7	15.4
Tamil	109	—	5.5	39.5	55.0
Muslim	124	2.4	19.4	67.8	10.4
Other	21	5.0	19.0	38.0	38.0
Total	699				

Note: Total number of households is 724. The data on income is available only for 699 households.

LAND AND HOUSING

Land is a limited resource within the location except for three social groups. In the early days, land was the most important resource for the indigenous professional groups. The *Walauwwa Land* (land owned by the Mansion) was fragmented due to marriages, and subsequently most of the land was sold out. By the 1930s, the land which was owned by the indigenous leading group was also fragmented due to marriages. The houses, and some business places which were owned by the indigenous leading group, were recently acquired by the government for political reasons. The company owners and upper level professionals bought land at the auctions of the balance of the land of the *Walauwwa* (Mansion) in 1965. The indigenous professional group and company owners have land with only a residential value while the indigenous leading group owns business premises in addition to residential land. To other groups, land is not a resource within the location. External land is a resource for some of the residents of other groups, and 35% of the residents have land internally, externally or both. Southerners have more land than others. For them external land, particularly in the village areas, is a considerable resource. External land is a real asset for some of the residents from the ideological point of view. They are proud of having hometown land they can claim for their roots. The residents of the poorest categories reside mainly on government land.

For the whole community, housing is the most important instrument through which they acquire other resources. These houses are direct resources to some outside residents. After 1956 and especially in the mid-1960s, most of the house owners auctioned their houses. Most of these houses were bought by the residents themselves and the rest by outside investors. As a result of this, some residents had to leave the area. On one occasion there was a conflict between these two groups, and the UNP (United National Party) supported the house owners while the SLFP (Sri Lanka Freedom Party) extended its support to the tenants.

There are twenty-one house owners who have one extra house for renting in this location. There are fourteen house owners who have at least two houses but no more than five. There are three residents who sublet a portion of their houses. Two house owners belong to the indigenous leading group while another three house owners belong to the indigenous professional group. Eighteen house owners do not reside in the location; they largely reside in peripheral rural areas such as

Kolonnawa, Wallampitiya, Gothatuwa, etc. Sometimes house owner–tenant relationships create conflicts when the owners ignore renovating the houses regularly and also when the tenants are asked to vacate their residences.

Land and housing are two of the main resources which influence the community structure. Land is very scarce in this community except for those who belong to the indigenous leading group and the indigenous landowning group. The land ownership of other groups is entirely limited to the land on which their houses have been built. The ownership of these people is as a result of either having bought land or the houses in which they reside having been vested in them. External land ownership is a significant characteristic of the migrants with 58% of them from the southern part of the country, owning land to the extent of one-quarter to four acres (this amount is calculated on the assumption that land might be divided equally among family members). The balance of 42% have not inherited or bought any land in their home areas. Twenty percent of migrants from other parts of the country own land; their individual portion does not exceed two acres. Those who have come from the hinterland of Colombo and from other parts of Colombo have no inherited land.

Although the indigenous leading group does not possess inherited land, they have acquired property. The land on which their residence has been put up is in the region of 20 to 40 perches. In addition to that, they have houses which have been rented to the migrants both within the location and outside. All these houses have been acquired during the period 1920 to 1950. They acquired this land and houses at very cheap prices compared with present values. Most of the houses owned by this group have been vested in the National Housing Department in 1972 and 1973.

The indigenous land-owning group has inherited land in the range of eight to forty perches. A few members of this group extended their land by buying adjacent blocks. Some of them have bought 20 to 40 perches in the peripheral rural areas.

Everyone in the leading business group (98% of them are southerners) has inherited land and most are able to purchase more land in their home areas. A very few original migrants of this group sold their land after their parents died. This group resides in Dematagoda and in the peripheral areas of Colombo. They have bought land and put up houses. Most of them acquired their property after 1940 in Colombo or the suburbs.

The company owners or shareholders of companies and upper level professionals migrated to the areas after buying land to the extent of 20 to 40 perches and erecting their houses. They bought land from the *Walauwwa* (Mansion) people at auctions during the 1960s.

The housing ownership pattern reveals that 267 houses are owned by the resident (including houses vested in them by the National Housing Department). Sixty-six are tenants of private house owners and 19 are tenants of the National Housing Department; 186 houses are government apartments and 157 houses are built on government land. The ownership status by ethnic groups is enumerated in table 3.10. This data indicates that 57% of Sinhalese, 85% of Tamils, and 71% of Muslims reside either as tenants of private owners or the government or reside in houses built on government land. A high proportion of southerners own their own housing while a small minority of the same group resides on government land or in government apartments. Tamils of Indian origin have shown a marked preference for government land, more so than other groups. The general tendency of the other groups is to look for rented and National Housing Department housing units.

As far as housing ownership status is concerned, it is important to note one striking feature in this community. Some residents in government apartments or residing in houses built on government land have a sense of disguised ownership though they do not have legal title to the land and/or house. This is due to the practice of transferability of houses from one tenant to another, particularly after 1970. This transferability takes the form of a buying and selling transaction. The prices are not according to formal supply and demand but rather arbitrary, depending upon the circumstances and the nature of the relationship of both parties of buyers and sellers. The total number of these transactions by type of houses is given in table 3.11.

Table 3.10

Ownership Status by Ethnic Groups

Ethnic Group	N	Own House (%)	Tenants (%)	Government Apartments (%)	Housing Department (%)	Government Land (%)	Other (%)
Sinhala	445	48.1	8.3	17.8	2.9	22.7	0.2
Tamil	109	13.8	17.4	34.9	3.7	29.3	0.9
Muslim	124	27.4	8.1	48.4	0.8	13.7	1.6
Other	21	19.0	—	42.9	4.8	33.3	—
Total	699						

Note: Total number of households is 724. The data on ownership status is available only for 699 households.

Table 3.11

Informal Transactions of Houses

Type of Houses	Before 1950	1951-1960	1961-1970	1971-1980	1981-1985
Permanent	6	9	27	46	31
Semi-Permanent	0	3	0	2	3
Improvised	0	0	0	0	5

HOUSING AND AMENITIES

Housing is a tangible and symbolic resource for everyone in Sri Lanka. Thus, it is important to enumerate the type of housing and its associated facilities. The type of houses in this community, in comparison to the Colombo urban sector, is given in table 3.12.

As far as main facilities are concerned, 9% of the permanent structures of this community do not have electricity, while the majority of semi permanent (85%) and improvised housing are not electrified. The main source of lighting in non-electrified houses is kerosene. But there are two types of lighting systems with kerosene oil: chimney lamp and bottle lamp. The people who use the bottle lamp represent, economically and symbolically, the bottom level of status in the community. Of the total, 18% use bottle lamp while 15% use chimney lamp. The source of lighting in comparison to the Colombo urban sector is given in table 3.13.

Pipe borne water is a luxury enjoyed by only 60% of the people living in Colombo, while pipe borne sewage is only available for 22% of the city's population. According to a 1975 survey, 69% of the improvised housing units did not have latrine facilities and more than 9% of households obtained water from a source outside the house. On the average for the whole city, one tap was used by 50 or more families. The type of accessibility to water and latrine facilities by type of housing structures in the study community is given in table 3.14. This indicates that 58% of the families have pipe borne common water facilities, 43% of permanent houses also do not have a private water source, and 2% of the families have access to their neighbors' private taps.

It is important to note the disparity of occupancy pattern in terms of ethnic groups. The majority of Sinhalese (70%) and Muslims (85%) are residing in permanent houses while the significant percentage of Tamils are residing in semi permanent and improvised housing units (table 3.15).

In terms of housing, the improvised housing units comprise structures built mainly of non-durable materials such as cadjan (woven coconut leaves), jute-husk or old zinc sheets, and are constructed by unauthorized occupation of private, government, and municipal land.

Table 3.12

Types of Houses Between Colombo Urban Sector and the Location

Nature of Houses	Colombo Urban Sector		Study Community	
	N	(%)	*N*	(%)
Permanent	145,140	75.0	490	70.1
Semi-Permanent	38,460	19.9	126	18.0
Improvised	9,772	5.1	83	11.9
Total	193,372		699	

Table 3.13

Source of Lighting

Source	Colombo Urban Sector		Study Community	
	N	(%)	*N*	(%)
Electricity	103,374	53.5	465	67.0
Kerosene	86,605	44.8	234	33.0
Other	177	.1	0	—
None	352	.2	0	—
Not Stated	2,864	1.5	0	—
Total	193,372		699	

Table 3.14

Sources of Water and Latrine by Type of House

	WATER				LATRINE			
Type of House	*N*	Public (%)	Private (%)	Neighbor (%)	*N*	Public (%)	Private (%)	Neighbor (%)
Permanent	490	43.8	54.9	1.3	490	45.2	54.4	0.4
Semi Permanent	126	93.1	4.6	2.3	126	88.2	3.9	7.9
Improvised	83	92.6	—	7.4	83	26.5	1.2	72.3
Total	699				699			

Table 3.15

Types of Houses by Ethnic Groups

Ethnic Group	*N*	Permanent (%)	Semi-Permanent (%)	Improvised (%)
Sinhala	445	70.1	16.9	13.0
Tamil	109	53.2	34.9	11.9
Muslim	124	85.5	8.1	6.4
Other	21	66.7	14.3	19.0
Total	699			

The scarcity of land and unaffordable prices cause overcrowding with improvised housing units. In the city of Colombo, the occupancy rate had grown from 7.11 in 1963 to 7.76 per unit in 1971. To make this situation worse, the number of housing units in the city of Colombo had increased during 1963 to 1971 by no more than a total of 0.6%, although the growth of population here reached 9.8% in the same period. (Quest 1980, 62:13) The occupancy rate in Dematagoda is 6.0%, but the rate of improvised housing units is higher (11.9%) than the Colombo rate (5.1%) due to the scarcity of land.

THE INTERNAL–EXTERNAL RESOURCE BALANCE AND CONTROL OF RESOURCES

This section mainly focuses on the examination of the resource structure in relation to its external and internal aspects. Dematagoda is viewed as one of the sub-systems of the Colombo resource base. These sub-systems are predominantly characterized by commercial activities with few individual employment opportunities. Dematagoda is a commercial center which is surrounded by a larger residential area. There are nearly seven centers which display such a configuration. The population of Dematagoda is 2.4% of Colombo's population. The employment at Dematagoda is nearly 2% of Colombo's total employment. Out of the total employment, nearly 70% are employed outside the area. Of this 70% figure, 90% are employed within Colombo city. Dematagoda has several individual employment avenues when compared with other areas of Colombo, but all these opportunities are not fully exploited by the residents of the area. The proportional share of the employment opportunities of the area is nearly 10%, and 20% of the total employed exploit the market opportunities in the area. A very marginal share of the Dematagoda market is exploited by outside residents and by the temporary residents of the area. Most of the goods flow into the area from the interior parts of the country via the central market. These goods are both consumer goods and raw materials. A small segment of the population provides various types of services to outside communities as well as inside the community. Twelve percent of all those employed exploit outside market opportunities of the small scale type. The Dematagoda market caters to both residents of the area as well as to outsiders, particularly from the peripheral rural areas.

A larger network of resources is based in Colombo, even in illegal activities. Even so, Dematagoda's share of this resource is considerable owing to the fact that those who control this are able to cover a larger area and have a prominent place in the wider network of the city. As an example, it is interesting to examine the network of resources by looking at the punting or bucketshop business in relation to its internal and external share. One family group dominates the bucketshop activity while five others are also engaged in it. These people belong to the indigenous leading group. This activity has a large network as 45% of the residents patronize the punting activity. They usually spend at least Rs. 2 per day. The sum expended goes up particularly on salary advance days and pay days. Sometimes the residents who are engaged in the punting activity mortgage their movable properties to the agents when they have no money for punting. One person in the indigenous group manages the betting and pays the winners. He has at least 35 agents collecting bets. In the early days he operated jointly with his brother. Today the two brothers engage in the activity separately. In those days the total collection per day was in the range of Rs. 10,000 to Rs. 20,000. At present it varies between Rs. 30,000 to Rs. 50,000. The average monthly income for the brothers is in the range of Rs. 5,000 to Rs. 10,000. There are nearly twenty collecting agents within the location with about ten agents from the peripheral rural areas and a few agents from government departments and corporations.

Besides the person who dominates this activity, there are about seven others. Patron–client relationships exist between the major collectors and their agents in the matter of collecting and keeping the bet money. The latter are given employment, commissions, credit, and other favors. They resort to the patron in times of crisis for favors such as protection from the police and the use of motor vehicles for urgent needs. These favors are reciprocated with service, respect, and continued employment under the patron.

The number of agents and the total collections of every other patron are less than that of the dominant patron. The number of agents varies between five and ten. They are also engaged in other activities such as lending money, running hotels, selling narcotics, etc. Their total income per month is in the range of Rs. 4000 to Rs. 8000.

The total collections per day from each peripheral area is in the region of Rs. 4000 to Rs. 8000. Kaduwela and Korathota are two of the highest collecting areas. The commissions paid to the agents depend upon the amount of collections. However, the commission is in the range of 10% to 20%. There are four agents who get 15% or more within the location; others get 10% or more. The large majority of agents are from Colombo and its hinterland.

The dominant patron provides employment opportunities other than as collecting agents. These employees are nearly 30 in number. Their duties are in bookkeeping and accounting activities. They are night workers. These employees are paid Rs. 25 per night with tea; the cashier is paid an extra amount which is usually more than Rs. 30.

COMMERCIAL AND INDUSTRIAL ACTIVITIES

The total business units in the selected community number nearly 200. Of these, 118 are in permanent or semi-permanent structures; the rest belong to the pavement business activities. Business activities of the area are largely handled by the Sinhalese, particularly the southerners. The Sinhalese account for 85% of the total business units (permanent or semi-permanent) while Tamils and Muslims account for 5% and 10% respectively. Pavement hawkers are mainly Sinhalese with a few Tamil women engaged in selling vegetables.

The retail business was handled in the early days by Indian Tamils who did not have citizenship. In the early part of the 1950s, *Kallathoni* (illegal aliens) were expelled from the area and those business premises were controlled by the indigenous leading group. Thereafter, Jaffna Tamils gradually obtained these premises and engaged in retail trade. However, the 1958 communal riots affected them negatively. Despite these effects, they were able to continue in retail trade until the 1978 communal riots.

The semi-permanent business premises, which come within the jurisdiction of the municipal administration, are largely controlled by the Colombo residents and by those who have come from the hinterland of Colombo. It is a fact that these business stalls were first acquired by these Colombo residents and subsequently sublet to the businessmen who have mainly come from the southern part of the country. The first acquisition of the stalls can only be accomplished through political links.

The business units can be classified into seven categories: (1) retail and groceries, (2) textile and jewelry, (3) perishable food items, (4) hotels and restaurants, (5) hardware, (6) manufacturing, and (7) services.

The distribution of activities by ethnic groups is given in table 3.16. The fixed capital, volume of trade, and the profit margin of main business activities are enumerated in table 3.17.

Most of the consumer items which are sold at the Dematagoda market, come through the wholesale distribution system of Colombo. Vegetables, fish, textiles, and hardware are some of these major items. There are few exceptions to the main distribution system. Coconut is one such main item. Coconuts are brought from the Negambo, Chilaw, and Kurunegala areas. The large scale intermediate businessmen exploit this opportunity. Ninety-five percent of the total quantity of vegetables to Dematagoda market is brought from the central market in Pettah. The other 5% constitute *keera* leaves which are cultivated within the area and the produce brought from the rural hinterland of the city. Fish is brought from the central market, and whenever there is a scarcity, some traders go to Negambo to purchase fish. Some seasonal traders come from Moratuwa and their output is between Rs. 200 and Rs. 500.

Retail trade depends on the Pettah main wholesale market. There are two to three intermediaries who bring chilies, onions, and dry fish from the dry zone and sell these items at low prices. However, they are not regular suppliers.

Firewood is brought from Padukka, Kaduwela, Hanwella, and Avissawella areas. The employment opportunities in these firewood depots are exploited by the people who belong to the marginal groups of the city and a few Tamils from Indian origin.

The fiber processing industry which is located in the area, uses about 25 to 30 tons of fiber per week. The fiber is imported from Negambo, Chilaw, and Wennappuwa areas. This industry provides employment for nearly 400 workers, of which 200 have been recruited from the peripheral rural areas of the city. Nearly 150 are from other rural areas and the rest from the same locality. In the early days the majority of the employees were from the locality. Once some employees attempted to form a trade union with external political connections; a dispute arose with the owner over the terms and conditions of employment. The management responded by retrenching workers from the locality.

Today the employer–employee relationship takes on the form of a patron–client relationship of a contractual nature. A male employee is paid Rs. 250 to Rs. 300 per month while females are paid on a piece rate basis. Each female worker can earn Rs. 100 to Rs. 200 per month.

Table 3.16

Business Activities by Ethnic Groups

Business	*N*	Sinhala (%)	Tamil (%)	Muslim (%)
Retail & Groceries	40	75.0	15.0	10.0
Textile & Jewelry	11	72.7	—	27.3
Perishable Foods	31	100.0	—	—
Hotels & Restaurants	10	70.0	—	30.0
Hardware	1	100.0	—	—
Manufacturing	5	60.0	—	40.0
Services	20	100.0	—	—
Total	118			

Table 3.17

Business Activities and Scale of Operation

Business	Fixed Capital (Rs.)	Volume of Trade (Rs.)	Profit Margin (%)
Retail/Groceries			
Medium	20,000 - 30,000	3,000 - 4,000	10-15
Small	10,000 - 2,000	1,000 - 2,000	10-15
Textile			
Medium	75,000 - 150,000	1,000 - 2,000	20-25
Perishable Food			
Fish	1,000 - 1,500	3,000 - 5,000	15-20
Vegetable	1,000 - 150	200 - 600	10-15
Hotels/Restaurants	3,000 - 50,000	2,000 - 5,000	25-40

Note: Volume of Trade equals the value of total sales per day.

Some workers are engaged in the personal activities of the owner. All these services are performed with due respect and loyalty and are reciprocated with money, credit, and other favors in various life crises of the employees. The labor regulations are not adhered to.

RESOURCE CONCENTRATION AND STRUCTURAL IMPLICATIONS

The majority of this community earn their living working as skilled–unskilled laborers in Colombo city. Thus, this area was referred to as a working class community. The internal economy provides the resource base for the people who occupy the apex of the hierarchy. They are the power holders and patrons of the community. They provide direct income or access to means of income for certain segments of the population.

The economic base of the indigenous leading group consists of both legitimate and illegitimate activities. The illegitimate, underworld activities bring them a disproportionately high income. Nevertheless, it is difficult to make clear-cut demarcation between legitimate and illegitimate income—both are complementary to each other.

The indigenous leading group enjoys more resources than others. Their earning capacity is very high. As a result, they play the role of patron not only to this community but also to peripheral areas. Their patronage cuts across various levels in Colombo. Even politicians, lawyers, and officials are patronized by them. This patronage is reciprocated with services provided by these politicians and officials. The degree of patronizing capacity contributes to the network of relationships which has direct implications on the community structure.

The total network of relationship emanating from the resource structure of the community takes a hierarchical form with vertical integration. The forthcoming chapters will focus on the process by which the total network of the community, particularly the urban institutional system, is operating in the context of given resource structure.

Chapter 4

Migration and Kinship

The pattern of in-migration has a significant impact on the total community structure of Dematagoda. This pattern can be analyzed in terms of the decision making process of the migrants. The economic conditions, the set of social and cultural values, and the social network of migrants are closely related to their decision making. The economic motive, given in the push-pull hypothesis, has to be viewed within a framework of differential perception and evaluation, situations involving possibilities of migration (Lansing and Muller 1967; Shaw 1985).

Four main elements of migrants' decision making process have been identified in the literature: (1) aspiring—migration is perceived and evaluated as an opportunity toward realizing ambitions and aspiration; (2) dislocated—migration is viewed as a recurring solution to limitations of the place of origin; (3) resultant—migration is perceived and evaluated as an alternative to factors such as unemployment or as a means to realize specific and limited objectives; (4) epiphenomenal—migration is viewed as means to contend with unique personal factors such as health problems and marriage (Taylor 1966, cited in S.R. Paul 1975, 107-108).

This pattern of decision making requires a structural explanation at the place of origin as well as the destination. Therefore, the examination of motivational types and factors which underlie the decision making of migrants in light of structural characteristics and the interactional system of respondents is the main focus of this chapter. Kinship relationship is given a prominent place in the interaction of the network system of migrants. The varying degree of this interaction has significant ramifications on persons' lives and the community structure.

REASONS FOR MIGRATION

There are five major reasons given by the respondents for their migration to Colombo: (1) occupation, (2) accompanied parents or joined relatives in Colombo, (3) runaway due to economic or unhealthy family environment, (4) marriage, and (5) education. Breakdowns within the sample are given in table 4.1.

Table 4.1

Reasons for Migration

Reasons	*N*	Percent
Occupation	14	38
Accompanied Parents	12	32
Runaway	5	14
Marriage	4	11
Education	2	5
Total	37	

Runaways due to economic or unhealthy family environment. The runaway group is characterized by economic difficulties and an unhealthy family environment. These adverse social and economic conditions push most of the young children from their homes. They possess hardly any land or the limited landownership is nonproductive. The respondents' recollections of their past reveal some kind of land disputes or encroachment by kinsmen on the paternal and/or maternal side. Most of these young migrants started their journey without knowing their destiny and were filled with uncertainty. Among this group, some came directly to Colombo while others spent some years in other parts of the country doing various things for their living.

A 57 year old Sinhala male businessman says:

> I was born in Gampaha (in Gampaha District) which is my mother's native place. My father is from Yakkala. He lived with mother in Gampaha. I went to a private college in Gampaha. I passed grade eight. My father's occupation was farming. My mother died when I was in grade six. After my mother died, I did not feel the need to go to school and study. There was no one to lovingly attend to my needs. I was the only child. Three years after my mother's death, my father got married to another woman. My stepmother did not treat me well. After three years of father's second marriage, I left home (ran away) and came to Colombo and lived with one of my mother's relatives who was living on Veluwana Road in Dematagoda (in this community). When I left home, I had Rs. 350 which I had earned doing various things. I started selling vegetables on the pavement at Dematagoda with the help of my relative. (07/01/1985)

A 54 year old male Sinhala and a self-employed person says:

> I was born in Kothmale Moratuwa (Nuwara Eliya). This was my parents' native place too. I went to the school in the village. I studied up to grade five. My father did farming and small business. My mother died when I was 11 years of age. I was the youngest of the family which consists of nine members (four brothers and four sisters). My brothers and sisters also did not get much education. We did not feel it necessary to get an education as farming was the occupation in this area. My parents had some claims to inherited lands, but there were other members who had

> rights to those lands. Therefore, we had rights only to a share of the harvest and the original house where we lived together. I left home when I was 11 years old. Only one of my sisters was married by then. None of the others had a job. My father had an affair with another woman even when my mother was living. He used to go to her home. This also caused the death of my mother. I did not receive love and compassion from anybody. Father did not look after the household expenditures. Yams, jack fruit and something picked up from the forest were the meal. If I ate rice for a meal, it was occasionally. I can't remember who gave me that meal. I can't remember exactly how others lived in my family. Under these conditions I decided to run away from home. Nobody influenced me. I left home and came to Gampola and told my situation to a boutique keeper who had rental camps. (05/02/1985)

OCCUPATIONAL AMBITION

The group with occupational aspirations could be divided into two categories: (1) migrants after obtaining a job, and (2) youths pushed out from their villages due to economic difficulties who then lived with relatives with occupational aspirations. The following cases are good examples for these categories.

A 38 year old male Sinhala, employed in the Ceylon Transport Board as a security person, says:

> My native place is Bentera-Matara District. My father was from Tangalla (Matara District). My father stayed in Beliatta. He was a postmaster in the postal department. He had come to Beliatta after selling his own inherited land. My mother had six acres of coconut land. I got through my S.S.C. examination in 1961 from Beliatta Central College. My mother had died by then. We did not have an economic problem. My father's intention was to educate us. Our fate did not lead us to get an education. Everybody studied up to S.S.C. We felt that it was enough at that time. We did not realize the necessity of education. I felt that it was better to do a job and to be independent. My age was then 18 years. I was about 12 years old when my mother died. I felt a big incompleteness in my life. My sisters dropped out halfway from the school when mother died. My sisters and myself had to look

> after household matters. After my S.S.C. examination, I was doing nothing for nearly one year. In 1962, my father was able to find a job for me through one of his friends at Bata Shoo Company at Ratmalana in Colombo. (05/08/1985)

In another example, a 41 year old male Sinhala unemployed person says:

> I was born in Payagala in Kalutara District. I studied up to eighth grade. My father was a farmer. My parents had land ownership; most of that is unpartitioned inherited land. Our income was not enough. I stopped my studies and helped my father's work for nearly five years. In 1962, I came to Colombo and lived with one of my distant relatives (he refers to this distant relative as a sister) who lived in Dematagoda. While I was staying with them I was able to find a job at a fish market in Dematagoda through one of their friends. Those days I earned Rs. 30 per day. I gave some money to my sister for my expenses. And I also helped my mother. I worked in this fish market and stayed with my sister until 1971. In 1971, I was able to find a labor job at the Colombo Harbor. I obtained this job with the help of Peter Kenaman who was then a Cabinet Minister. I helped him in his political campaign when I was staying with my sister. (06/30/1985)

ACCOMPANIED WITH PARENTS

Some of the migrants who accompanied their parents also reveal the economic difficulties faced in their village setting. One such example is as follows.

A 44 year old Sinhala female, dependent on her children, says:

> My native place is Radawana (Gampaha District). My parents are from Pasyala. I was two years of age when my father died. No one from my mother's side looked after us. After my father's death we were in my native place nearly six to seven years. In those days only my grandmother (father's mother) helped us. My mother went for labor work, and prepared food for selling. But her earnings were not enough to feed us—myself and my sister. In those days one of my mother's aunts was living in Dematagoda,

> Colombo. They asked us to come over to their place. They had said to my mother that she could do a job in Colombo. My mother went to work in tailor shops as a helper. After some time we rented a house and lived separately. (05/29/1985)

Another variation to this category is due to transfers of their parents who were working in government departments. Most such employment transfers took place in the Ceylon Government Railway. One of the CGR quarters is located in Dematagoda and some migrants, as a result of employment transfers in 1970, put down permanent stakes in this location or surrounding areas.

MARRIAGE

All the migrants with marriage reasons are females. The bottom line of this migratory pattern is also connected with the hard economic realities. This study reveals that women in the lower economic strata in the rural setting fell in love with strangers from Colombo and entered into a marriage. It is interesting to note that most of these marriages were deviations from the acceptable rural norms, even though the marriage partners received parents' consent.

A 45 year old Sinhala, self-employed woman says:

> My marriage was a love affair. In those days, he used to come to our village to collect vegetables to sell in Colombo. Both sides of parents gave consent to our affair. In 1962 we got married. After that we came to this *garden* for residence. My husband had been born in this garden. (05/29/1985)

If they belonged to the upper strata in the rural setting they were forced to arrange marriages which largely tend towards rural migration rather than rural to urban. The poor economic condition and the practice of dowry make room for alternative marriage patterns and rural to urban migration. Rural to urban migration could be a possibility even in arranged marriages if a partner has a strong economic tie in the urban setting. There is one such example within the sample. A newly married Muslim couple migrated to this location renting out a house in 1982. The husband is a jewelry shop owner in Pettha.

It is interesting to note that there is only 21% of direct migration to the location from their rural setting; 79% of total rural migrants stayed in Colombo before they arrived in this location. The duration of stay in other areas of Colombo is generally varied from five to fifteen years. Some migrants tend to show high geographical mobility within Colombo. This high geographical mobility is largely correlated with high occupational mobility. This characterizes the pull factors with low quality employment opportunities of the urban sector. In other words, migration from one place to another is connected with the changes or instability in occupations.

Rural to urban migration is largely characterized by surplus rural labor. The absence of landownership, or unproductive land ownership, unhealthy family environment, and lack of rural employment pushed this rural labor out from their home areas. Within the sample, southern migrants possess some land when compared to the migrants from Sabaragamuwa province and the western province. This ownership of small plots of land among southerners did not retain them in their home areas due to large families and low income. Nevertheless, there was no magnet of employment opportunities to attract these rural laborers. Only those who were able to secure either a kinship connection or any other type of connection from the urban end migrated to Colombo. Some of those migrants initially were able to secure employment opportunities under their distant kinsmen. They worked as helpers in their kinsmen's business ventures until they secured employment elsewhere. In this process of establishment in Colombo, most of the migrants tend to experience instability and high occupational mobility.

Kinship Relationships

By recognizing the limitation of the conventional anthropological method, I did not repeat the collection of genealogical data in the community of Dematagoda. I did explore, as Epstein (1980) did in her study in Africa, the significance of kinship under urban conditions. The main focus is on categories of kinship interaction or the ways in which kinship relationship is used for various purposes. In agreement with Clyde Mitchell, Epstein said that kinship means quite different things in rural and urban context. It is a category of interaction within the wider urban system.

The circumstances that prevail in a town, however, may be quite different so that kinship relationships under urban conditions may become in a sense "destructured," stripped of much of their customary content; kinship here consists rather of broad categories of persons who stand in different degrees of blood and affinity to one another and acknowledge among themselves bonds of a rather diffuse solidarity (Epstein 1981, 192).

Five categories of relationships emerged from the empirical data of this study. They are: (1) strong relationship, (2) mutual dependence, (3) selective relationship, (4) limited to essential matters, and (5) severed or distant relationship. These categories indicate a continuum from intimate relationship to the severed relationship so that this typology is arbitrary and does some violence to each respondent's own concepts of social distance. However, I tried as much as possible to standardize these categories using my own judgment of the facts given on kinship relationship. These categories can be used for comparison.

Strong relationship. The respondents of this category generally maintain strong connections with most of their immediate relatives. This group observes more traditional practices in kinship relationship, visiting each other on ceremonial occasions and helping in family crises. They emphasize the importance of maintaining *Nedakama* (kinship) and *Sahodarakama* (brotherhood). They are not supposed to consider status gaps in terms of economic and occupational differences. The violation of these norms tend to sever the relationship. In fact, those who have a property base in their kinship relationship are more vulnerable. Nevertheless, the poorer partner generally tends to play a subordinate role in this relationship for economic gain, security and sympathy. In turn, he/she respects, shows loyalty, and gives his/her labor on important family occasions.

Mutual dependence. People in this category are more emotionally involved with each other. Their relationship is not confined to important life crises. The mutual help also goes beyond the economic terms and takes the form of very close affection, giving advice, and showing sympathy to each other. As in the first category, the established norms are very profound and the violation of these norms will end up with either severed or distant relationships.

Selective relationship. This category is characterized with many types such as strong, mutual dependence, limited to essential matters and severed or distant relationships. People of this category tend to maintain certain types of relationships with their relatives on a selective basis. There is a high degree of variability in their criteria of selection.

Limited to essential matters. The relationship in this category is largely confined to the important life crises such as funeral ceremonies, death anniversaries, wedding ceremonies, puberty functions, and serious illnesses of a relative. This relationship takes the form of formal visits in such life crises. It is confined to formal practices without having emotional involvement, but still maintaining *Nedakama.* There is no economic base or characteristics of mutual dependence in this relationship. Both parties may be economically independent either with equal or unequal status.

Severed or distant relationship. The absence of any connection or only very rare visits characterizes this relationship. The violation of norms, pertaining to the previous categories, changes those relationships into this category. The extreme level of poverty and the time and distance may also cause this type of relationship. The extreme version of this relationship is that both parties are not known to each other.

PROFILE OF KINSMEN CONCENTRATION

Family types. Forty-seven percent of this community's households are extended family units in which the respondent is living with at least one or two immediate relatives such as parents, brothers and sisters of either side or both sides of the married partners.

Ethnicity and kinship. The ethnic distribution by family type is as shown in table 4.2. This data indicates only slight differences among ethnic groups. This study reveals the majority (88.2%) maintain kinship relationships. Table 4.3 illustrates the type of relationship by ethnic groups. Of the total sample, 27% of Sinhalese, 19% of Muslims and 11% of Tamils maintain strong relationships. Muslims have the highest severed relationships, with Tamils and Sinhalese taking the second and third place, respectively. However, Muslims have the highest

Table 4.2

Family Type by Ethnic Groups

Ethnic Groups	*N*	Nuclear Family (%)	Extended Family (%)
Sinhala	60	53.3	45.7
Tamil	9	44.4	55.6
Muslim	16	56.3	43.7
Total	85		

Table 4.3

Kinship Relationship by Ethnic Groups

Ethnic Groups	*N*	Strong (%)	Mutual (%)	Selective (%)	Limited to Essential Matters (%)	Severed (%)
Sinhala	60	27	18	29	18	8
Tamil	9	11	22	45	11	11
Muslim	16	19	25	12	19	25
Total	85					

percentage of the mutual dependent type relationship compared to Sinhalese and Tamils. The selective relative relationship is more common among Tamils. Sinhalese and Muslims take the second and third place in maintaining selective relationships.

Place of origin and kinship. As far as kinship relationship by origin is concerned, the majority of the rural born people belonged to the strong category (30%). The mutual dependence type is highest among urban born. A relationship that is limited to essential matters is more common among locally born people than those in the urban born category. Among rural born, only 17% fall within this category. Maintenance of selective relationships is more or less equal between locally born and rural born. As far as severed relationships are concerned, they are highest among the urban born (23%). Among rural born it is only 8% while there are none in the category of locally born (table 4.4).

Table 4.4

Kinship Relationship by Origin

Origin	*N*	Strong (%)	Mutual (%)	Selective (%)	Limited to Essential (%)	Sev-ered (%)
Location Born	15	20	20	33	27	0
Rural Born	40	30	15	30	17	8
Urban Born	30	17	27	20	13	23
Total	85					

Kinship Types and Structural Dynamics

STRONG RELATIONSHIPS

The property base is a more profound factor for the maintenance of strong connections among southerners than among other migrants. This property relation is largely based on inherited landownership. The empirical evidence reveals two types of property connections in maintaining *Nedakama*: (1) Migrants who obtain a share of harvest, regularly or occasionally from their unpartitioned bilineal inheritance. (2) Migrants who have assigned a guardian role over their property to some of their relatives. The guardian relative is responsible for farming, protecting and sending the harvest for his/her urban relative. In turn, he/she gets a share for the guardian role. The *Nedakama* is usually strengthened by this property relation.

It is possible to identify two subcategories of migrants within the first type of property relations, in terms of their actual behavior. The first group is satisfied with their present relationship having regular or occasional harvest from their unpartitioned inheritance. The second group is aspiring to the partition of their inheritance before their parents' death. Therefore, a frequent visiting pattern before their parents' death is common among this group, whatever the given reason on customary grounds. However, it is interesting to note, even without materializing the aspiration to inherited land, the majority of migrants still tend to maintain *Nedakama* even after their parents' death. For example, a southern migrant, leading businessman who has stayed in this community more than 30 years, reduced his frequent visits to important family crises after his parents' death, but he still enjoys the *Nedakama*. He says:

> When my parents were alive, I used to go to my native place every two or three months. After their death, there was not much need. I have my unpartitioned inherited land. My younger brother looks after those. I am not going to claim my position (rights). I receive my share of the harvest once a year. (03/31/1985)

There are a few possible explanations for this decision. First, he might have had the intention to get partition of his inheritance by way of parents' intervention, if he considered that the total inheritance is big enough to share among brothers and sisters. Second, initiation of the partition idea, after their parents' death, would disrupt the *sahodarakama* which is relatively more important than the potential share of inheritance. Furthermore, the partition may run the risk of losing a trustworthy guardian role, presently played by his younger brother. Third, the initiation of partition idea might damage his position in his family circle, by showing unnecessary greediness. He has a fairly sound economic position, as he was identified in the category of leading business group in this urban community. Fourth, he gains more status within this community through his external kinship network.

The inherited land, in most of the cases, is not big enough to partition among relatives. For example a migrant from the southern province of the country, a 36 years old male, employed as a foreman in a public sector organization, gives his explanation in his case:

> I go to my native place once a month to visit my parents. My father's side inherited property which has been transferred to my father's brother. That land has two acres of paddy and one acre of highland with a house. My father's inheritance has also been transferred to him. We do not like to claim for this inheritance. Then we might lose *Nedakama*. He enjoys all of the family inheritance including the share of my aunts. No one can get benefit if it is divided into small pieces. (06/23/1985)

This implies the choice between a small portion of inherited land and the *Nedakama*. In this case, *Nedakama* is relatively more important than the inheritance. Furthermore, he intends to go back to his native place and settle down there, after his retirement from his government job. This decision is realistic for him as he has sole ownership from his maternal side. Therefore, his frequent visits to his parents and relatives have more economic logic than traditional customary practices.

> When I go to my native village every month I give Rs. 100 for my parents. My parents and sisters look after the paddy land and enjoy the harvest. But every season my mother sends rice for me. (06/23/1985)

The strong kinship relationship largely operates on an equal basis. A variation to this equal pattern can be seen between poorer migrants and their relatives. One or two relatives usually enjoy the inheritance. The economic position of the relatives at the native place is a little higher than the migrant. Therefore, the relatives who enjoy the property are obligated to give a portion of the harvest when the migrant visits them. However, it is not a contractual obligation, so the property inheritance is not the basis for a strong relationship.

Another variation in this category is characterized by a dependency relationship of respondents with their relatives. These people are largely dependent economically on some of their relatives who can help them in their life crises. However, the degree of dependency is varied from one case to another. On the one hand, the degree of dependency is shaped, to a certain extent, by the nature of the relationship that the respondent maintains with the community. On the other hand, the degree of dependency has an impact on the community shaping the household position in the community. The following is a good example of the importance of the dependency on external kin. A 38 year old Sinhala female is a non-migrant. She works as a clerk at the general hospital. According to her perception, her father was a businessman and had high status in this community. When she was in high school, the economic prosperity of the family began to fall. As a result, they lost the social status that they were enjoying in the community. Therefore, they wanted to regain the lost status. This was a family crisis. In this crisis her father's brother, a wealthy person living in Kandy District of Central Province helped them out by constructing a two story house which is one of the few in this community today. They consider construction of this house as a symbolic step in the process of regaining social status in the community.

A 34 year old Muslim male is another example for this category. He was born into a Sinhala family and was given to a Muslim family for adoption when he was an infant. He is a Muslim and married to a Muslim woman within the same family circle (it was a cross-cousin marriage proposed by foster parents). He is totally dependent on his wife's family. He has limited decision making in the family circle. His voting behavior is also influenced by family decisions. However, he is economically and socially secured by his wife's family. He plays a subordinate role to the family and maintains a strong attachment and connection within his family circle.

The kinship connections with native places of the leading group are more intense economically than any other group in this community. This group was able to obtain more land in their native places in addition to their inheritance. This group enlists the help of kinsmen to cultivate their land. They make frequent visits, at least three or four times a year. They make special visits and help kinsmen in their life crises. In addition to these visits and help, a share of produce is reciprocated with the kinsmen who play the guardian role and labor. The leading business group, to a greater extent, patronizes kinsmen in their home areas. They recruit young labor from among their kinsmen as assistants in their business in Colombo. Furthermore, they encourage and provide necessary initial assistance to those who want to migrate to Colombo from their home areas.

The leading business group also has a large kinship network within the city and in the suburbs. Most of their relatives are also engaged in business activities within Colombo or in the periphery of Colombo. This kin group is largely characterized by mutual dependency and cohesiveness. They assist each other in their business ventures and in their life crises. They borrow money from each other for their investment activities. Cross-cousin marriages are taking place within this kin group. The leading business group tends to avoid marriage partners from Colombo residents. They stick to either their own kin group or to their own business group who have come from the southern part of the country.

Migrants in the first category, with rural origin, tend to maintain *Nedakama* as much as possible even without having property or economic base. The majority of this group is from the districts of Western Province (Kalutara, Gampaha, and Colombo). They are very proud about this relationship. They enjoy social status through this relationship and tend to look down on the others who do not practice kinship relationship. One of my informants expressed, "We are not people who have just dropped from the sky as some of the people living in this community."

The respondents in this group emphasize the necessity of maintaining kinship relationship in many different ways. They do not want to behave in an unacceptable manner. They observe traditional practices as much as possible to continue this relationship. For example, a middle age community leader who has migrated from Gampaha district, expressed his fear of violating certain norms related to marriage rules.

> There is no caste problem. I do not consider it at all . . . but caste has to be considered in a marriage of a child. Otherwise, we can't face our relatives. Perhaps our relatives will shun us. We have a certain fear about that. (04/30/1985)

Even the younger generation of the indigenous professional group desire to maintain *Nedakama* without any economic basis. A twenty year old college student expressed his views:

> I feel that we are not alone. Among relatives we have participation and cooperation. I can obtain unknown information from our kinsmen. We have strong connections among our relatives. (04/26/1985)

The underlying logic of this relationship directly relates to their total social network in the community. This group is deriving more status from their kin network and tries to maintain a superordinate position in the community.

LIMITED TO ESSENTIAL MATTERS

Four major reasons are expressed by the respondents for the confinement of their relationship to essential matters. They are: (1) close relationship will lead to many problems and disrupt the *Nedakama,* (2) time and distance, (3) the economic difficulties of both parties, and (4) social distance among relatives. Those giving the first reason are very sensitive to maintaining relationships with their relatives. This particular way of behavior is adopted in order to continue the relationship. There is a necessity of maintaining kinship relationships confined to essential matters. For example, a 40 year old Sinhala male respondent says:

> The close affection will not last long. There should be a limit. It is necessary to participate in a wedding function and funeral with or without contributing. If we intervene with each other in day to day matters we will lose *Nedakama.* (06/09/1985)

Three reasons could be drawn for this type of behavior: (1) The absence of property transaction among relatives, (2) both parties are economically independent from each other, and (3) each possess a certain degree of social status through this kin network.

Both the time factor and the geographical distance prevent close kinship relationships. The members in this group are busy with their daily economic activities. The majority in this group has a very tight monthly budget. Travelling far away to visit their relatives will affect their living conditions. Time is an important factor for those who are engaged in self-employment activities without having substantial income.

The third group is characterized by extreme poverty. Both parties are not able to help each other or visit each other. They are largely engaged in unskilled types of work and do not have regular income. A 54 year old respondent's case best exemplifies the nature of this relationship.

> I have five brothers and sisters. I do not go to any one of them. We live.... If we have, we eat, otherwise we do not, we do not like to go and bother them. We visit them only on weddings and funerals. There is no way to visit them without any reason. (05/02/1985)

The fourth group tends to maintain relationships only for essential matters as their relatives have a higher status in terms of economic position, education and/or occupation. Even though their position in the family circle is relatively low, they do not want to maintain unequal relationship with their relatives. Therefore, the social distance with their relatives is common. A 43 year old Muslim male respondent describes his social distance in this manner.

> They are educated people. We did not get an education. They do not treat us properly.... Some of my wife's relatives visit us. But I do not expect any help from my relatives. I go to my friends. I do not go to my relatives even though I may starve. I do not like to be second in front of my relatives. It is better to go to my friends who help me before I ask, than go to my relatives. (05/05/1985)

This behavior indicates the protection of personal dignity in relation to his relatives. In this case his friendships are an alternative or substitute for his kin network. Therefore, he is in a position to maintain a social distance with his relatives.

MUTUAL DEPENDENCE

The empirical evidence reveals two types of relationship within the category of mutual dependence: (1) mutual dependence with equal relationship, and (2) playing a superordinate role to relatives. The socio-economic background of the first type has high variation. Economically it is possible to identify low income groups and middle income groups who maintain mutual dependence with equal relations. The middle income group within this type consists of both professional categories and minor employees and blue collar workers. Helping each other in their mutual distress is the common practice within this type of equal relationship. Many examples can be traced to illustrate these practices. One respondent in this study was interdicted from his work as a result of participating in a general strike which was held in 1980. During that period of nearly one year he was economically looked after by his relatives, brothers and sisters, and wife's relatives.

The second type within this category is characterized by entrepreneurial and/or leader types in the community. Their position in the family circle is relatively higher. They help economically in the family crises of their relatives so that they enjoy a superordinate role. However, this superordinate role has no contractual basis. The emotional involvement with each other is very high.

MAINTAIN DIFFERENT TYPES OF CONNECTIONS

The people who practice selective relationships place their emphasis largely on the established norms, and tend to give justification for their selection. The empirical evidence reveals generalized categories of relatives for this selection rather than individual relatives. These categories are: maternal side, paternal side, brothers and sisters, and spouse's side. The given issues for strong relationships and severed relationships are: property matters, help in crisis, practicing the norms of *Nedakama*, distance and economic difficulties and other reasons. Table 4.5 shows the given issues and the relative categories of selective relationship.

The expectation of help in a crisis situation is strong. The violation of these norms causes conflict among brothers and sisters and it perpetuates throughout generations. This is more applicable in an urban environment with a loose kinship ideology. Splitting up of relationship among relatives may start even with a personal reason. There is a good example for this type of relationship. A Sinhala male 44 year old respondent says:

> I had an objective when I was a young boy, in my life to achieve a certain position in the society. All of my aunts and their children united together. They did not love us, and father raised us with many difficulties. The aunts who had a certain level looked down upon us. My mother worked to give us an education. My sister got through only J.S.C. I had the interest to study. I got my J.S.C. certificate in 1957. My mother had told one of my aunts to find a job for me. Then my aunt had told my mother that there were no jobs and asked me to be a peon. (04/08/1985)

This might start with personal jealousies among in-laws. However, it persists through the next generation. One of this respondent's cross-cousin brothers occupies a political leadership position in the area (he is the ward member representing the municipal council). This episode implies some hidden conflict with his relatives in maintaining family status.

He has a severed relationship with his wife's side. His marriage was his own decision. He was not able to get his wife's parents' consent for his marriage. According to his opinion the reason was that his family was large. He did not allow his wife to continue relationships with her parents. On the part of the parents, usually the accepted practice is to reestablish the relationship after a child is born to their married children who broke the marriage rules. In this example, his wife's parents did not visit them after the first child.

These norms are the ground rules for choice among kinsmen. Usually if the parents visit after a first child, there is a tendency to transform the severed relationship to a strong relationship. In another example, a 37 year old Muslim male respondent was able to enjoy a strong relationship with his wife's side after his first child was born.

Table 4.5

Reasons for Selective Relationship

Reasons	Maternal Side		Paternal Side		Spouse Side		Brothers/Sisters	
	Strong	Severed	Strong	Severed	Strong	Severed	Strong	Severed
Property	3	2	1	2	0	0	0	1
Help in family crisis	1	3	0	2	1	0	0	0
Practicing the norms of *Nadakama*	3	1	0	1	9	3	9	8
Distance and economic difficulties	0	0	0	4	0	0	0	1
Other	0	1	0	1	1	2	0	1
Total	7	6	1	10	11	5	9	11

Some of the severed relationships with bilateral kin are caused by issues over property matters. In most of the cases either their bilateral relatives or own brothers and sisters enjoy the total inheritance forcefully or are transferred the rights by cheating the relatives.

Unequal status among kinsmen is one of the strong reasons given by some of the residents for their severed or distant relationships. Their complaint is that their relatives do not respect them as kinsmen when they visit them since their relatives have economically or occupationally higher status than they do. All the reasons for severed relationships are given in table 4.6.

A kinship network contributes to each person's (or each household's) position in the community in terms of status, resources, social security, attitudes and values, and linkages to a wider network in the urban setting. Therefore, it is possible to argue that the kinship relationships of each individual or household has resources, power and ideological implications which have significant impact on neighborhood, religion, and political networks. For example, as illustrated under the mutual dependence category, in an urban setting kinship network is a sanctuary for political victims. However, the kinship network has no linear connection to the individual attributes and other networks. It has more reciprocal connections. The nature of this reciprocity can only be understood by looking at other networks. The coming chapters will be devoted to examining the neighborhood, religion, and political relationships of the community.

Table 4.6

Reasons for Severed Relationship

Reasons	Total	Percent
Violation of Marriage Rules	5	22
Violation of Other Kinship Norms (Ex. Puberty Function)	2	9
Status Gap	3	14
Property Issues	3	14
Gratitude	1	5
No Help	4	18
Distance, Economic Difficulties	2	9
Other	2	9
Total	22	

Chapter 5

The Neighborhood Relationship

In the preceding chapters, I have focused on the socioeconomic setting of the community, patterns of regulation of resources, and the kinship relationships of households under urban conditions. The relationships associated with a household have many dimensions. This chapter will focus on neighborhood relationships in a spatial context.

As outlined in Chapter Two, houses in this community are grouped into sections that are identifiable as discrete residential units, and each unit has clear demarcations on the ground. Almost all the houses of each unit are of the same type. Most of the residents of these units share certain amenities such as communal latrines and bathrooms. This provides a common contour of resource proximity within which a pattern of relationships emanate and exist. The important questions which are raised therefore are how residents of Dematagoda respond to this situation, what kind of relationships they have established among themselves, and what the various factors are which help to explain the pattern of neighborhood interactions.

NEIGHBORHOOD PROFILE OF THE COMMUNITY

The intensity of neighborhood relationships, for the sake of conceptual convenience, can be categorized into three: (1) high, (2) moderate, and (3) limited. The study reveals that 44.7% of the sample maintains a high degree of neighborhood relationships, 30.6% moderate, and 24.7% have limited relationships (table 5.1).

The high level neighborhood relationship is characterized by mutual dependency in life crises as well as in daily matters. This category interacts heavily with a selected number of families, while maintaining a healthy relationship with all others. The families in this category visit very often and help each other frequently. This close relationship is referred to as either friendship or brotherhood. They have developed strong emotional attachment for each other. Privacy is almost nonexistent among these families. The social milieu of interaction basically pivots around normal life crises such as sickness, death, emergency situations, and ritual ceremonial functions.

The content of reciprocity is varied from one family to another, and it depends on the nature of the crises. It is possible to identify a generalized normative priority order of these life crises. They are: (1) death and funeral functions, (2) sickness, (3) life threatening emergencies, (4) weddings, puberty, ritual offerings, (5) self-help reciprocal activities such as replacing a roof or a small construction for a neighbor, and (6) extending credit facilities for urgent needs.

The nature of interactions varies from formal visits to tangible help (money, material labor, emotional attachment and sharing griefs and happiness). Decisions are largely dependent on the nature of the relationship of both parties and the level of need that is required by the person who is in the crisis situation. In a funeral situation, it is customary to visit and pay respect to the dead body. Everyone in the neighborhood is expected to do so unless there is serious tension and severed relationships between parties. Therefore, usually this is the time for many people to forget enmity with their neighbors.

Neighborhood interactions vary in terms of their content and form, depending on the socio-economic characteristics of households. This study reveals different degrees of interactions among neighbors.

Social distance, ethnic tolerance, conflicts, competition, and reciprocity are important dimensions in this interaction process. The empirical evidence shows a dynamic characteristic of neighborhood relationships in the daily life of the community.

This data indicates that the majority of Tamils fall within the high category while none are within the limited category. The limited category is higher among Muslims than Sinhalese, while a significant percentage of Sinhalese fall within the high category. However, a little over 30% of all three ethnic groups maintain a moderate level of neighborhood relationships.

NEIGHBORHOOD RELATIONSHIP AND POLITICAL AFFILIATION

Neighborhood relationship does not directly correlate with political affiliation. The data indicates that only the Sri Lanka Freedom Party and indifferent category have above 25% of households with limited neighborhood relationship. Irrespective of political affiliation most of the respondents tend to maintain either a high or moderate level of neighborhood relationship. However, the majority of United National Party (the ruling party) affiliated and no affiliation groups have higher neighborhood connections than the Sri Lanka Freedom Party and the Marxist groups (opposition political parties since 1977 up to now) and indifferent groups (table 5.2). This phenomenon has a kind of political logic that cannot be easily explained through the numerical data.

NEIGHBORHOOD-KINSHIP MATRIX

In most cases, the neighborhood relationship is a substitute for kinship in this community. A small percentage of households have kinsmen residing in the vicinity (for example, in the same neighborhood and in other neighborhoods of the location). As shown in table 5.3, only about 9% of the sample have both high and moderate level kinsmen concentration in the same neighborhood, while it is only about 5% in other neighborhoods. As far as neighborhood-kinship matrix is concerned only about 6% of the sample maintain both at a moderate level, 19% maintain both at a high level, and only 8% maintain both at a limited level. The majority prioritize one over the other (table 5.4).

Table 5.1

Neighborhood Relationships by Ethnic Groups

Degree of Neighborhood Relationship	*N*	Sinhala (%)	Tamil (%)	Muslim (%)
High	38	71.1	15.8	13.1
Moderate	26	69.2	11.5	19.3
Limited	21	71.4	—	37.6
Total	85			

Table 5.2

Neighborhood Relationships by Political Affiliation

Political Affiliation	*N*	High (%)	Moderate (%)	Limited (%)
UNP	35	54.3	25.7	20.0
SLFP	14	28.6	28.6	42.8
LSSP/CP	6	33.3	50.0	16.7
No Affiliation	16	68.7	18.8	12.5
Indifferent	14	21.4	50.0	28.6
Total	85			

Table 5.3

Space Dimensions of Kinsmen Concentration

Degree of Concentration	Same Neighborhood (%)	Other Neighborhood (%)	Other Locations (%)	Other Parts of Colombo (%)	Periphery (%)	Other Districts (%)
High	1.2 (1)	3.5 (3)	2.4 (2)	9.4 (8)	7.1 (6)	56.5 (48)
Moderate	8.2 (7)	1.2 (1)	4.7 (4)	14.1 (12)	17.6 (15)	16.5 (14)
Low	28.2 (24)	18.8 (16)	18.8 (16)	22.4 (19)	20.0 (17)	9.4 (8)
Zero	62.4 (53)	76.5 (65)	74.1 (63)	54.1 (46)	55.3 (47)	17.6 (15)

Note: High = More than 5 family units. Moderate = At least 3 family units. Low = 1-2 family units. Total sample is 85. The categories of kinsmen concentration are not mutually exclusive.

Table 5.4

Kinship–Neighborhood Matrix

	Neighborhood			
Kinship	High	Moderate	Low	Total
High	16	9	11	36
Moderate	9	5	2	16
Low	14	12	7	33
Total	39	26	20	

Sixteen percent of the respondents have placed importance on neighborhood relationships. The majority of this category substitute neighborhood relationship for kinship relationship. The Sinhala majority tend to maintain kin affinity with their neighbors. The poorer Tamils and Muslims, particularly those who do not have kinsmen in the location, have no choice but to maintain a high degree of relationship with equal neighbors.

The deviant cases to this substitution of neighborhood relationship could be categorized into two groups. In the first group are residents among recent migrants, the company owners, shareholders of companies and professionals who have limited or severed relationships with their relatives due to a variety of other reasons. The life style of this category, at least at the surface level, is more Westernized. Even though they have limited neighborhood relationships, they do interact with the community at another level. They make financial contributions to the community activities (political, social, and religious) at the request of the members of the community. The second group is comprised of people who are frustrated with their previous involvement in politics and other community activities, as well as maintaining limited relationship with their relatives due to the reasons given in previous chapters. The frustration of this group is very frequently associated with the shift of political power which affected their social network in the community.

The neighborhood interactions of the indigenous professional group is largely confined to the matters of importance in life such as funerals (except politically active members of this group). They reside in their own separate houses with their own land and facilities. Their immediate neighbors, in most of the cases, are their own kinsmen. Therefore, the normal frequent interaction with the rest of the community is not a necessity, which is common among those who maintain high neighborhood relationships. However, this group tends to maintain a superordinate relationship with the poorer neighbors who live in adjacent gardens. They occasionally seek their services. For instance, the households of the indigenous professional group send their poorer neighbors to the market to bring their food stuffs for which services are paid or help given in their emergencies. However, attitudes towards their poorer neighbors are not positive. This group generally thinks that close interactions with them would make some trouble. The social interactions of this group with the community are largely on a selective basis except in the case of leadership interests. Nevertheless, financial contributions to the common activities of the community and emergency situations of the poorer people of the immediate environment are unavoidable.

Some of the residents in the indigenous professional group have somewhat distant relationships with their neighbors. They are worried about the congestion around them due to rapid increase of population. According to them, this area is socially polluted, though they are used to it and tolerate it. For example, with regard to filthy language that they hear everyday and the illegal activities taking place around them, a retired school teacher from a highly westernized family said:

> There are no disturbances for us, we are used to this language. This is a form of entertainment. . . . Once a *kassippu barrel* (illegal liquor) was hidden in our garden. I destroyed it. Then it was never repeated. Nobody asked about it. (05/04/1985)

This example indicates a fair degree of social tolerance between the indigenous professional group and their poorer neighbors.

Political intervention is a significant factor in certain conflictive situations in the neighborhood between these social groups. One of my informants revealed one such instance. He said:

> Some migrant residents add an extension for their kitchens in their row houses. The roofs of these kitchens were laid over the garden of one of the original families in this location (a family of the indigenous professional group). Then they sent a petition against this action to the municipal council. Then the municipal council sent a notice to the migrant residents, informing them that their authorities would come to demolish these extensions as it was an illegal act of violating the building codes, and they were informed that the municipal council would charge a penalty of Rs. 25. Then a ward member informed the vice mayor of the municipal council who is well known to him and prevented the act of demolishing the extensions of the kitchens. (02/10/1985)

The social interactions between the indigenous professional group and the indigenous leading group exist at a very marginal level of social distance that, maintained on the basis of the legitimacy of the major income sources, prevent interactions between these two groups. The indigenous professional group does not consider families of the indigenous leading group as respectable families, though they enjoy more resources and play a significant role in politics and in community activities. The social distance that prevailed between the indigenous leading group and the leading business group began to disappear gradually after the 1977 general election. In 1977, the power shifted from the Sri Lanka Freedom Party to the United National Party. The indigenous leading group played a political agent role to the United National Party while the leading business group is directly affiliated with the Sri Lanka Freedom Party. Therefore, these political changes have affected the neighborhood relationship between social groups of the community.

Social Interactions in Ethnic-Caste Mixed Neighborhoods

There are no ethnic enclaves in this community. All three ethnic groups live side by side. Nevertheless, different degrees of ethnic tolerance, conflict, and reciprocity are the ingredients of neighborhood interactions. The food exchange on the days of ethnic festivals is one of the symbolic ways that residents show their tolerance in this community. Food exchange is the usual customary practice. Sinhalese exchange food plates on the new year festivals. A modified form of this practice has been adopted between different ethnic groups. Almost everyone in this community sends a food plate on their festival day to the households of the other ethnic groups in the neighborhood. There is an exception to this practice of food exchange. The poorest people and the lower caste people receive food from other ethnic groups in their neighborhood, but they do not make a return according to the customary practice. The poorest people cannot afford to participate in these customary practices while the lower caste people are not supposed to return food plates as it is considered that they will pollute the superior caste. One of the Sinhala respondents expressed this practice saying:

> There are three *sakkily* households in front of my house. We give food for them on our festivals. We do not take food from them. They also do not try to give. They know that it undermines our position. (07/19/1985)

Sinhalese and high caste Tamils generally do not interact with these untouchables, but they help them in their life crises.

Some Sinhalese try to maintain a somewhat closer relationship with lower caste members than others are willing to do. One Sinhala respondent has expressed his non-caste attitude, saying that his children are friendly with the children of these *sakkily* families. However, children of both parties playing together is not sufficient enough to conclude that there is a tendency towards intimate and equal relationships with these untouchables. In some cases this social distance is based on status. A 42 year old male said:

> We do not interact with two *sakkily* families in this neighborhood. The Tamil family whom we interact with has status like Sinhalese. (06/23/1985)

These cases indicate the high caste consciousness and the subservient position that is occupied by the low caste Tamils in this community. If both groups are extremely poor and if there is no caste identification, there is a tendency to develop more equal, intimate relationship between Sinhalese and Tamils in the same neighborhood. Then this relationship is characterized by mutual dependency for daily needs, such as borrowing money from each other.

Estate Tamils with South Indian origin are scattered in the community numbering about three or four families. They represent South Indian castes, primarily from the lower end of the spectrum. In this community, the majority of them are kinsfolk with a high degree of social interaction. The conflictive instances between different castes have also been noted by other neighbors. These conflicts are mainly taking place at common water taps and toilets on the ground of contamination. For example, the conflict between two untouchable castes: *Sakkily and Panikkar* was revealed by one of the informants.

It is important to note that more middle class type Jaffna Tamils vacated their residences, numbering 15 in this community, as a result of the 1978 and 1983 communal riots. A few poorer Jaffna Tamils still remain in this community since they have limited options for geographical mobility. Despite their vulnerable position, they still retain the superior consciousness as Jaffna Tamils in their neighborhood relationship with Indian Tamils. Most of the conflicts between these two groups at the neighborhood level, however, emanate as a result of lack of common facilities such as water and toilets.

Tamils behave harmoniously with their Sinhala neighbors. They occupy subservient positions under the communal tension prevailing in the country. During the communal riots, these Tamils were protected by Sinhala neighbors from outside mob attacks. Tamils appreciate this task of protection though they do not have equal social interaction in the community. A poorer Indian Tamil expressed his view in this manner:

> Sinhalese do not invite us for their wedding ceremonies. I do not know why. Even if they invite us we have nothing to offer them as gifts. Whatever the reason is, it is a great thing that they protected our lives. (06/02/1985)

The poorer Tamils perceive themselves as innocents, though the northern Tamils are trying to divide the country. During communal violence, it is the common practice that garden leaders and area leaders with the help of their followers protect these innocent Tamils. In some neighborhoods, a *thug* leader performed this role. There may be a variety of motives behind this protection, but there are two possible and explicit reasons. On the one hand, the leaders have to perform their role in conformity with the desire of the state to maintain law and order by protecting Tamil civilians. On the other hand, they are supposed to protect the community and neighborhoods from outside attacks. Any type of exterior threat potentially demeans and is a challenge for the community power. Despite these reasons, selective attacks have been noted. There is one such case in the sample. An Indian origin Tamil had not been protected during the communal violence in 1983. His house had been demolished and households goods had been taken away. Initial protection had been given to him by one Burgher family. As a result, the Burgher family had been threatened and this Tamil family had gone to a rescue camp. These incidents could be explained as a result of nonconformity to the community and neighborhood norms. Sinhalese usually expect their Tamil neighbors to play a subservient role. They are expected to adopt the self-perception of *innocence*. If Tamils try to exhibit equal or high status, they face some negative consequences. On such occasions, exterior elements are permitted to creep into the community on a selective basis.

ETHNIC INTERMARRIAGES

Intermarriages between different ethnic groups are numerically negligible in this community. The basic survey of the study revealed that there are only fifteen ethnically mixed households. The type of ethnic mix is given in table 5.5.

Table 5.5

Ethnic Mix Households

Type	*N*	Percent
Sinhala and Tamil	11	73
Muslim and Sinhala	2	13
Burghers and Sinhala	1	7
Burghers and Tamil	1	7
Total	15	

The degrees of tolerance for these intermarriages are varied from one family to another depending on the economic situations and other social factors. It is important to see the reactions to such intermarriages. For example, consider a 32 year old male Tamil with an Indian origin, who married a Sinhala girl from a family in his neighborhood. This girl was living with her sister and brother-in-law. She had fallen in love with this Tamil man. Her sister and brother-in-law did witchcraft to prevent them from getting married. But they ran away from this community and lived with the respondent's relatives in Colombo. They got married in 1975 and they came back to the community in 1982. The two families have no social interaction but the respondent and his wife's brother-in-law talk to each other as both of them are involved in community activities as leaders.

In this case, he enjoys more equal relationship with his Sinhala neighbors than other poorer Tamils in the community. He is invited for birthday parties, puberty functions, and weddings by his Sinhala neighbors. In this neighborhood, it is important to note that Tamils are the numerical majority in ethnic composition. This numerical factor, along with his leadership role in this garden and his marriage relationship to a Sinhala family has smoothed the social distinctions between him and his Sinhala neighbors. This example is an exception to the common reality of social distance of neighbors and potential hostility between two ethnic families as a result of ethnic intermarriages.

The Sinhala-Muslim relationship is more equal than the Sinhala-Tamil relationship in the neighborhood. The caste element is totally absent in this relationship. The exchange of food plates on their festivals is a visible phenomenon without having any racial attitude. Sinhalese do accept food plates from Muslim neighbors. However, this practice is absent between Sinhala professionals and upper level business families of recent immigrants. Most of these families in both groups are highly Westernized. They have limited social interactions, confined to occasional chats and children playing together on the access road.

Except for this Westernized group, others, both Sinhalese and Muslims, interact heavily in community functions, ritual festivals, and political meetings and gatherings. They contribute money and labor despite their religious differences. Nevertheless, minor conflicts at the individual level are unavoidable. Whatever the immediate issue which causes these conflicts, Sinhalese tend to show racial superiority and look down upon Muslims. The word *hambaya* is very commonly used for such inferior references. This type of conflictive relationship is possible either at an economically unequal or equal competitive level. However, these unequal, unhealthy relationships do not last long. There are a few instances where the poorer Sinhalese maintain a somewhat dependent type relationship with rich Muslims for emergency purposes; usually these poorer Sinhalese borrow money from their Muslim neighbors.

Healthy relationships between Sinhalese and Muslims are largely governed by political factors. There are two tangible reasons in a political context: (1) The electorate, which this community comes under, is represented by a Muslim and he holds a position of cabinet minister; furthermore, the Muslims are the second numerical majority in this community. (2) Under the environment of Sinhala-Tamil tension prevailing in the country, maintaining a healthy relationship with Muslims as a minority group is a political necessity on the part of the Sinhalese. This healthy relationship contributes to the pool of state legitimization with regard to equal rights.

CASTE AMONG SINHALESE

Among the Sinhalese, caste is generally an unknown factor in this community. The greater anonymity with regard to caste prevents the community from strict maintenance of the caste system. The phrase of *Colombo Goyigama* is used to pretend higher status; however, some people of this community are very inquisitive in finding out the caste identity of their neighbors. People generally tend to say that "we do not consider caste differences in this area" as a response to an initial stereotype question. But the intensive interviews have revealed their caste consciousness and their limited interactions with each other. The following few statements illustrate this caste consciousness:

> In this garden, there are many *Daubi* (washermen) people. But there is no such distinction. When people conflict they refer to caste affiliations. (05/29/1985)

> I do not know the caste of my neighbors. I know only three families. Only those three families are the same caste as our family. I do not know about others. (06/11/1985)

This chapter presented a profile of neighborhood interactions and dynamic characteristics related to the neighborhood's pattern of behavior in this heterogenous community. This behavior is largely determined by individual position in the total network of the community. The political reality is of paramount importance in understanding these characteristics.

Chapter 6

Political Behavior

This chapter will describe the nature of the political behavior of Dematagoda in terms of respondents' affiliations and reliance. The logic of this behavior and its impact on the total community, particularly in terms of patronage politics as a means of regulating resources, will also be examined.

According to Eisenstadt, political behavior at the community level reflects "a distinct mode of regulating crucial aspects of institutional order" (Eisenstadt 1980, 49) and individual life within a framework of patronage system. The patronage system has either been built into every sphere of social relationship or impacted upon them. Each person at the individual or group level is forced to choose, strategically, a patronage network for his or her own ends. In this process, some are able to have direct access to politically institutionalized patronage or have indirect access through dyadic networks. The patronage is founded on reciprocal relations and characterized by a vertical chain from neighborhood to community and to the external economic, legal, administrative and political institutions. The vertical patronage system has the attribute of inequality in power relations, in spite of the exchange of different types of resources: economic (employment, housing, and urban services) and political support, loyalty, votes, protection and the promises of solidarity. Thus, this system is a kind of, as Pitt-Rivers (cited in Eisenstadt 1980) termed, *lopsided friendship* network focused upon influence and dependency. Hence, the patronage system and associated political behavior of Dematagoda is compatible with the argument developed by Eisenstadt and Louis. This system:

> creates a paradoxical combination of elements that are a major feature of the patron–client nexus. The most important contradictions are first, a peculiar combination of inequality and asymmetry in power with seeming mutual solidarity expressed in terms of personal identity and interpersonal sentiments and obligations; second, a combination of potential coercion and exploitation with voluntary relations and compelling mutual obligations; third, a combination of the emphasis on these obligations and solidarity with the somewhat illegal or semi-legal aspects of these relations. (Eisenstadt and Louis 1980, 50)

Political Affiliations by Ethnic Groups

The respondent's political affiliation is enumerated in table 6.1. As far as Sinhalese are concerned, the majority are not affiliated with the ruling political party, the United National Party. Thirty five percent of the Sinhalese are affiliated with the United National party, and 23% are affiliated with the Sri Lanka Freedom Party while only 10% are affiliated with Marxist political groups: the LSSP (Lanka Equal Society party [the Trotsky group] and the Communist party [Moscow wing]). A significant percentage expressed that they were either not affiliated to any political party (11.7%) or are indifferent, not having any ideological commitment (20%). Contrary to the Sinhalese political affiliation, the majority of Tamils and Muslims (nearly 56%) are affiliated with the ruling party, while not anyone is affiliated with the Sri Lanka Freedom Party and Marxist parties. The no affiliation group is relatively high among Tamils and Muslims when compared to the Sinhalese. Eleven percent of Tamils and 12% of Muslims tend to hold indifferent views.

Table 6.1

Political Affiliation by Ethnic Groups

Ethnic Groups	*N*	UNP (%)	SLFP (%)	LSSP/CP (%)	No Affiliation (%)	Indifferent (%)
Sinhala	60	35.0	23.3	10.0	11.7	20.0
Tamil	9	55.6	—	—	33.3	11.1
Muslim	16	56.3	—	—	31.2	12.5
Total	85					

Sri Lanka as a highly politicized country; political affiliations are generally perceived as channels which bring tangible benefits to individual families and to members of groups. These benefits are usually in the areas of employment, promotions, business, and housing. This community is not an exception to that reality. However, the degree of political reliance ranges from no dependence to dependence. Four categories of people have been identified in this study in terms of political affiliation and political reliance (fig. 6.1). Of the total sample of 85, 44.7% are not dependent on political channels.

The dependent groups could further be categorized into three subgroups: (1) people who have already achieved some benefits and aspire to obtain more (27.1%), (2) people who perceive potential benefits in the near future (15.3%), and (3) people who are already disappointed with their political affiliations (12.9%).

	Non-Dependents	Dependents
Affiliated	A 18 21.2	B 37 43.5
Non-Affiliated	C 20 23.5	D 10 11.8

Fig. 6.1. Political Affiliations and Reliance

POLITICAL AFFILIATIONS AND RELIANCE

The distribution of political reliance by political affiliations is given in table 6.2. Forty-three percent of the UNP affiliated group achieved some benefits while 25% are perceiving potential benefits; 5.7% are disappointed and 25.7% do not rely on political channels. Contrary to this behavior of UNPs, among those who are affiliated with SLFP and Marxists groups, 40%-50% do not rely on political channels. This attitude is more compatible and a reflection of the descending order of power. Among SLFP's 28.6% achieved their goals through political channels while it is 33% among Marxist groups. These data indicate that the UNP's achievement rate is higher than the SLFP and the Marxist groups, while the disappointment rate is higher among the latter groups. Two explanations are possible for this phenomenon. First, there is a commonly held notion that the UNP government made available more employment opportunities. Second, as the UNP presently holds the power, there is a natural tendency to have a higher rate in the category of potential benefits than in the disappointed category.

As far as no affiliation and indifferent categories are concerned, a striking feature is noted. A small percentage of these two categories have achieved some benefits and aspire to potential benefits through political channels. Around seven percent of each category has achieved benefits and aspire to obtain more and 13% from the no affiliation group and 6% from the indifferent group perceive potential benefits in the near future. Except for one Muslim, all the others who behave in this manner are Sinhalese.

The ethnic breakdown of political reliance is given in table 6.3. Of the total of five Tamils who are affiliated with the ruling party, only one has no dependence on political channels for their individual goals. The majority of Tamils who are affiliated with the UNP (60%) perceive potential benefits in the near future. Only 20% of this category have achieved some benefits. As far as Muslims in this category are concerned, they are either not dependent or have already achieved benefits. None is aspiring to obtain benefits or is disappointed. However, of the non affiliated Muslims, the majority are disappointed in this regard. Only one Muslim respondent, being indifferent, was able to achieve benefits through political channels. Not one of the Tamils in the no affiliation group or in the indifferent group was able to achieve his or her individual goals through political channels.

Table 6.2

Political Affiliation and Political Reliance

Political Affiliation	*N*	No Dependence (%)	Disappointed (%)	Perceive Potential Benefits (%)	Obtained and Expect More (%)
UNP	35	25.7	5.7	25.7	42.9
SLFP	14	42.9	21.4	7.1	28.6
LSSP/CP	6	50.0	16.7	—	33.3
No Affiliation	15	53.3	26.7	13.3	6.7
Indifferent	15	80.0	6.7	6.7	6.6
Total	85				

Table 6.3

Political Reliance by Ethnic Groups

Ethnic	*N*	No Dependence (%)	Disappointed (%)	Perceive Potential Benefits (%)	Obtained and Expect More (%)
Sinhala	60	41.7	13.3	16.7	28.3
Tamil	9	55.6	—	33.3	11.1
Muslim	16	50.0	18.8	—	31.2
Total	85				

It is important to raise a few questions with regard to this political behavior. Despite losing political power, why do a small percentage of Sinhalese in this community affiliate with Marxist political groups? Why do not minorities affiliate with Marxist groups at all? Why are most of the minorities affiliated with the ruling party, while the majority keep away from the ruling party? Why are all three ethnic groups represented significantly in the no affiliation and in the indifferent categories? How could some people be able to live without political reliance? What attributes in terms of their social networks and resources keep them away from community politics, though they are self-identified with a political party or with a political ideology? What is the nature of political reliance in this community? What mechanisms operate in this process of political reliance? In order to answer these questions it is important to see the respondents' backgrounds, experiences, perceptions and attitudes regarding their political affiliations and behavior.

AFFILIATED NON-DEPENDENTS

As far as occupational distribution is concerned, this group has two striking features. First, no white collar job holders from the private sector are politically affiliated with UNP and LSSP/CP parties. Second, all the respondents in this category who are engaged in business are UNP affiliated people.

As shown in table 6.4, this group has a diverse origin. Though the majority is from Colombo (33.4% from other parts of Colombo, 16.7% from Dematagoda—both from the community and the adjacent communities—and 5.5% from the Colombo periphery), 16.7% are from peripheral districts such as Kalutara and Negambo of Western Province, and 22.2% are from other districts (including up country). Only 5.5% are Southerners. The people from Western Province and Southern Province in this group are affiliated with Sri Lanka Freedom Party politics, while the people from up country and other parts of Colombo are affiliated with the United National Party.

As far as per capita income distribution is concerned, 50% has over Rs. 400; 16.7% are in the range of Rs. 200 to Rs. 400 which can be considered a moderate level per capita income; 27.7% fall within Rs. 100 to Rs. 200 and only 5.5% have below Rs. 100 (table 6.5). Of the total of nine who are affiliated with UNP, six (66%) respondents have

Table 6.4

Place of Origin by Dependent Categories

Place of Origin	*N*	Southern Province (%)	Western Province (%)	Up Country (%)	Other Districts (%)	Periphery (%)	Other parts of Colombo (%)	Other location/ Same garden (%)	India (%)
A Non-Dependents Affiliated	18	5.5	16.7	11.1	11.1	5.5	33.4	16.7	—
B Dependents Affiliated	37	10.0	15.0	5.0	—	10.0	20.0	35.0	5.0
C Non-Dependents Non-Affiliated	20	27.0	5.4	5.4	5.4	—	13.5	43.3	—
D Dependents Non-Affiliated	16	30.0	—	20.0	—	10.0	20.0	20.0	—
Total	85								

Table 6.5

Per Capita Income Distribution by Political Affiliation and Dependent Categories

Dependent Categories	*N*	Below 100 (%)	100-200 (%)	201-400 (%)	401-500 (%)	501-750 (%)	Over 750 (%)
A Non-Dependents Affiliated	18	5.5	27.7	16.7	16.7	16.7	16.7
B Dependents Affiliated	37	10.0	25.0	20.0	10.0	10.0	25.0
C Non-Dependents Affiliated	20	13.5	13.5	48.7	8.1	5.4	10.8
D Dependents Non-Affiliated	10	50.0	10.0	30.0	—	—	10.0
Total	85						

the above moderate level of per capita income. Only 50% of the SLFP respondents fall within this category while none from the LSSP/CP are in this category. However, there is only one respondent who has below Rs. 100 per capita income and he is a UNP affiliated person.

The majority (77.8%) of respondents in this group own their residence; 16.7% are tenants and only 5.5% who are affiliated with LSSP/CP are living in government land without having housing ownership (table 6.6).

It is interesting to note that, of the total 18, 72.2% have no membership in any community organization, political or otherwise. They are politically self-identified. Five respondents have formal affiliation to some of the community organizations which are considered non-political. Four of them have a leadership role in the community. They are not affiliated with the ruling political party.

This data suggests that there are two subdivisions of this group: (1) people who cannot separate their ideological faith from their family tradition, and (2) those who have placed their ideological faith in government policies. However, the majority has no formal or informal link to the community politics. Their sound economic position permits them to be aloof from community politics. As a result, they tend to be critical of certain political activities and behaviors of the community (these criticisms may not necessarily be open to the community). The first subdivision tends to be more status oriented with their political faith. An adopted Sinhala person in a Muslim family says:

> I do not affiliate to any organization. I voted UNP every time. All of my Muslim relatives are UNP. I never expect anything from the government. (05/18/1985)

This statement implies his independency from politics. He is proud of it. In another example a Sinhala businessman who is largely satisfied with his achievements, described his political affiliation.

> Since 1921, I am a right wing person. There was a time when I was heavily involved in politics; I spent my own money. My father had worked in an estate owned by J.R.'s father (President of the country). I had a friendship with the present prime minister and president. (06/19/1985)

Table 6.6

House Ownership by Political Dependent Categories

Dependent Categories	*N*	Squatters (%)	Owners (%)	Tenants (%)
A Non-Dependents Affiliated	18	5.5	77.8	16.7
B Dependents Affiliated	37	20.0	60.0	20.0
C Non-Dependents Non-Affiliated	20	15.0	70.0	15.0
D Dependents Non-Affiliated	10	40.0	40.0	20.0
Total	85			

Another person in this category says:

> Since the day I remember I voted UNP. My father also had given money to Mr. Kaleel for his election campaign. (07/20/1985)

Regarding local politics some respondents in this category tend to be critical of certain community leaders. The present MC (Municipal Council) ward member was the target of such criticisms.

> MC ward member is taking bribes to secure employment. His leadership is useless; he has only his body strength. He does for both his family and friends. He is not concerned about the people who live in flats. But they are the people who helped him in his election campaign. Now the young people are angry with him. (05/06/1985)

This respondent further says:

> I am only a member of one community organization. I am not interested in those activities. It is not necessary that others enjoy benefits while we are degrading our status. (05/06/1985)

The ideological faith and the legitimacy of the second subdivision of this group are directly connected to their family stability and to the national level government policies. A UNP affiliated, retired Muslim person, who has stable income and secure family position says:

> The present government should continue. They have done some good things; we don't need any help from them. My children are educated, we have no need to go after them (politicians). (06/09/1985)

In another example, a Sinhala respondent expressed both his faithfulness to the UNP and his aloofness from local politics.

> I am not a member of any organization, political or otherwise. I do not know whether there are such organizations in this community. . . . Since I was eligible for the vote, my father was telling me to vote for SLFP. But during the 1977 election time, I thought that there was no use if the country was going like that. Therefore, I voted for UNP. (04/10/1985)

The SLFP and LSSP/CP affiliated people who fall within the group of affiliated non-dependent are largely ideologically oriented toward keeping away from local politics. They perceive the local situation as opportunistic politics. The lower and middle level professionals in this group tend to criticize the activities of the present government. A few of those statements concerning the racial strife are:

> It is very difficult to live. The Northern problem has a great impact. I have to say that the present system of government is not suitable. It is difficult to say that there is a leadership. Sometimes there may be a leadership which submerges their opinions. (06/09/1985)

> The country's matter is disappointing. Prices are increased, there is corruption, and we have to compensate in the form of prices. About the Northern problem, there is very little effort to correct the situation. I am not saying that the previous period was good, but this period is much worse. Because of the open economy, there is malpractice, theft, corruption. I am really wondering that at this rate where this will end up. (06/21/1985)

A person who was tremendously involved in leftist politics both within and outside the community, who is presently inactive, expressed his ideology as the usual Marxist does.

> There are no solutions to the problems of the country or to the racial issues from these capitalist governments. (05/02/1985)

In another example, a leftist who is active in local politics expressed his views on competitive political tension in the community.

> I am a leftist. We established a community organization for these flats after 1977. What we suggest through this organization is submerged by UNP people. (05/22/1985)

AFFILIATED AND DEPENDENTS

This group consists of 43.5% of the total sample. Of the total number of Sinhalese in the sample, 48.3% fall within this group, 44.4% are Tamils and 25% are Muslims. Seventy percent of the Sinhalese in this group are affiliated with the ruling party, 21.6% are SLFP affiliated people, and 8.1% are leftists (LSSP/CP).

In this group 24.4% are engaged in lower level white collar jobs, mainly clerical and allied; 27% are unskilled workers. Only 16.2% are in each category of skilled, business, and dependent. Of the total of 26 UNPers in this category, 23.1% are white collar employees; 12.5% of SLFP, and 66.6% of leftists are white collar employees. All the business people in this group are affiliated with the ruling party. Of the total SLFP in this category, 37.5% are unskilled workers; 33.3% of leftists and 23.1% of UNP affiliated people fall within the unskilled category.

As far as place of origin is concerned, a significant percentage (43.3) were born in the same location or are from the adjacent locations. Southerners, people from other parts of the country, people from other districts and people from Western province are the second (27%), third (13.5%), fourth (10.8%) and fifth (5.4%) categories, respectively. None are from the periphery in this group.

The politically affiliated and dependent group shows a dispersed per capita income distribution pattern, while still forming the highest group within Rs. 200 to Rs. 400 (48.7%). The lowest group (5.4%) is Rs. 501 to Rs. 750. In this group, 10.8% have over Rs. 750 per capita income while 13.5% have below Rs. 100 (table 6.5).

The majority (73%) have house ownership while 13.5% form a category of residents in government land and tenants. A small percentage of the respondents in the ownership category are not the real owners. The ownership is in the hands of their relatives, such as in-laws or spouses.

Of the total number of 25 UNP affiliated respondents in this category, 15.4% are area leaders, 15.4% are community leaders, 19.2% are garden leaders and another 15.4% are members. A significant percentage, 34.6%, are non-members. Among SLFP affiliated people, 25% are leaders, 25% are community leaders, 12.5% are garden leaders, 25% are members and 12.5% are non-members. Of the three leftists, one is a member, one is a community leader, and one is a leader.

There are three types of respondents in terms of expectations (explicit or implicit) through political activities and channels: (1) Those who need employment, promotions and housing, (2) political agents who seek balance between income and status through politics, and (3) minorities who need protection for life and personal benefits.

Employment, promotions and housing. Certain types of employment, promotions and housing through political channels have become an acceptable norm in Sri Lanka. It is a quite obvious fact for both parties that there will be an obligation, when an unemployed person supports a political campaign. In certain cases, this obligation takes a verbal contractual form in the process of political campaigning at the community level.

This study has revealed that many jobs in the Ceylon Transport Board were made available to the community to fulfill political promises. This was possible as the member of the parliament in this electorate occupies the ministry of transportation. The following few statements are evidence for these political transactions. A 28 year old Sinhala male is a member of the UNP youth organization. He says:

> I got this CTB job on 15th December 1977. I did political work and through them, I went for this job. Two members in my family were not given jobs as they are SLFP affiliated people. I worked for the UNP with the hope of employment and with that promise. (06/18/1985)

A 37 year old Muslim male is trying to get a job for his brother. He says:

> My mother knows the minister. We can get a letter too. We have asked for a job for my brother. The minister said that he would look into it and find something. During election time I worked for the present MP (Member of Parliament). I hung flags and helped him in his political meetings. I am affiliated with the UNP youth organization, but I am not a member. (07/24/1985)

Some respondents were not successful in using political connections at the local level and they are now in the process of contacting external political channels. The following case is a good example:

> I am trying to get a job for my son in the electricity board. I am going to get this job through a CMC member (Colombo Municipal Council) of Maligawatta. I asked a leader (one of the political agents), but it did not work out. (06/23/1985)

Another unsuccessful respondent who needed a job in CGR (Ceylon Government Railway) and a house says:

> We voted for the present MP. I went canvassing for him. An MC member led us. From those days, we are UNP supporters. We voted for UNP with the hope of good things for the country and for us, a good job. This government has done something good for the country. . . . In 1977, I was given a job in the CTB. I asked for one in CGR. I couldn't get that since I was over age. I did not like to go to CTB. Instead of me one of my friends went for that job. I wanted to go to CGR, because it has a pension. . . . We do not have a house. We went to the MP and told him. He gave letters to give to the prime minister and the minister of local government and housing. But there is not much consideration for that. (05/05/1985)

However, he is not a disappointed person. This example indicates that the MP of the electorate channels the needs of his jurisdiction to the respective ministries. The possibility of accomplishing these needs depends on three factors as the MP has no controlling authority over other ministries. (1) The strength of the relationship between the needy and the MP in the context of local political process. The strength of this relationship is determined by the contribution made by the needy or the political agent who speaks on behalf of the needy. (2) The relationship between MP of the area and the minister of respective areas of considerations. (3) The flexibility of government and ministry policies and regulations.

People who have not used their political channels, keep their connections smooth with the hope of potential benefits when they have a need. For example, a *garden* level leader expressed his views in this manner.

> I am the organizer of the UNP youth organization. I do not get involved in politics heavily. I am with the party as a member. I go to introduce youths of this garden when they look for jobs. In addition I participate in *Shramadana* (offering labor in common activities). Actually I did not get any benefits, yet, from these activities. In the future, I will use these connections for the needs of my children and my sisters. (06/23/1985)

A fish seller in Dematagoda market area, residing in government *flats*, says:

> Still I do not need any help or advice. If I need anything I will obtain it, if I know them. We were brought up together. I voted for the MC member. (04/21/1985)

A person who is aspiring to promotion maintains his political connections and party identification in the working place as well as in the community.

> In the work place, I joined Philip Gunawardane's trade union at the beginning. When he crossed over to the UNP, we also automatically crossed over. I have one more grade to obtain. For that matter, I hang on to the same union, but I do not participate in political activities in the community. I vote for UNP. (05/27/1985)

This example indicates his assessment of internal-external balance of political affiliation in terms of his objective.

Political power changes have a potentially adverse effect on people's lives in the community. Under such circumstances some people adopt strategies and alter political relationships. For example, a 42 year old Sinhala male works as a laborer in the government hospital. He is a SLFP affiliated person and has a membership in the Communist Party trade union in his work place. He describes his difficult situation in this manner:

> During the last presidential election I supported SLFP. I drew posters, hung flags and distributed political leaflets. After the election some people told me that I was going to be transferred (as a punishment). They have gone even to the MP. From the beginning, I was leaning towards the left. My father is UNP. I do

> not know who went to inform him of my political activities. . . . During the Colombo municipal election I supported the UNP nominee. He is one of my contemporary students and we have lived together in this community since our childhood. Therefore, I welcomed him, putting a garland around his neck in front of my house. I gave money for his political campaign. We friends put together a list and collected Rs. 100 from each person. His opponent from Sri Lanka Freedom Party also is an unacceptable person. The present MC members interest about the local matters is not adequate. But we can't neglect him because he is a poor person like us. . . . I told him about a job for one of my brothers-in-law. But still I did not get that help. He said, "We'll see." (04/28/1985)

Despite their political identification these people are trying to get access to the present political channels using personal friendship, locality feeling, and belonging to the same neighborhood group. Some of the respondents are already disappointed in this effort. One person who was dissatisfied with his SLFP affiliated political history, tried to use *friendship* as a means to gain access to the power centers outside the community. He says:

> I do not have connections with politicians, but I know Boomananda from his childhood. We have drinks together. But he does not introduce us to the big people, in order to get something done. He asked us to come again. The ward member of the adjacent ward also joined us to have drinks. (07/23/1985)

Political disappointments are an inevitable outcome of this process since political channels are not always able to look after all the needs. Under such circumstances, the reciprocal relationships tend to be disturbed. The following statements illustrate such disappointments.

> I am a member of the UNP party. I had had enough harassment from SLFP. I was sent on compulsory leave and transferred. But, now I do not have any help. After facing such harassment, I was not given a promotion even from this government. Now I have grade 2, I was in grade 3. I did not get even that promotion because of politics. All the promotions are given to the office bearers of UNP trade union. I have received all my salary increments in this grade. The only thing I can apply for is special

> grade, but it will not come to me. When they recruit for that grade, leaves without pay are taken into consideration. I take leaves without pay very frequently. It is difficult to live on my present wage. I get only about Rs. 1050. If they would allow us to resign from the job with compensation, then I will do that. I pay Rs. 400 rent for this house. My water bill is about Rs. 300. I paid one of them. Since nobody pays the water now, I also do not pay it. I requested a house from the government, at least a *flat*. They say that it cannot be given. They say that shanty dwellers should be given the priority. But I know that those who do not live in shanties are also given homes though I was not given a house. I am disappointed with this government because of these things. (05/26/1985)

Another disappointed person expressed his views in this manner:

> I looked for several jobs. I tried to get a driving job in the CTB. I told the MC member. He said that my name was included in the list. I worked in politics, but it was no use. Before 1981, I was involved in politics and worked hard. I went to every meeting and I helped to put up UNP political stages and hung flags. I was fired in 1980 (as a result of a strike). I am not a leftist. I tried my best to get my job back. The MC member is a friend of mine. But it did not work out. I decided on that day I will never go into the political field and work for them except giving my vote for the party which I like. (05/22/1985)

These statements indicate several things about community life in the context of scarcity of resources and the political channels which are the main controlling mechanism of resources internally and externally. The following characteristics could be inferred from this evidence. First, it is quite obvious that there is no rational way of distributing scarce resources. Second, a system has been developed through practice in the relationship between community people and the people who control the political channels. This is more of a reciprocal arrangement which is socially acceptable. This socially acceptable norm is that the people who support a particular party in their election campaign are eligible to get something tangible as a return once the party gets into power. The scarce resources such as employment, housing, and infrastructural facilities are distributed in this fashion based on the degree of contribution made available to the political campaign individually or by a group as a whole. Even though there is no contractual form in this reciprocity, most people's behavior and expressions indicate such things.

> After 1977 I did not receive a position that was equal to the support I gave to the politics. . . . I blame the minister as he did not help us. I told them that if he does something we will help. (03/31/1985)

Third, there is a frequent violation of this norm. Malpractice, corruption, and nepotism have crept into the system and created tension, unhappiness and disappointments within the community. Fourth, there is an adverse effect on the other areas of relationship within and outside the community. It creates neighborhood tensions and leads to adverse relationship between community people and governmental service organizations such as the Colombo Municipal Council, the Housing Authority, and the Common Amenities Board.

Political agents, patronage and status. Political agents are expected to patronize the supporters distributing party directed benefits. They engage in organizing, contributing and leading the supporters, bringing political allegiance to the respective parties and politicians. Political agents as mediators have attributes of both clients and patrons. In order to stabilize their income sources and status position, they seek political patronage from external politicians while they develop clientele from the community.

A political agent's patronizing capacity is determined by their own resources and networks as well as party directed benefits. Personality attributes and skills of these agents and their direction in life also are factors which determine the nature of the role of political agents. As far as agents' occupational backgrounds are concerned, it varies from entrepreneurial attributes to professional elements. These political agents are identified in this study as area leaders and community leaders. They have influential power over both clients and their own patrons. Their behavior is largely characterized by favoritism, political manipulation, reciprocity, networking and status consciousness. Their whole strategy aims at a balance between income stability, status and politics. It is necessary to trace a few cases as illustrations of political agents' patronage capacity and status consciousness.

Case No. 1. A 40 year old male, an area leader type, married, has two children born in this location, and he belongs to the indigenous leading group having a medium scale business. He has had several businesses. Presently he owns an illegal liquor bar. He describes his experiences and difficulties in business and his expectations as follows:

> My daily profit is around Rs. 400. I run this business on commission basis. I pay commissions to my core workers. This business is not a stable one. If it is stable I can manage to pay wages and an employment provident fund. I requested a license from the previous government to do this business. They refused it since I am affiliated to the UNP. The present government says that they do not issue new licenses.
>
> Most of the income that I earned had to be spent for fines. Every month I have one or two court cases. I allot money from my monthly income for these court cases. I send my employees as defendants on a rotational basis. I allot Rs. 800 to Rs. 900 for these cases. I contribute money for New Year festivals and for police festivals. I allot another Rs. 200 to Rs. 250 every month for these festivals. Now, I do not have as many disturbances from the police (they do not raid frequently) as I am affiliated to UNP.
>
> I help my neighbors. I give my cars for weddings. I buy coffins for poorer people, those who cannot afford it. CMC gives little money for a coffin for poorer families. It is not enough. Sometimes, some people from Boralla electorate come and ask for loans. Most of them do not settle this money back. Some people do repay on installment basis. Some pavement hawkers in Dematagoda come and ask for money, ranging from Rs. 3000 to Rs. 5000 to resume their businesses after they get released from prison (the assumption here is these people got caught for various illegal activities they engaged in other than their legal businesses.) I do not take interest. Once they get established, they return this money. At this moment nearly ten people from Dematagoda market area owe me money.

After this government came into power I helped some children of poorer families to get jobs. I did my political activities strongly in North Boralla, and Dematagoda. I got nearly 500 jobs for this area. It is about 100 for Dematagoda ward. They have in mind the feeling of gratitude that they got these jobs because of me. They call me *aiya* (elder brother - fictive kinship).

My priority expectation is to obtain a license for this bar. It is my known job. I did gem mining in 1978. I bought those lands from an auction in Lunugala. It was not successful. I could not manage both businesses here and there. When I went there, activities here went down. I have to manage everything, others do the work. I had a friend of mine in Balangoda, we jointly did this gem mining. I cannot say that I lost money, I got back what I invested.

The minister (MP of the area) accompanied me to the minister of finance to get a license for my liquor bar, but I could not get that license, because there was a president's law not to issue new licenses. I can do hotel business. But in order to obtain a place for that, I have to put a big down payment. The minister's public relations officer told me to start a hotel taking a bank loan. I was given a place in Boralla supermarket on the third floor. I can't do anything there. Therefore, now it is closed. It is difficult to do these things (liquor bar) in unknown places.

I did canvassing within the whole Boralla electorate. I am the treasurer of the Boralla UNP *polite bureau.* I was offered *anusasaka* positions (patron-advisor) in the *village* temples, Weluwanaramaya and Gnanawimala. But I did not accept any one of these positions, it was not necessary for me to take these positions, if the *Rajakariya* (duty) is fulfilled. Those are bogus positions. I contribute for all the festivals and functions of these temples. Every month I do *alms-giving* (offer food) for twenty monks of Weluwana temple. I contribute to the churches when committee members come and ask for help. I am the *anusasaka* of the youth society. I help this society every time when they participate in *yowuna puraya* (district youth camps). I am also the *anusaska* of the community development organization. I am assigned as *anusaska* in any of the activities of the ruling party in this electorate. According to my knowledge, I do not have any opponents. In common activities I join with leading businessmen.

> Before 1977, the minister appointed me as an organizer to one of the adjacent MC wards. I refused it. I do not need to become a *member* (MC ward member). I do a similar service like a member does to the area. According to my opinion, in order to do a service, it is not necessary to have a position. Sometimes I think that I am more respected (or treated) than a ward member. A position of ward member is both gained and lost. (04/29/1985)

Case No. 2. In another example, an area type leader, affiliated with the Sri Lanka Freedom Party, belonged to the leading business group. Now he spends the latter part of his life in a relaxed fashion, but his interests in business and politics still lurk in his mind. He migrated to this location in 1950 after serving in World War II as a soldier. He was from down south. He started several businesses in Dematagoda and in the peripheral areas while he was working in a government factory as an artist. Now he is retired from his government job. Some of his businesses closed down and the rest have been transferred to his two sons. The following description reveals some of his past experiences and present activities.

> I was involved in political activities since 1954, soon after government workers were given political freedom in 1956, I joined openly in political activities. First I joined the SLFP trade union as a committee member. I was the treasurer of the Dematagoda branch of the SLFP. (Still he is considered as treasurer, but these political organizations are inactive at this moment as their opponents are in power.) I was a secretary in Mutual Aid Funeral Society in this location. I faced many threats because of my political involvement as a businessman. My opponents always exaggerated that, saying "SLFP treasurer is doing black market." I contributed to almost every social function and festival in the area. We established "Dematagoda United Traders Buddhist Association." We celebrated *wesak* festivals through this organization. I was able to get significant number of jobs for some unemployed youths in Dematagoda ward, irrespective of their political affiliations.
>
> Still my interest is to do business, but I have not enough time left in my life to do that. I have transferred these businesses to my children and I do some community activities and art work. I am the *anusasaka* of community development organization of this *garden*.

> After the establishment of TV, I started to work for them as an artist on a contract basis. I earned about Rs. 1500 monthly. I felt that the letters on TV were not good. I thought I should go and talk to the president of the TV. First I went to the MP's PRO and got a letter to go to the president of the TV. That's how I got that job. I worked there until last month. Still I earn Rs. 250 to Rs. 300 doing contracts on my own.
>
> After the power shift in 1977, the SLFP affiliated people face difficulty in continuing in politics. After 1977, SLFP affiliated political organizations began to be diluted. I spent my own money for garden committee meetings. I spent nearly Rs. 6000 for the political activities of SLFP organizer of the ward. Then he escaped also. After that, I was disappointed with politics.
>
> Everybody in this community now is on good terms with me. Even the UNP *Kattiya* (group) has a respect for me. Because now I do not affiliate with either side. I have made a decision that I will not go for political activities but this is not firm. I help the public and community development activities. Even in those activities, there was a political influence, as I am a SLFP person. But after awhile, they themselves decided unanimously that I must be in the Community Development Organization. I told them to hand over these things to youths, while I would be an *anusasaka* (patron-advisor). In this area I am accepted strongly. Other members in these organizations are not motivated enough. Recently, I shouted at the secretary. The operation of the organization is in his hand. (03/31/1985)

Case No. 3. In another example, a leftist (LSSP affiliated person) explained his experiences. He migrated to Colombo in 1949 and to this location in 1964. He was a clerk in the Department of Education and a member of the General Clerical Socialist Union (GCSU). He was involved in the 1980 general election and lost his job.

> I am involved in enough social activities. I was involved in the activities of a community organization organized by Buddhists (they conducted a Sunday school and vocational training center, needle work and music for young children). Now I am devoid from many things. I played a leading role in many activities at Dematagoda. I was the organizer and secretary of the New Year festival

> committee for nearly five years. I was the president of the *Sama Mandalya* (the Board of Peace—a new institution, a judiciary board, introduced by the SLFP government to settle small disputes at the local level). We have done enough. We should retire now. If there is something necessary we will come forward. We maintain friendships and necessary connections. Now we do not engage in these activities very much. I am not taking an active role in the Community Development Organization, but I have a membership. People of the Dematagoda junction respect me more than the people of this side. I have friends living outside this area. I am in a position to obtain Rs. 5000 immediately just by sending a message. I have friends in Dematagoda, Kollonnawa, Maligawatta and Pettha. One of my friends is a contractor. His long term fixed deposit in a bank alone is Rs. 35 million. He is a Roman Catholic person. He is in a position to give Rs. 200 per day as offerings.
>
> I encountered some political problems because I am leaning towards the left. I have now decided to take an indifferent position in public activities and political affairs. No need to take leading positions. I think we have done enough services during our lifetime. But there is no appreciation for that. It is not appropriate to expect something in return for help that we did. But there should be appreciation at least in the minds of those who obtained that help. I am not worried about those things. I helped some people to enroll their children, nearly 300 to 400, in schools. (05/20/1985)

Case No. 4. A 30 year old male, born in this location, is another example. Unlike the other three cases presented above, he is an ambitious man of achievement, strongly pursuing a political career. He is in a competing position in the political setting of the area. His personality with this political ambition can be traced through his life history.

> First, I went to St. Johns College at Dematagoda. I studied there up to grade 10. Those days we were poor. My daddy tried to give me an education. We had a simple life, and were poor. But my daddy gave me all that I needed. I did not get through my GCE (General Certificate of Education) examination the first time. The second time I got the best result. Then I got a scholarship to Nalanda College. When I was preparing for my examination in

December, I did tutoring for one person for Rs. 20 per month. In 1976 I started doing tutoring, with six benches. At the beginning I had eight students. I charged Rs. 15 per person. I taught all the subjects, except English, for the GCE (OL) examination. After the first month, the number of students went up to 20. At the end of the first year it was 90. I employed other tutors. In 1978 I wanted to sit for the Advanced level examination, but I could not do that, as I was busy with this tutoring. By this time my monthly income was about Rs. 20,000. I didn't have enough space at my house. I moved certain classes to the temples, Weluwana and Gnanawimala. In 1979, I rented out a building in this location.

Gradually my social interactions began to be changed. I started to have friendships with the children of big people. I bought a car. After I bought this car, my downfall started. I spent a lot of money for this car. In 1980, my monthly income was about Rs. 20,000, but my expenses were about Rs. 24,000. I expanded my tutoring business to other areas. I started classes at YMBA Boralla, Butharamulla, Ambalangoda, down south. My name became popular, but my control over the business began to be decreased. My discipline was decreased. I started going to clubs. I had to change my lifestyle in order to face the society (to cope with the high society).

After some time, the number of students began to be decreased. Gradually my downfall was started. I closed classes at YMBA Boralla, Batharamulla and down south. I handed over Dematagoda schools to some other people and took some money for my "good will." I requested a visa to go to France. I couldn't get that. In 1982, I went to Pakistan with my own money. I got some pocket money from the Seventh Day Adventist Movement. My sister was a member of this group. I started doing business studies in one of the universities in Pakistan. But I couldn't continue. After six months I came back. I tried to get a visa to go to France when I was in Pakistan, but it did not work out.

Since my childhood, I have had political interests, becoming popular, and taking leadership. I had several positions in school societies such as the president of science society, president of Buddhist student organization, secretary of literature society. I won a gold medal in a speech contest.

> During the presidential election and the referendum, I was in Pakistan. Before the MMC election (Member of Municipal Council), I told the party strongly that I would be going to contest this seat. Then they told me that they would give me a place next year. Therefore, I helped, at this time, the party nominee for his election campaign. I spent money for that campaign. After he won, the MP asked me what I would like. I told him that I need a position of the Justice of the Peace. Then he gave me an island wide position of the Justice of the Peace. My sister had married the MP's PRO (personal relations officer). (05/06/1985)

It is possible to identify from these cases three types of political agents with the following characteristics: (1) Entrepreneurial political agents having the objective of income stability and/or self-esteem and status consciousness, (2) political entrepreneurs who are pursuing a political career, and (3) political agents having strong status consciousness. These cases indicate the following characteristics: (1) Political agents face difficulties when they are in opposition, and the opposition group is rather politically inactive or tends to make alliances with those who hold power. The indifferent attitude and passive behavior is the strategy in this direction. Under these circumstances, non-continuity of party organizations within the community is a significant feature in this political process. There is a tendency to weaken the politics of an ideological kind in the face of strong patron-client ties of dyadic contracts, quasi-groups, and other social networks. The vested interest of both parties contrasts with political ideologies. (2) These political agents play a mediating role between power centers and the community having attributes of both patrons and clients. (3) Networking is an essential task for them to play this patronage role and enjoy self esteem and status. (4) Crossover politics and cross channeling of benefits are also by-products of this patron-client relationship.

Minorities who need political reliance. The Tamils in this group have political faith in the ruling party, but they do not get involved in political activities. There is only one deviant case for this behavior. Non-involvement of the majority is a protective strategy which they adopt under the present communal tensions. Most of these Tamils struggle to live, expecting both economic and political protection. In this respect their choices are extremely limited and they have the fear that the political involvement may create an unsafe environment. However, they try to maintain their political faith in the UNP politics and use those political channels smoothly.

For example, a 32 year old male Tamil has not only political faith in the UNP but also direct involvement in political activities. In order to understand this behavior it is important to trace his background and his neighborhood environment. He is a young Tamil married to a Sinhala woman in the same *garden*. His marriage brought some tension between him and his wife's family. His wife's family is actively engaged in UNP politics. The majority of residents in this *garden* are Tamils and UNP affiliated people. His income is unstable and he is aspiring either to get a permanent job in the government sector or to establish a stable business using political channels. Under these circumstances, he is taking a *garden* level leadership position affiliated to the ruling party, though he is not totally satisfied yet with regard to his expectations. He expressed his feeling:

> I asked the ward member to get a job for me. There is no effort yet. They have to do it. I am a leader of the UNP *garden* committee. Yet there is not any use. (06/09/1985)

The non-involvement behavior has to be understood in the context of neighborhood politics and the individual's personal circumstances. The following two statements reveal this non-involvement:

> From the beginning we did not do political work. We vote for the party. In some instances, we go to the MP and get some help. He usually helps us. (06/09/1985)

> We received a letter from the MC ward member to get a job for my wife. . . . We voted for UNP. We only give our vote and keep quiet. If we work for one side we will lose our protection. (05/19/1985)

NON-AFFILIATED AND NON-DEPENDENTS

The data show 54% of the Sinhalese in this group are white collar workers mainly employed in the government sector. None among the minorities are white collar workers. Minorities in this group are either blue collar workers or totally dependent on their children. Among Sinhalese, there are about 15% blue collar workers, 15% are engaged in business, and another 15% are dependents.

As far as place of origin is concerned, the Sinhalese have diverse roots while minorities are from other parts of Colombo, other locations and a few are born in this location. Only one Tamil person in this group of the sample is of Indian origin.

There is a marked difference in terms of per capita income between majority and minority in this group. All the minorities, except one, fall into the below Rs. 400 per capita income group. About three quarters of the Tamils fall below Rs. 200. Sinhalese are by and large dispersed among all income groups. However, of 13 Sinhalese, 38% fall within the category of over Rs. 750.

As far as housing ownership is concerned, the majority in all three ethnic groups are house owners. Only four live on government land and the other four (three Sinhalese and one Tamil) are tenants.

In the case of age distribution, the majority in this group fall in the middle age group or old age group. Nobody is in the young age group.

The majority who are engaged in white collar jobs were rather reluctant to talk about politics. One respondent, retired from the government sector, said "There are no political conflicts nowadays. People do not worry about political matters. They don't want to discuss them." (06/22/1985) This implies his feeling about the necessity of avoiding politics. A middle aged woman who is employed in the government sector expressed her views.

> We live pretending to be indifferent about political status. Therefore, there is no disturbance for us. When I vote, I consider the personal qualities of the candidate. If an IRC person goes to parliament, then it is no use for me, no use for the government and no use for the country. (04/20/1985)

The following inferences can be drawn from these statements: (1) The white collar category perceives a potential disturbance as a result of political affiliations, and (2) there is a social distance between this group and those who control political channels.

There are seven non-white collar Sinhalese with no political affiliations and no dependence on political channels for individual benefits; two of them are females. A 51 year old widow, dependent on her children, has reasonable savings and property ownership. Her family enjoys a fairly good living condition. The per capita income of this family is Rs. 1000. She is aspiring to move out to the periphery where one of her daughters is living. But she wants to keep the ownership of her present residence considering the increasing property value in this location. She has a more pessimistic view about political affiliations.

> We do not have membership in any community organization, political or otherwise. We know that there are organizations in this community. We do not get any use by following them. It is of no use for the country either. (07/08/1985)

A 65 year old male is another example in this category. He is a retired person from his government job and presently has no specific expectations. All his children are employed and have a secured income. Per capita income is a little over Rs. 450. This family resides in a house for which he will get a deed in the near future from the national housing department. He also holds a pessimistic view regarding community politics as in the previous case. Another person in this category is a 38 year old male, not married, who works as a laborer in General Hospital. Per capita income of this family is Rs. 100. He is still a tenant, participating in activities that are carried out by the community development organization but has no affiliation to political organizations. He also has no specific expectations in his life. He casts his vote more on the basis of personality attributes than on political ideology. He says:

> It is good if the country is developed without having political divisions. I can't say that there is an improvement in the community. Five fingers are not the same. (05/13/1985)

His pessimistic view is more of a response to the political disunity. He is trying to rationalize his own personal behavior in this political context.

> I cannot have an expectation because of times that we live in. (05/13/1985)

Unacceptable leadership is another reason for avoidance of politics. In one such example, a skilled worker employed in a private company says:

> We do not go to the MC ward member's society. They also do not come to us. Political party organizations should know how to increase the membership. Members should not go after political party branches. Once we get membership, it is a disturbance for us. We waste our time. Political party organizations operate only in opportunistic ways. Those days I had a friendship with both sides. Both sides got separated. They do not try to resolve problems easily. Both sides tried to show their own power, and did not get any benefit. (05/20/1985)

Minorities with no political reliance. There are four Tamils and three Muslims in this group. Muslims do not reveal their views on politics. As I noted earlier, the Tamil minorities' non-involvement is a strategy for their own protection in the context of neighborhood politics. They have no intention to get personal benefits through politics. They totally depend on their labor for living; political avoidance and having indifferent views are much safer for these people. However, this political avoidance indicates the powerless and subservient position of Tamils in this community. There is a social constraint for the freedom of expression. The following are some of those statements:

> I never participated in political activities. If you go for that, then people from one side get angry. I vote without expressing my ideas. I do not go to anybody to ask any help. (06/02/1985)

> We are not affiliated to any organizations political or otherwise. It is difficult to live in this area while having connections to those. (07/15/1985)

> In this *garden* there are both UNP and SLFP affiliated people. If we take a side others will get angry. Then we cannot have connections with them. If we live as ordinary people, then we can have a relationship with everybody. If we do not behave good there will be troubles. We do not go for political activities. We say yes to everybody who comes for canvassing. When we vote, we consider who is going to help, at least a little, Tamil people and who is going to give consumer items at lower prices. I got my citizenship in 1977. Thondaman (one of the national level Tamil leaders in the country) asks us to vote for those who help Tamils. Most of our Tamils vote for Sirimavo Bandaranaike (prime minister of the country during 1960 to 1965 and 1970 to 1977) as she promised, in her election campaign in 1970, rice coming down from the moon. As Thondaman became a minister in the government (in the UNP cabinet), Tamils thought that they would get help. But I have not decided that I should be with these people. In the next election, we have to vote looking at the situation. Nobody forces us to vote. (04/05/1985)

NON-AFFILIATED AND INDIFFERENT GROUP WITH POLITICAL RELIANCE

Of the total of ten in this group, six are engaged in an unskilled type of work and three are dependent on their children. Only one person is engaged in business activities. As far as their place of origin is concerned, there is no marked difference. These represent by and large a diverse origin. The majority is over 50 years old. As far as monthly per capita income is concerned, 50% of this group fall below Rs. 100 category. There is only one person over Rs. 750. Three people fall within the Rs. 201 to Rs. 400 category. Forty percent of this group live on government land without having housing ownership. Another 40% has ownership of residence including those who obtained ownership from the National Housing Department as a result of Housing Ceiling Act. The rest (20%) are totally tenants.

Six Sinhalese are politically dependent. Two of them are old female widows who struggle for their living. Their living conditions are very poor in every respect. Their main concern is to get employment for their sons using political channels, though their family members have no formal political affiliations. A 46 year old female describes her effort for this objective:

> We do not have membership in any of the community organizations political or otherwise. In order to get a job for my son I made an effort by obtaining letters from the MC ward member who resides in this community and the MP of the electorate, a cabinet minister in the government. But he did not get a job yet. (07/04/1985)

The youngest respondent (33 years old) in this category has already used the political channels to obtain his job though he has no formal affiliations to any political party. Unlike the two female widows, he is rationalizing his non-affiliated behavior.

> I was never affiliated with a political party and I will not ever be affiliated with one. I obtained UNP support in order to get my job through a friend of mine. But I did not work for them. If we work for a political party, then people become enemies. The other reason is that there is a secret ballot, but before we vote, we were identified and labeled. It is difficult to be without enemies once you work for a party. People talk to me on the way from here to the junction. But I have moderate connections with them. Because of that reason, some people might say that I am proud. However, it is better to have moderate connections. (05/28/1985)

He further rationalized his non-affiliation, going beyond the community level:

> The Government uses Armed Forces, not for our protection, but for their own protection. If something happens, we have to die irrespective of Tamil or Sinhala. Poorer men have to give their necks for everything. The Government raises the prices of consumer items in the face of terrorism. They do not raise wages, all of which are troubles for us. (05/28/1985)

Politically non-affiliated, a Sinhala respondent who is totally disappointed with political channels described his views in this manner.

> There is no use of organization. Office bearers of these organizations get jobs for outsiders by taking bribes. It is difficult to get jobs for the boys in the *village* (referring to the community). Only relatives and friends of the leaders of organizations get these jobs. *Nana* (the inferior reference to the MP of the electorate, as he is a Muslim) helps in those. We did not get membership. It is

> not necessary to pay a membership fee as they provide jobs for outsiders. Every organization is a political one. Therefore, we do not affiliate with any one of those. (06/17/1985)

This behavior reflects a disappointment. This is an outcome of his efforts regarding his children's education and employment. He made an effort to secure employment for his young child after his education ceased. His older son got through General Certificate of Education (ordinary level) and wanted to continue his education. The ambition of continuing education was a failure since his son was not accepted by Colombo schools due to bureaucratic corruption prevalent in the school system. He further says:

> Two major schools in Colombo ask Rs. 5000 to secure my son's enrollment. I did not have that much money. Therefore he has to stop his education. All the other schools said that there was no room. I informed the Department of Education of this situation. We did not even get a reply. That is the system of free education. (06/17/1985)

The necessity of political reliance for certain people is unavoidable. They always try to use political channels strategically. Once they fail in their strategies they are disappointed, but their avoidance from community politics does not necessarily mean that they are no longer reliant on politics. It may be a temporary setback from a strategic point of view. For example, a 29 year old male, a more energetic, entrepreneurial type of person is pursuing personal family advancement. He takes initiative in *garden* level community activities, particularly on the matters of maintaining infrastructure facilities. He has a vested interest pertaining to this entrepreneurial ambition. He is a landlord, owning three extra houses in this garden. The improvement of infrastructure facilities increases the value of his property and strengthens the relationship between him and his tenants. Improvement of these infrastructure facilities has a lot to do with the intervention of Colombo municipal bureaucracy and the community politics. His efforts so far in this connection are failures. He expresses his disappointment saying:

> I do not go after politics. I do something depending on the circumstances. Once or twice I worked for politics as this is an essential thing (to improve toilet conditions). It did not work out. Therefore, I avoid politics and try to make success in our life. (06/23/1985)

Political avoidance is a strategy for the group who is non-affiliated but with reliance. Their voting behavior is largely determined by personal attributes which are approachable to them rather than ideological commitment. This behavior is best exemplified by the following statement made by one of the respondents in this group.

> I do not work for political parties. I vote for a person whom I think is deserving, a person who can do something and through whom I can get something done. (06/21/1985)

Of the four Muslims in this group, three are disappointed. One Muslim woman said that she was not affiliated to any political party but she had approached both political parties through political agents of respective parties, to obtain jobs for her children. The following statements indicate some of the disappointments of this group with regard to their personal expectations.

> All those who worked for the MP obtained houses. We did not. My sister applied. She sent an application for a house and ran here and there (this means contacted political channels) but still she couldn't get a house. (05/12/1985)

> Nobody in our family works for politics. The UNP did not do anything for the flats. They did not give even a job. They gave only for political stooges. I did not go to the MC Ward member. Other people are going. Some people say that he helps only for his known people, who spent money for his political campaign and for his political stooges. I heard that he also takes bribes to get employment for some people. We did not see this, but people say it. I am not ready to do political activities. The reason is there is no unity among the people of this area. I do not like to go voluntarily. (04/21/1985)

> We can't get anything done from the government. Sometimes, I get angry about the activities of the government. They have no respect for people. (05/23/1985)

The analysis of the different manifestations of political behavior of Dematagoda clearly illustrates the complex and paradoxical nature of patronage politics. Even the cases of the politically non-affiliated, non-dependent and people with indifferent attitudes regarding politics reflect a characteristic of dependency and obligation to the patronage system. This obligation has explicit dependency particularly at the community level and at the national level in general. The adaptation of non-involvement behavior is one of the outcomes of integration where the patronage system is highly pronounced. Thus it is a form of obligation to the community structure by the people who have less power in community affairs. However, the patronage system frequently does not operate smoothly, but dissatisfactions, tensions, and conflicts are outcomes of the basic social process of the community.

Chapter 7

Community Conflicts and Politics

Community conflicts and patronage politics have structural manifestations. As political behavior is interwoven into the social fabric, the macro level political changes have a great impact on the community structure. In the context of macro–micro political structure, community conflicts over the issues of resources provide the basis for outside intervention. The political parties and authorities directly or indirectly are involved in these matters. The level of involvement and the method of intervention have significant impact on the community resources structure and the network of relationships. Community conflicts are dramatized by political factionalism and alliances, flavored with ascriptive demands such as locality, kinship, ethnic, religious and symbolic festivities.

Small disputes between families over infrastructural facilities and personal matters are very frequent incidents in the Dematagoda community. These disputes produce temporary tensions between respective families. In addition to these small disputes, 19 major conflicts have been noted during the period of 1970 to 1985 in the household interviews. The types of issues upon which these conflicts have occurred are enumerated in table 7.1. These conflicts are serious enough to have external institutional intervention for settlement between parties.

Table 7.1

Major Community Conflicts During 1970 to 1985

Issues Over Conflict	Number of Conflicts	Percent
Housing (Landlord/Tenant)	2	10.5
Boundaries	1	5.3
Toilet Facilities	3	15.8
Water Taps	1	5.3
Business	3	15.8
Political	4	21.0
Other	5	26.3
Total	19	

POLITICAL DYNAMICS

Housing is one of the major areas that some of the relationships revolve around. Soon after the political changes occurred in 1956, some house owners made an effort to sell their houses to outsiders at higher rates. As few tenants could not afford high prices, they prevented house owners from selling these houses to outsiders. This act led to conflict and tension between landlords and tenants.

In 1964, one of the house owners who owned a fair number of houses attempted to sell them. His tenants offered Rs. 5000 for each. The owner refused that offer as his price was higher than the offer. He threatened the tenants, saying that he would not sell these houses to them as they were SLFP affiliated people. But there were a small percentage of UNP affiliated tenants, too. This house owner made the arrangements to have an auction for these houses. The residents got wind of this arrangement and took the matter up with the then prime minister, the leader of the SLFP, Sirimavo Bandaranayaka. She gave her assurance that the government would acquire the houses to ensure that the tenants would not be evicted. The owner, unaware of this development, set a date to auction the houses. On the day of the auction the residents picketed the venue of the auction carrying placards notifying prospective buyers that very shortly the houses were to be acquired by the ministry. This was an instance where people of diverse political affiliations put aside whatever political differences and interests and showed unity as tenants.

During the SLFP political regime, 1970 to 1977, the National Housing Department acquired most of the houses under the Housing Ceiling Act. The government acquired these houses and began to transfer them to the residents. As a result, some of the house owners who were affiliated with leftist politics for a long period crossed over to the UNP in the 1977 election.

There is an interesting political dimension in the effort of evicting shanty dwellers from the crown land which was set apart for a school building by the Education Department. The effort of the Education Department to evict the residents created tension between these two parties. Therefore, the residents of this land expected the local politicians to solve their housing problem. Over the period of 1975 to 1985, several attempts have been made to evict them with little success. One such attempt made during the previous political regime is a good illustration. The government authorities acquired crown land in the suburban area where these residents were to be resettled. Several members of the community made a reconnaissance mission to have a look at the area and also to assess the feasibility of resettling there before they actually committed themselves to move. They returned with a decision not to make the move. The explanation of the mission for this decision was that the people of the suburban area, where the resettlement land is located, were under the impression that this land was meant to house the overflow from their increasing numbers. As such, they were antagonistic towards any outsiders moving in. In the context of political reality, this explanation was somewhat exaggerated. There are two possible underlying reasons which can be presented for the decision of not moving. First, the mission explanation is rather a political manipulation than an authentic reason. The ulterior political motive is to prevent moving these residents out. The numerical strength of these shanty dwellers was a political base for certain local politicians. Second, there was no clear resettlement plan on the part of the government. The intended resettlement was not feasible. On the one hand, such a move would definitely cut off the easy access to the economic base of these dwellers. On the other hand, there was no plan to integrate these dwellers into the local community of Colombo suburbs.

The numerical preponderance of urban population is closely associated with the reality of political factionalism. The lack of housing, low income, and the scarcity of land are thriving factors for the establishment of poor quality sub-standard housing in any urban environment in most of the larger cities in Sri Lanka. This situation creates a ground for patronage politics. In this community, the overflow from government *flats* began to encroach on the playground and erected temporary housing structures with political permission. This permission is an example of bypassing the housing regulations and all the sanitation codes of the Municipal Council. In this case there was a mediating patron, a Buddhist monk, who wanted to establish a temple in this location with a new clientele, as there were already two well established temples within the community. Therefore, the needs of three parties, the need of houses, local politicians and the mediating patron, were satisfied by overruling the regulation. The outcome was the establishment of congested and unhealthy shanty dwellings around the government housing scheme during the period of 1977 to 1985. This was one of the reasons which aggravated the conflict between residents of these government *flats* (majority UNP affiliated) and the older residents (the majority are politically left oriented) of the west bounds of Gnanawimala Road. According to the evidence of both sides violent acts of attacking each other were frequent between these two groups.

These conflicts, most frequently, started with personal rivalries at an individual level and ended up involving the majority of both parties. The older residents of this community, particularly from the west boundary of Gnanawimala Road, stigmatized the residents of the government *flat*s as uncivilized people. They always blame these residents of government *flats* for these major conflicts. The residents of the government flats are of the opinion that they were not considered as human beings and were treated as animals by these older residents of the community. However, this hostility is gradually fading away and improvement of relationships in recent years has been noted by both parties.

Many explanations are presented for the improvement of the relationship between these two groups. It is interesting to note two contrary views presented by some residents of this community. First, there has been a high mobility rate of the original residents of these government *flats,* transferring their houses to newcomers. Newcomers are considered more civilized than the original residents. Second, the increasing trend of healthy relationships is not due to civilized newcomers but due to the attraction of the younger generation of the older residents by the illegal activities done in the government *flats.* Some of these activities are prostitution, narcotics, and blue (pornographic) films.

In addition to these two contrary views the following reasons could be drawn from the interviews. (1) Some people from the older residents of Gnanawimala Road have also crept into the shanty areas putting up temporary dwellings. (2) Some intermarriages have taken place between families of these two groups. (3) The political allegiance mainly among the community political leaders of the ruling party.

As far as intermarriages are concerned, it can be safely assumed that there was a tension between these two stigmatized groups as civilized and uncivilized. Such a tension was revealed when there was a relationship developed by a man from the older residents of the civilized group with a woman from the government *flats.* It is noted in one interview that a person who was trying to escape without marrying a woman whom he has affection for, was threatened by a group of people from the government *flats*. His house was attacked in 1983 when this group was threatening this man. The final outcome of this threat was that he had to marry this woman.

Some *intra-garden* conflicts were aroused between family groups over matters of illegal business. Two such incidents are recorded in the interviews. (1) A fight over the competition of punting business between one of the *gardens* and government *flats*, and (2) a fight over an illegal liquor business between two family groups of *flats* and another *garden*. These conflicts caused severe injuries to some members of the family groups.

Most of the other intra-group conflicts are over the issues of using infrastructural facilities, such as pipe borne water and toilet facilities. Political factionalism and interference revolve around these issues. In certain cases, these inner group conflicts are power battles between political opponents rather than genuine quarrels over infrastructural issues. One such battle which took place in one of the *gardens* of this community is a good illustration. A migrant from Kalutara district in the western province, married to a woman from older residents in this *garden*, was the key actor in this conflict. He was affiliated with leftist politics and an active member of the community. He describes this battle.

> In front of our house, there was a road tap. We used this tap as our own, fixing a water pump. We maintained the tap well. We imposed an order to our neighbors that they must fix the pump after taking water. We thought that it was an obligation on their part. After some time of this order, CMC (Colombo Municipal Council) officials came and asked us to remove this pump. My neighbors had informed this situation to the mayor and asked him to take action to remove this tap from this location. At that time the government was in the hand of UNP, but CMC was occupied by the leftists. The mayor ordered engineers to remove this tap. Despite this order, we did not allow the officials to remove it. We went to ward members of the Colombo Municipal Council ward members and were trying to cancel the mayor's order. The mayor was in a difficult setting, that he was pressurized by both sides. The UNP supporters influenced him to reinforce the order several times while we influenced him to cancel this order. This war continued nearly four years. During this period, some of our

> neighbors tried to demolish this tap at night. We were able to prevent those efforts. Leftists help leftists in such incidents, though they do not help in personal matters. (04/06/1985)

In another example, the conflict over an infrastructural issue was settled through political intervention with adding facilities to the people who were involved with that conflict. In one of the gardens, there are two housing lines. The majority of one line of houses in this garden is affiliated with the UNP, while the majority of the other line is affiliated with SLFP. Before 1976, the residents of line number two were allowed to use the common toilets which were allocated for line number one, as there were not enough toilets for line two. The year 1976 was a time when the political tension was reaching its peak due to the forthcoming election in 1977. As a result of this political tension the people of line number two closed down the common toilets for the residents in line number one. The police intervention in this matter was a failure. Then the residents of line number one made an appeal to the SLFP organizer of the area. As a result, the SLFP organizer built two toilets with his own money.

In a highly politicized community, conflicts and politics are magnets to each other. Conflicts may start purely on a personal basis free from politics, but these largely end up with political manifestations. The same is true for the conflicts which have direct political origin. Those conflicts are flavored with characteristics of personality, locality feelings, issues over infrastructural matters, family clashes, religious and community functions. The economic activities of the bazaar cannot be isolated from politics. The community festivals such as the religious and new year festivals cannot be performed without having political connections. The community development organizations' activities cannot be separated from the politics of the area.

Inter and Intra-Political Rivalries and the Trends

It is interesting to note a dynamic nature of the political drama to reveal inter and intra-political rivalries and the trends exhibited in this community. Let me present this political drama through one of the case histories of this study. A 39 year old Sinhala male was a politically active person in this community.

My father was from Weligama (down south), mother from Meethotamulla (Colombo suburb). I am a plumber. My father had migrated to Colombo when he was 17 years old. I have been to my father's village several times, but we do not have any economic connections with our relatives there. My aunt's children live there. My father's brothers and sisters died. My uncles have had a hotel in "Dematagoda." My father told me that he was staying in this hotel while he was working in Colombo as a laborer. He was helping their activities in this hotel whenever he was free. My mother's *Mahageya* (original main house) is still there in Meethotamulla. My mother had seven members in the family—four brothers and three sisters. Some of them had lived in one of the adjacent locations of the study area.

I studied up to the eighth grade. I went to Dematagoda *Anuruddha Maha Vidyalya.* Those days there were no kinds of popular schools. I stopped going to school in 1953 when I was in grade eight. Tuition masters were brought into our house to educate us. But we didn't have the talent to learn. Not because of economic difficulties. I started work while I was going to school. After school I worked for my father. My father was a plumber. I liked to go to work. I worked for my father nearly one year. Then I worked for my brother. When I left my father, I had some skill as a *workman.* My father paid me Rs. 2.25 per day. My brother paid me Rs. 4.00. After some time I joined with my brother-in-law. He was a contractor. He gave me Rs. 5.00 per day. I went from place to place for both money and learning. He (brother-in-law) had a company (building construction) at Ratmalana (suburb in Colombo). I worked for him for two years until 1956. With his help I went to the technical college. I followed a one year course in plumbing. After this training I worked again for my second brother as a skilled worker *bass* (implies a supervisory role in addition to his skill). Then my age was about 20 years. He paid me Rs. 7.50 per day. By then I was married. By 1959, even after my marriage, I worked for my brother for some time.

I married from Kandy (capital city of the central region of the country). This was a love marriage. She was a poor woman. Her parents were not alive. At that time she didn't have a guardian. Since my young age, I was thinking that I would bring (would marry) a woman from a poor place (poor family). I did dislike dowry. My father-in-law has had a second marriage from Colombo. Her father had died in an accident. They were in an adjacent location. No one from my family disagreed about my marriage. I had a very simple marriage ceremony because my sister's wedding was coming up. We had to take her marriage ceremony. (It is customary that sisters should get married first, and brothers are supposed to contribute to the sisters' marriage ceremonies.) I did not save money by then. But I had a savings book. By that time even Rs. 300 to Rs. 400 was big money. I spent about Rs. 200 for my wedding. My friends gave me the necessary transportation. After my marriage, I stayed in my sister's house in this *garden*. After six months of my marriage I fell down from a building at fort where I worked. Therefore, I had to face many economic hardships. My spinal cord was damaged and I couldn't stand for nearly one year. My sister helped me for food. This was a very unhappy situation. Even my brothers neglected me. After that I decided not to work for wages under anybody. They didn't give me money even for my medicine.

I got off to the road, even before I was fully recovered. I met one gentleman who was in Grover Street (one of Colombo's locations). He had buildings. I started to work for him. He helped me. I worked for him four to five years. Generally, he paid me whenever I did some work. After that I met another gentleman. He then was an engineer. I worked with him as a contractor.

I started a current account in 1963. By 1964, I achieved a certain level. I earned money. Nearly 30 people worked for me. I employed them. Some of my employees were from this community. During this time some people who were engaged in politics, a number of nasty people, came to me and insisted that I take a leading part in some activities in the area.

I had a feeling to work for the poorest even during the period of the father of the previous leftist member of the municipal council. Lanka Sama Samaja party was then popular. Therefore I started politics with them. My father objected. But I didn't stop. My father objected as he felt that my prosperity was disturbed by this. I had in my mind to continue in politics. The gentleman whom I worked for became unfriendly. I stopped totally my contract work. I couldn't manage my contract work as I didn't go to the work sites. Then workers did whatever they wanted.

By then I was the Secretary in the Youth League and a member of the *Local* (intermediate level party organization—one of the representatives of the ward). I became a party member in the *Local*. Then I had certain commitments regularly. I faced the problem of economic backwardness. My wife also supported me in politics.

The secretary of this *Local* was also from this community. I also had some followers. At one point, as a result of a communication breakdown (orders from the secretary didn't reach me in time), the secretary was upset. But I did party activities in time. In the meantime, an order was given by the party that one member from each youth league, for every month, had to be appointed as a representative to the local. Because of this the party could charge Rs. 1.00 for every month.

I was a little bit nervous about this. I told the secretary of the local about this situation. He wanted to discuss it with me. I argued with him on certain issues. He informed these things to the party incorrectly. A *mudalali* (a trader, a leading businessman in the area, and one of the key figures in this area, who is a member of the United National Party—opposition political party at that time) had signed for my current account as a guarantee. On that basis, the secretary gave a wrong impression to the party that I was going to join the UNP. The party submitted an alleged complaint against me. As a result of this, I resigned from the party and came home.

In the meantime, the government changed, political power shifted from left to the right. Then UNP was in power. In 1965, during the period of UNP, I was silent nearly one year. No politics. I did one or two small contract works here and there.

Then, again another group came to me (one of the directors of the flour milling corporation under the regime of the previous government, one of the SLFP members, and several others). They suggested to form a SLFP organization within the area (SLFP—Sri Lanka Freedom Party). We formed a SLFP organization. By then there was no SLFP organization in this community. By 1968, the LSSP party became unpopular in this area. Then the secretary of the local and others came behind me. They had forgotten all the previous happenings and unfriendliness. By 1969 we worked jointly (SLFP and LSSP came into a non-contesting pact having in mind to form a coalition government). By 1970 I took the leading position in the area. I was the main polling agent of Dematagoda. After about one month of the victory, the cut-throats were started. I was labelled as SLFP member. Boralla electorate in which this community comes under, was represented in the state assembly, by the LSSP, under the non-contesting pact. The LSSP member won the political seat and the secretary of the *Local* intentionally made the MP unhappy about me.

I didn't drink alcohol those days. One day Munidasa and some others came to me and suggested me to join with them for a drink. Because of them I also got used to drinking.

The SLFP government passed a Housing Ceiling Act in 1972. As a result of this the people who had money in this country stopped housing construction. Therefore, no work was available during that period. I had to suffer without many meals. I had to face the situation without rice for many weeks, though I occupied such a significant leadership role.

In the meantime, I met one of the leading SLFP members in the electorate. He accompanied me to his own estate in Kuliyapitiya [this is in one of the districts in the intermediate zone of the country]. I distributed some of the jobs properly among SLFP members of the area. The SLFP member understood my honesty and my economic hardships and he brought me the necessary foodstuffs weekly. The roof of my house started leaking and it was deteriorated. I just managed to maintain the roof only in the kitchen area and the veranda.

By 1976 all my enemies of the area were united. They decided that they would either kill me or do bodily harm and expel me from the area. In a small way a riot occurred. One day when another leader was coming to see me, he was threatened at the entrance of this *garden* (this leader was one of the traders at Dematagoda Bazaar who was in this community. He was also a SLFP supporter). A person in 65 *Garden* was murdered by one of my present enemies, on an issue of land dispute. For that matter, one of the leading UNP political actors and others got caught (the defendants of this case are UNP affiliated politically active people. The victim was affiliated with leftist politics). I saw this incident. I gave the eye witness. Because of one of my weak statements they escaped. After they escaped they came and tried at me. During the SLFP period the present MC ward member lost his job in CTB (Ceylon Transport Board). Some members of the SLFP in this area were trying to make arrangements to re-employ a leading UNP political actor who was one of the defendants. All the SLFP political actors made a joint effort. They didn't ask any help from me. I didn't go to help them voluntarily. I kept silent. When the defendant was about to be reemployed, something happened and he couldn't get his job. They suspected me regarding this. One of the SLFP political actors was saying that I had done something to prevent reemployment of the defendant. He (defendant) started to hate me. Everyday, since morning, I was very scared. One day the members of one family of my opponents house passed some sarcastic words and laughed at us, saying that tonight was *meat and rice for the dinner*. I used to come home early. I heard that there was a gang (crowd of about 30 to 40 people) gathered near the *flat*. I have only my two nephews to take to the front. I do not have weapons too. I have only an ordinary saw. It is not sharp enough. I also had a knife used for fish cutting. I asked my nephews, "Let's go to the middle of the crowd and we catch leaders and attack them. I will attack one. You attack the other leader." I took them. First we crept into the next *garden* through the back side of our *garden*. We went to the crowd. Then one person ran and the crowd also ran. The following day the situation was terrible. I had no money in my hand. I had only my bicycle which was given by Salusala on a loan. (Then, I was working at Salusala. By about 1975, the SLFP representative of the area created a new job for me at the Salusala. It was called "plumber and masonry technician." I mortgaged my bicycle and I bought three bombs and put those softly underneath the backyard of my house. And I prayed I would not have to use those. However, the news that I bought bombs was spread. Then my enemies became silent. Then that problem was over. In 1976, a corporative manager had a problem with my nephews. He brought a gang and attacked my sister. Then I took an iron bar and attacked them back. But they put a complaint first in the police station. But the police didn't sue me because eye witnesses were contradictory.

The cooperative manager had friendship with stubborn (cruel) people in this *garden*. In 1976 on Christmas day, I went somewhere with one of my brothers-in-law and we had a drink. In the evening, I thought we could come home quietly. But my brother-in-law started shouting in front of our *garden*. One of my enemies was there in front of the garden. Then I told one of them, once I am understood, then you would follow me. The cooperative manager was standing like a thug in the middle of the *garden*. I got angry. My brother-in-law was holding his hand. I attacked the cooperative manager. He went to the house where the gang was. There were some more thugs in a hut across the canal. Those thugs came over and beat me with a big stick. I also had a weapon in my hand. My wife was stabbed. I got upset. Then suddenly the police came. I was trying to come out of the crowd. One constable was injured unintentionally with my weapon. I couldn't recognize him because he was without a uniform. I was remanded for 14 days. I thought my wife was dead.

After I came back from remand I went to meet the LSSP municipal member and told him that I didn't have a lawyer for my case. Economically I had difficulties. He sent me to a lawyer who was the brother of the then Speaker of the National State Assembly. But he was not in politics at that time. The LSFP municipal council member told this lawyer not to charge me.

The second day on which I met him, he was sarcastic to me. After that I didn't go to him. There was a school teacher at the Central School Dematagoda who recently got through his examination. I went to him and explained my situation. Then he promised me that he would appear free for me, but finally I pleaded guilty. I was again remanded for 14 days and I was under probation for two years. The court decision was given early in 1978. By that time UNP (United National Party) was in power. The Sri Lanka Freedom Party was defeated in 1977 July election. I was silent in the 1977 election. Right after the election, the whole area became silent. I was thinking when I was in remand. I took a decision not to do politics. We are only political stooges. You earn enemies because of politics.

When I was silent before the election, the nephew of the UNP minister (then candidate) came to my house and asked me to work for them. I didn't go. I was still working in Salusala.

The following day after the election, some people have had plans to attack me. The UNP political nominee of the community has had objected straightaway. There were also hidden enemies. There were one or two persons like that. All these plans were their decisions. "Man's absolute duty is to serve the man." That's what I did.

One of my close friends was the president of the UNP Trade Union at Salusala. He was the purchasing officer. During the SLFP regime he was transferred to Jaffna. (Transfers to Jaffna are regarded as punishment because in that area terrorism is going on. The Tamil Liberation Movement is fighting for a separate government.) I told the management not to transfer him to Jaffna. Therefore, he was transferred to Hatton, on my word. (Hatton is a safer area in the up country.)

It seemed to me that SLFP was going to lose. I had a good organization based on friendship. We decided to come to work whether we won or lost. We did so. Although the UNP won, they couldn't laugh at us, because we were more powerful. One week after the election I was asked to work on a dangerous machine. My finger was injured. My good friend (the UNP Trade Union leader) fired 238 employees from their jobs. Those employees worked on a casual basis. My job was permanent. Therefore, I was not fired. Management was trying to put me out. They were seeking a reason for that. I had difficulty. After six months of the election I felt I couldn't work. Lots of troubles. Then I put my leave and I told them that I was going to resign. By then a report was given to chairman of the Salusala against me based on the incident that took place in my community in December 1976. They took up the point that I injured a police constable. After that I was fired from the job in early 1978. I filed a case in the Labor Tribunal. I lost the case. Then I appealed. I won the appeal. The organization was ordered to pay me the compensation. But it was only Rs. 3000 because I had a brief service in that organization. Then I again started my own private job. There was a break for a few months after I was fired from my job. Even now I don't have continuous work. I don't possess basic capital.

The people in this area do not like to make me join in politics now. Because they do not like to give an opportunity to a talented person. Then people will follow me. The leadership in this area at this moment does not allow me to take the leadership.

Although I didn't vote for the MP of the electorate, he helped me. Since the beginning, I was one of his opponents. All the people around him consult him not to take me closer to him. I can go to his bungalow and meet him. If there was a strong organization against him in this area, it disappeared as I became closer to him. Now the leftists have difficulty in organizing in this area. What I did was not jeopardizing the leftist movement in this area.

There was an opening *Pirith Ceremony* at the Weluwana Terrace for distribution of 21 houses for MC ward member and others. I went for that. When I was there the Minister saw me. He talked to me. Whenever he sees me he calls me *Bass* [literary meaning is skilled and experienced worker; it implies supervisory skill]. If he has any kind of work in his bungalow—carpentry, masonry, plumbing, etc.—he gives me the responsibility to organize and complete this work. He built faith in me. He totally relies on me. Whatever valuable things he has, he allows me to look after those.

The following day after the opening ceremony for the distribution of houses, I had to go for some work in his bedroom. Then he asked me about the houses, whether those houses were beautiful and chief or not. I said those houses were good.

> Then the minister told me, "I will give one for you also at Kent Road." I didn't say anything. I was silent. Then the minister asked, "Why, do you have a house?" I told him that I was constructing a house and therefore, I didn't want one. If I was ready to accept it, then there would be more enemies for him. Yet, the presidential election was also not held. It was coming up. In such a situation, you must respect a person who deserves it. The MP's [he addresses MP as *Mahathmaya*, meaning gentleman] birthday was on June 17. Two days before his birthday, he saw me on the Duplication Road when I was crossing the road. The following day his bodyguard told me that the minister was talking about me when he saw me on the Duplication Road. The minister had told him that I had become a good person after I was close to him.
>
> The birthday was organized by the official UNP political nominee of the community. I didn't do any help for that. I asked them what could I do for that. They told me that everything was all right. For this birthday function, one of the leading betting shop owners, the owner of the wine store, and others were helping. I was just present.
>
> Since 1960 I was a member of one of the community organizations (in which religious teaching, and teaching of some handicrafts, are done). For some time I was a committee member in this. In 1970 to 1972 I was the secretary. After that I gave up these. There was no particular reason. When I was doing well others were trying to disturb me. After 1970, I was the secretary of the Cooperative Divisional Committee for one year. Now I am not going to that community organization at all. (05/08/1985)

It is possible to make few generalizations from this individual case. (1) When a person has attained a certain level of economic position and has acquired a capacity for patronage within the community, there is a tendency to exploit that capacity of patronage by the external political actors. This connection, in turn, reinforces the power of the person. (2) In the process of this interaction among actors, the *political cutthroats* are inevitable due to the competition for power within a political party. It is also possible in this political game to develop alliances between political opponents. (3) The decisions of individual political actors are very strategic in accordance with both external and internal political changes of the community. Different types of decisions, in different points in time are possible and are determined by the personal circumstances and choices available to the actors. Decisions are also affected by personal aspirations and the structural conditions at a wider level. For example, the changing voting strength and power of a political party and national political policies on economic and welfare issues are attributes of wider structural conditions. The person in this example aspires to an economically comfortable life balanced with political and social recognition. Thus, his decisions are outcomes of the internal–external structural conditions. Nevertheless, his strategic decisions are given personal and ideological justification. (4) Employment, employment promotions, employment terms and conditions, and housing are political goods. These are the resources which give rise to political patronage and conflicts. Both internal and external political actors are operating within this system of patronage and embark on a continuous struggle of incorporating the democratic ideals of new nations. Thus, paradoxical elements in this process are inevitable. The negativist reciprocal effect on individual and group life at both the community level and outside organizational level are a possible outcome of this patronage system. (5) Political actors are engaged in a game of risk which has direct impact on their positions (ups and downs) and on their quality of life. (6) Community behavior is characterized by conflicts and alliances between factional political groups, with vertical and cross-channeling patronage elements.

In summary, conflicts in Dematagoda have arisen due to a number of reasons. (1) Substantive conflicts center around the question of who gets what share of scarce resources, (2) who controls these valued and scarce resources, and (3) these issues are associated with political instability both at the national and local level. The political instability exhibits a variety of faces under different structural conditions. For example, factionalism, alliances and strategic integration among factions are some of these political faces in the community. These political attributes have ideological manifestations which provide the symbolic language both for community integration and conflicts and controversies.

Chapter 8

Religion and Politics: Behavioral Manifestations

This chapter examines religion and politics, and their behavioral adaptations, in Dematagoda. The prime concern of this study is to identify these behavioral adaptations in relation to the network of relationships emerging from the socio-economic and political structure of the community. The following specific questions are addressed in this chapter: (1) What is the pattern of religious behavior? What variations can be identified? (2) Is this pattern of behavior fixed or fluid? (3) Is there a correlation between different types of social categories (ethnic, status, political) and different types of behavioral adaptation? (4) What is the changing nature of this behavioral adaptation? (5) What connections, if any, exist between political affiliation and religious behavior? (6) Do connections exist between politics and religious institutions in the community? (7) What is the underlying rationale of behavioral adaptation and the operation of religious institutions?

There are two schools of interpretation of macro, analytic, social science studies of religion and politics which have been applied to Sri Lankan society. The first school of interpretation deals with the role of religion as a tool of political legitimization in an historical context—in our case, pre-colonial, colonial and post-colonial Sri Lanka. Most of these studies began in response to the conflict between Sinhala and Tamil that took place after Sri Lanka's 1948 independence (Houtart 1974; Gunatilleke 1984; Apter 1963; Tambiah 1986). These studies reveal the political indoctrination of Sinhala-Buddhist chauvinism which has negatively contributed to the contemporary ethnic conflict in Sri Lanka. The second school of interpretation focuses on behavioral transformation. These studies are largely based on Weber's theoretical formulation of the transformation of doctrinal Buddhism on the behavioral level (Ames 1963; Gombrich 1971; Leach 1962; Obeyesekere 1972; Wriggins 1960; Yalman 1964).

While neither of these approaches has been applied to the relationship between religion and politics in a dynamic community context at the micro level in Sri Lanka, the latter school of interpretation has some relevance to this analysis. Two levels of behavioral transformation have been identified: first, at the level of belief and practice, making accommodations to meet the religious needs of the laity, and second, at the level of religious organization, making links with secular authorities whose backing was necessary for the propagation and establishment of Buddhism in different communities (Malalgoda 1976, 1). These behavioral transformations were explained with regard to the social and political changes that have occurred from 1800 through the mid-20th century. Two major concerns have been noted in this historical context: first, the difference between interests of the newly emerging social elites or status groups, and those of the traditional peasantry, and second, the effect on Buddhism of these changes in the traditional system of stratification. It has been examined the ways in which these changes affected Buddhism, and how Buddhism changed itself to meet the new circumstances (Malalgoda 1976, 2). Also, the significance of recent changes in Buddhism in the context of the broader concerns of the study of "new nations" has been examined (Wriggins 1960). A few anthropological studies have traced these behavioral transformations at the village level (Leach 1962; Yalman 1964).

Obeyesekere (1963) shifted the focus from the village to the urban context. His main focus was on the transfer of political power to the Ceylonese with the granting of independence. He examined the movement of the political power and social "conditions" that produced changes in Buddhism on the behavioral level and, more importantly, the transformation of doctrinally orthodox Buddhism to the concrete "needs" of behavior and their satisfaction. Following Weber, he writes: "Such doctrinal transformations, it can often be presumed, occur under the pressure of human needs or motives and/or through the operation of social structure and economic variables" (Obeyesekere 1972, 56). Today, this changed religion is known as popular Buddhism. One specific interest of Obeyesekere's was the symbolic significance of moving statues of Buddha from the traditional isolated repositories to the "market place" in urban settings. Obeyesekera examined these shifts in the context of socio-political changes in urban settings.

All these social science studies neglected micro level behavior in heterogeneous communities. Macro level behavioral transformations do not necessarily parallel individual, group, and organizational levels of behavior in urban community settings. Variations can be found in urban communities because they exhibit a high degree of behavioral dynamics in response to the processes of social networks. Beliefs and practices are closely associated with the changing structural dynamics of urban communities. Therefore, I propose to examine behavioral adaptation rather than transformation, as it is difficult to draw parallels between macro and micro levels. Nevertheless, I will interpret macro level transformations as they contribute to the structure of micro communities.

Popular religion is the national trend in Sri Lanka. According to Apter's analysis (1963), most of the new nations adopted *political religion* in order to mobilize the people to strengthen the political power as well as to legitimize their political process. Nonetheless, the micro-level phenomena at the community level is grounded in such social conditions as ethnicity, the politics of ethnic composition, the characteristics of regional politics, and the socio-economic and infrastructural conditions of the community. In the final analysis, the distribution of power has great bearing on the life changes of individuals and groups, their aspirations and decisions. And, in turn, these individual and group decisions determine religious behavior. Thus, the changing adaptations of behavior are closely associated with the changing power structure of the community.

VARIATIONS IN BELIEFS

Four types of religious behavior have been identified in this study: (1) those who practice orthodox religious behavior, (2) popular religion, (3) religious plurality (going beyond one's own religious jurisdiction), and (4) no faith.

ORTHODOX BELIEF AND PRACTICE

Those who practice more orthodox behavior comply as much as possible with the original teachings of their respective religions. In the case of Buddhism, this is closer to the Theravada doctrine. This requires one to follow the path taught by the Buddha to attain enlightenment. Dumoulin describes:

> By reflecting on the transitoriness of our existence, one should endeavor to search for that which shines beyond us--that is, eternal life. Through the wisdom which comes from reflection on the transitoriness of life by following the path taught by the Buddha, every one can attain enlightenment. (Dumoulin 1976, 7)

The more orthodox Buddhists in this community believe this, though they do not practice it in a strict sense. In their practice they are confined to the concept of the *triple gem*—seeking refuge in the Buddha, in the Dhamma (universal laws which govern human existence and may be known by reason), and in the *Sangha* (monastic order). They do not worship god with the hope of help in life crises. They rely on fundamental concepts such as reincarnation and *karma* (the effect of good or bad deeds). Theravada Buddhists believe that the nature of the universe was shaped by *karma* and rebirth. They discard all the ritual elements centered around many gods. For life's crises they highly depend on *Pirith Chanting*, which is usually performed by the *Sangha*, but laymen are also allowed to do this. This is a silent rehearsal of Buddha's meritorious characteristics, with the belief that it brings spiritual power and will remove all evils from laymen.

POPULAR RELIGION

Popular religion provides hope for unsophisticated laymen. It has ritual elements such as devil dancing, witchcraft or charming, and *Seth Santhi* (elaborate rituals performed by a priest in order to assure success or remove evil spirits). Buddhists who practice popular religion believe in many gods and highly depend on their power. In the case of Buddhism in Sri Lanka, Hindu elements have been incorporated into popular beliefs throughout history. Robert Knox, a 17th century observer of Ceylon, noted the co-existence of two levels of Buddhist worship, saying, "Budu for the soul and the gods for this world." (Knox 1958, 130) According to Dumoulin:

> Today a Buddhist no longer needs to go to a Hindu temple *devale* to worship the gods. There is at least one *devale* in most Buddhist temples of Sri Lanka. The Buddhist monk, nevertheless, still does not officiate at this *devale* cult or offer sacrifices to the gods; that would be a blatant violation of an old Theravada tradition. Instead, he employs paid Hindu priests called *Kapurala*. (Dumoulin 1976, 75)

In recent years, popularization has gone one step further, even to the officiation of *devale* by Sinhala Buddhist *Kapurala* in many temples. The characteristics of popular religion are not confined to Buddhism and Hinduism. Some of the traditional cultural elements have been absorbed into both Ceylon Catholicism and Islamism.

RELIGIOUS PLURALITY AND NO FAITH

Those who believe in religious plurality tend to think that all religions are the same on the teaching of morality. Unlike those who believe in popular religion, they do not confine practice to their own religious jurisdiction, either in terms of basic beliefs or temple attendance. However, they adopt popular elements of several religions in their behavior. This complex behavior reflects a religious syncretism (Silva and Athukorala 1991, 147-149). People in the "no faith" category hold no particular religious views.

RELIGIOUS BELIEF: A PROFILE

Fifty-four percent of the total sample fall within the category of popular religion, while 28% lean towards orthodox practices. A marginal percentage (9%) adopt religious plurality Another small percentage of the sample have no faith and do not practice religion (table 8.1). The majority of Roman Catholics (62.5%) are among the more orthodox in their beliefs and practices. A few Roman Catholics practice either popular religion or religious plurality. Only a marginal percentage of Roman Catholics affiliate with the "no faith" category. This is quite a contrast to the Buddhists and Muslim people. Sixty percent of Buddhists and 63% of Muslims people practice popular religion. Only about 25% of Buddhists and 25% of Islamics practice a more orthodox religion. It is interesting to note that Hindu Tamils in this community usually believe in religious plurality, while in other religious groups, only a marginal percentage falls within this category (table 8.2).

POLITICAL AFFILIATIONS AND RELIGIOUS BELIEFS

Those who adopt a religiously orthodox attitude fall into three political categories: (1) a more socialist oriented group (29%), (2) people who do not have political affiliation and hold indifferent views (42%), and (3) the remainder (29%) identified with and in alliance with the ruling party. A substantial percentage (47%) of those who practice popular religion are identified with the ruling party, 20% are identified with the Sri Lanka Freedom Party (which is the left of center group), and 33% of those who practice popular religion fall within the no affiliation category and the indifferent category. None is in the Marxist group (table 8.3).

There are 20 subjects (23% of the sample) affiliated with socialist-oriented political parties. Of this 23%, 70% (14 subjects) are affiliated with the Sri Lanka Freedom Party, which is identified as left of center, while the rest are affiliated with the Marxist groups: Lanka Sama Samaja Party or Sri Lanka Equal Party (Trotsky group) and the Communist party (Moscow wing). There is a marked difference, in terms of religious behavior, between the Marxist groups and the group which is affiliated with the Sri Lanka Freedom Party. All of the

Table 8.1

Type of Belief

Type	*N*	Percent
More Orthodox	24	28.2
Popular Religion	46	54.1
Religious Plurality	8	9.5
No Faith	7	8.2
Total	85	

Table 8.2

Religious Belief by Respondent's Religion

Religions	*N*	More Orthodox (%)	Popular Religion (%)	Religious Plurality (%)	No Faith (%)
Buddhists	58	26.0	60.0	5.0	9.0
Hindus	3	—	—	100.0	—
Muslims	16	25.0	63.0	6.0	6.0
Christians	8	62.5	12.5	12.5	12.5
Total	85				

Table 8.3

Religious Belief by Political Affiliation

Religious Belief	*N*	UNP (%)	SLFP (%)	LSSP/CP (%)	No Affiliation	Indifferent
More Orthodox	24	29.2	12.5	16.6	12.5	29.2
Popular Religion	46	47.8	19.5	—	19.6	13.0
Religious Plurality	8	62.5	12.5	—	25.0	—
No Faith	7	14.3	14.3	28.6	14.3	28.5
Total	85					

Marxists tend to have either more orthodox religious beliefs and practices or no faith in religion. Of the Marxists, 67% believe in orthodox religion, while the rest hold no religious faith.

All Marxists in the sample are Sinhala Buddhists. This is not surprising in the political context of Sri Lanka. It has been pointed out that nothing is incompatible between Buddhism and Marxist socialism (Thambia 1992, 16). One of these Sinhala Buddhist Marxists belongs to the indigenous professional group, and he is still active in community activities. The Marxist group has no political power. Except for one, Marxist group interviewees were previously active in community activities and politics. Now their lives are characterized by frustration, and they are almost aloof from community affairs. The majority of the subjects (64%) who are affiliated with the Sri Lanka Freedom Party believe and practice popular religion. Twenty-two percent lean towards more orthodox practice. Only 7% have no faith and another 7% practice religious plurality.

As far as minorities in this community are concerned, there are striking features of their political affiliation and religious behavior. None of the minorities fall within the socialist-oriented categories, 56% of the minorities in the sample are affiliated with the ruling party, and the rest claim either no affiliation or are indifferent in their political behavior (table 8.4). Five of the nine Tamils (56%) are affiliated with the ruling party. Three of them practice religious plurality. One falls within the more orthodox category, while the other believes in popular religion. Two of the Muslims who are affiliated with the ruling party practice popular religion. Of the other two, one is more orthodox, and the other ascribes to religious plurality. There are eleven minorities who have no affiliation and indifferent political views (four are Tamils and seven are Muslims). Two of the Tamils practice religious plurality, one is orthodox, and the other one falls within the category of no faith. Of the seven Muslims in this category, none goes beyond his own religious jurisdiction. Three of them practice popular religion, another three are leaning towards orthodox, and only one has no faith.

The above data suggest that orthodox believers tend to be outside the ruling political party, while a substantial percentage of the believers in popular religion are identified either with the existing political power or are in the no affiliation and indifferent groups. Only a little less than one fourth of the popular believers are identified with the Sri Lanka Freedom Party, the left of center group. None of the Marxists believes

Table 8.4

Religious Beliefs, Political Affiliations by Ethnic Groups

Ethnic Group/ Political Affiliation	*N*	More Orthodox (%)	Popular Religion (%)	Religious Plurality (%)	No Faith (%)
Sinhala					
UNP	21	24.0	66.0	5.0	5.0
Leftists	20	35.0	45.0	5.0	15.0
No Affiliation and indifferent	19	31.5	63.2	—	5.3
Tamil					
UNP	5	20.0	20.0	60.0	—
Leftists	0	—	—	—	—
No Affiliation and indifferent	4	25.0	—	50.0	25.0
Muslims					
UNP	9	11.0	78.0	11.0	—
Leftists	0	—	—	—	—
No Affiliation and indifferent	7	43.0	43.0	—	14.0
Total	85				

in popular religion. The Marxist groups tended to discard popular religion to become either more orthodox or to become non-believers, probably in reaction to the loss of dominance they had finally exercised in popular temples and in the community. The category of "no affiliation and indifferent" are powerless people in the community. They might see potential negative consequences of political affiliation. Their non-affiliation gives them access to any political party whenever they need help. The adoption of religious plurality on the part of minorities gives them a sense of security in the community despite the pressure of communal tension in the country. None of the minorities are affiliated with socialist political groups. The majority of minorities (about 55%) are affiliated with the ruling party, while the rest have no affiliation or indifferent political views. The majority of the Tamils are very flexible in religious behavior and tend to practice Hinduism, Buddhism, and Christianity. The no faith category is very small among minorities.

Structural Analysis

This section provides a structural explanation with qualitative illustrations. Five structural conditions are identified as underlying factors for behavioral adaptations in Dematagoda: (1) religious plurality and strategic decisions, (2) poverty and orthodox belief, (3) chance and popular religion, (4) losing power and orthodox overtones, and (5) Buddhist temples, patronage, and politics.

RELIGIOUS PLURALITY AND STRATEGIC DECISIONS

Only two in the sample who are not minorities fall within the category of religious plurality. One is a Sinhala Buddhist, who was born locally, is 30 years of age and has a moderate level of education (i.e., in both English and Sinhala). He enjoys an above average standard of living and owns his own home. Presently he is an island-wide Justice of the Peace and has the ambition of pursuing a political career. He adopts the belief that at their foundation, all religions are the same. He has tolerance for many beliefs and participates in religious functions of all religions. In his case, the adoption of a non-biased attitude with a cosmopolitan character is a good political strategy. The other Sinhala respondent in this category is an ordinary member of this community, a Buddhist, and married to a Roman Catholic woman. In this case, the religious plurality is a reflection of compromise between husband and wife to maintain a healthy relationship within the family.

The adoption of this particular religious behavior by minorities has a wider structural meaning that goes beyond issues confined to the individual and family. For example, the Estate and Colombo Tamils residing in Colombo communities have no choice except to maintain harmonious relationships with the majority. All the Tamils maintain either high or moderate level neighborhood connections. Very few Tamils maintain external kinship connections. Their kinship connections are confined to the one or two related families in the *garden.* They have very limited choices because of their network, occupation, income, and total wealth. Their social and physical mobility are totally constrained. Under such circumstances, neighborhood and community interaction is the dominant mode in their social relationships. Relationships between the Sinhala majority and the Tamil minority at the neighborhood level exhibit inequality in a variety of ways. Extremely poor Tamils maintain dependent relationships with their Sinhala neighbors who have a higher income status; if economically equal, they maintain symbolic distance. The social relations between these two ethnic groups are characterized by different degrees of ethnic tolerance, conflict, and reciprocity. These structural elements could be best exemplified through a few cases.

> *Case I.* A Hindu Estate Tamil, 42 year old male, lives in a temporary house constructed on government land. He is illiterate. He was born in Kandapola (Nuwara Eliya District) of central province. He was brought to Colombo by his father when he was a child. He has no permanent job but works as a laborer for a Muslim contractor. His monthly income ranges from Rs. 150 to Rs. 200. He is related to one family residing in a separate house in the same *garden.* His kinship connections are very selective and limited. Nevertheless, he maintains a good neighborhood relationship, though it is of a more subordinate and dependent type. He votes for the United National Party, the present ruling party. He was protected by Sinhalese neighbors during communal violence of 1983. He has no alternative place to live, and he is community oriented (i.e., he has a sense of belonging to the community and does not intend to move from this location). He has no sympathy

towards terrorist activities in the northern part of the country. He says, "Because of the activities done by Jaffna people, we have to live with fear of death." His living conditions are very poor. He possesses no wealth except a few kitchen utensils and mats for sleeping. He says, "We are Hindus, we practice Buddhism, too. We go to Buddhist Temple. Both religions are the same. We go to Weluwana temple." (06/02/1985)

Case II. An Indian-origin Tamil male who claims to be a Roman Catholic, was born in the same *garden* he currently lives in. His mother is a Colombo Tamil. He is 32 years old and is married to a Sinhala Buddhist woman from the same *garden.* His house is a semi-permanent structure, owned by the department of housing, which is expected to transfer ownership to the tenants. He has no permanent employment. He works as a tailor for a few tailoring shops. His monthly household income is about Rs. 8000. Presently his wife is employed in the Middle East. He is engaged in community politics and has a moderate level affiliation with United National Party. He maintains a selective kinship connection and a high level of reciprocal-type neighborhood relationships. His living conditions are somewhat better than the previous case. The value of his household goods is about Rs. 6000. He prefers to have a permanent job, and if that is not possible, he is willing to start a small business once his wife comes back with some savings. He was protected by Sinhala neighbors during communal violence. He is also a community-oriented person. He is actively engaged in all religious ceremonial functions taking place in the community. He says, "Whichever deity is, we should have a faith. We go to church, to temple, and to Hindu kovil." (06/09/1985)

Case III. A Tamil female Buddhist, 43 years of age, is married to a Christian man. She lives in government *flats*. She is educated up to the fifth grade. Her husband was a laborer; now he is unemployed because of chronic illness. Her son is the breadwinner of the family. He collects trash (papers, aluminum, tins, etc.) and sends it to a recycling factory in the Northeastern province. His income is not regular. He earns Rs. 30 to Rs. 35 for a few days work each week. This family maintains strong kinship connections and a moderate level of neighborhood relationships. They do not have any political affiliations. They vote secretly. They were protected by a thug leader of the area during communal violence of 1983. They are community-oriented people. (05/22/1985)

These cases indicate the close association between the social network that Tamil minorities enjoy and their acceptance of religious plurality and flexible practices. The practice of religious plurality by estate Tamils may be a reflection of their subservient position, due to the circumstances of communal pressure in the country. The acceptance of Sinhala dominancy and rejection of the rebellion activities of Northern Jaffna are reciprocated by protection from external racially motivated mob attacks. The poor estate Tamils have nothing to offer except through legitimizing Sinhalese behavior and attitudes both at the community and national levels. The practice of religious plurality is one of the possible strategies of legitimization. The absence of complaints and agitations from estate Tamils at community levels strengthens the Sinhalese position, in a political context, with regard to the communal tension and conflict in the country.

POVERTY AND ORTHODOX BELIEF

Most of the non-leader type of Sinhala Orthodox Buddhist believers economically fall within the marginal categories. Their standard of living is very low. Most of them are squatter settlers on government land living in poor quality houses. They choose a combina- tion of kinship, neighborhood, and political networks depending on their perceptions and capabilities of maintaining relationships with others.

This group's beliefs and practices are close to doctrinal Theravada Buddhism. They are in a helpless situation and have no belief in gods. Women in this category have a relatively greater belief in religion than men. The following expressions illustrate their practices and views. A 34 year old married male says:

> We go to temple only on *Poyadays* (religious holidays), we light lamps at home everyday to Lord Buddha, and to *Seewali Hamuduruwo*. I do not have any belief in God. We do not go to *Devala* at all. I do not believe in rituals. (06/13/1985)

Another 33 year old married male says:

> I worship Buddha at home. I light a lamp for him. I do not have any belief in *Thovil* ceremonies and in God. These are lies. Who can find that God exists? No point believing in God. It causes us to spend money out of our own pocket. (05/28/1985)

A married female 44 years old says:

> I light lamps to Buddha at home, too. I pray for God (offer righteousness to God) but do not make vows. And I do not go to beg from him. I worship Buddha and offer righteousness to God. We do not believe that God can do something for us. I do not believe *Thovil* (rituals) at all. (05/29/1985)

The level of poverty and hopelessness in their lives prevents them from believing in such a God or practicing the rituals which are common in popular religion. The Orthodox Buddhism is more acceptable to these very poor than is the popular belief in Gods. They believe in a rigorous Karmic concept. Whatever the sufferings and enjoyments they have are predetermined or shaped by the deeds of a previous life. According to Theravade Buddhism, the gods are not supreme beings. They are not greater than truly enlightened human beings.

CHANCE AND POPULAR RELIGION

Random chance is an unavoidable element of life. Belief in popular religion is one of the laymen's instruments used to reduce the chance element in their daily activities. There is a popular view that the greater the risk in life, the higher the intensity of religious and ritual practices. This study reveals that those who have unstable income tend to seek more superstitious help. Regardless of the level of earnings, the people who engage in self-employment activities are more sensitive to religious beliefs and practices, as their income is unstable. The intensity of this type of belief and practice is much higher among those who have illegitimate income sources such as bootlegging, loan sharking, and drug dealings. For example, the leading indigenous group that falls within the high income categories is highly dependent on ritual practices such as devil dancing, witchcraft, or the use of charms and *Seth Santhi* in order to remove evil elements (the common belief is that these are disruptive) to gain individual economic prosperity and success in life. Some of the major events and related common religious and ritual practices among popular believers, particularly among Buddhists given in table 8.5.

Table 8.5

Religious Events and Practices of Buddhism

Event	Practice
Sickness such as high fever, stomach ache, prolonged headache	Chanting oil is applied to the head Chanting water is spread over body and inside the house; chanting threads are put around the neck
Disease caused by virus or evil spirits and serious illnesses	Major vows promising alms-giving to monks, to mothers, and to beggars Promising to offer objects to temples Promising to release a cow from the slaughterhouse
Desire for social and economic mobility (success in business, politics, occupation, education, renouncing evil characters and protection from enemies)	Make various vows, depending on affordability
To resolve neighborhood conflicts and to defeat enemies in the neighborhood	Pray to God Witchcraft
To protect newly built houses, new extensions or renovations from acts of pollution and evil characters	*Bodi puja* offerings to temples Stop eating meat in the house

The extent of these religious practices vary from one household to another, depending on the degree of belief and the level of affordability. The volume and degree of glamour of these ritual activities are positively correlated with symbolic value to these families. Thus, the greater the level of affordability, the higher the symbolic value to the household in the community. In the context of symbolic value, the leading business group and the indigenous leading group enjoy a superior position when compared to the other categories.

Beliefs and practices of religious and ritual activities are also sources of political legitimacy. This is the national trend in mainstream politics in the country. This community is not an exception to the national trend. Those who engage in mainstream politics frequently practice and perform religious and ritual ceremonies at individual and group levels to obtain legitimacy. The common belief is that it reduces the risk element in politics at the community level, since this is highly competitive and produces tension among people.

LOSING POWER AND ORTHODOX OVERTONES

The causal associations between political and religious behavior of the respondents cannot be explained by their expressed ideological commitment without looking at more structural dynamics of the community. Individual case histories have revealed some fluidity in religious and political behavior. For example, some of the present orthodox believers used to practice popular religion. It is necessary to see what structural factors contributed to the change in their behavior. It seems to be that, for certain cases, the political changes at the national level have affected their lives at the community level. These political changes have altered the political power of the community and have caused shifts in ideological commitment accordingly.

It is important to see the respondents' community involvement in relation to their political and religious behavior. Five categories have been identified in terms of their involvement: (1) area leaders—active beyond community level, (2) community leaders—confined to the community activities, (3) *garden* leaders—confined to neighborhood matters, (4) membership—contribute money and labor whenever necessary, and (5) non-members—no membership but participate in activities that have a direct effect on their lives, upon request of the organizers.

It is possible to infer from the data that a significant ideological polarization exists at the level of area leaders and community leaders. The two "poles" each contain two religious orientations. On the one hand, Buddhist orthodoxy is, surprisingly, linked with no faith to form a "pole" around which half the area leaders and community leaders tend to congregate (table 8.6). The other half congregate around the second "pole," that of popular religion and religious plurality. This second pole also attracts the three lower levels of political participation, namely the garden leaders, ordinary party members and finally, non-members. The difference between these two poles should be emphasized. The lower levels of political activity are overwhelmingly drawn to the second pole, whereas the two higher levels are exactly divided between the two poles.

It is interesting to note that some of the leaders who are affiliated with socialist political groups had practiced popular religion up to a certain point and then shifted their faith towards orthodox religion or adopted no faith. The question arises as to why they adopted this new practice. It has a direct connection with the political reality both at the national and the community levels, rather than with ideological commitment.

At the national level, a majority trend is characterized by a popular belief. At the community level, departure from the national tendency is closely associated with the dynamic structural complexities in relation to the distribution of power. The individual perceptions and motives have to be traced within this structural reality. Some of the important questions include the following: Why do some people depart from popular trends and adopt orthodoxy or no faith? Who are these people? How do they rationalize their behavior? With whom do they have an alliance? What choices do they have in terms of their network?

In order to address these questions, it is important to trace a few individual cases. Let me begin with a person who has no faith in religion. He is 56 years old, of Buddhist background, male, and a community leader. He is politically affiliated with the Sri Lanka Freedom Party, left of center. He says:

Table 8.6

Type of Faith by Type of Leadership

Leader Type	*N*	Orthodox Religion (%)	No Faith (%)	Popular Religion (%)	Religious Plurality (%)
Area Leader	8	50.0	—	37.5	12.5
Community Leader	8	25.0	25.0	50.0	—
Garden Leader	9	44.4	—	44.4	11.0
Membership	10	10.0	10.0	70.0	10.0
Nonmember	50	26.0	8.0	56.0	10.0
Total	85				

> Until I was 50 years of age, I accepted and practiced religion well. This was until 1978 to 1979. I realized that a certain class put forward the philosophy for their own benefits. Politicians take sides. However, we live in a religious climate. Every morning, I light a lamp before I leave. But those things are not worthwhile tasks. Since it is a tradition, we have been addicted to those practices. We do these things because we should train our children and pass these things on to our younger generation. Generally, it is not a bad thing. I do not go to temple. I go once in several years. Temples are no use. They have been put up as a means of living. The Gnanawimala temple is a *Mudalali* temple (entrepreneurial type). I hate that much. Cheating money has been increased. People have not developed. This has become a barbarian era. People still worship trees, rocks, and statues. We can't publicize these things. It is like a cutting of our own throat by ourselves. We live quietly. That is the way we have to live, be in a nest, if we go out, we are finished. I did welfare to these *flats* during the period of 1969 to 1980. I worked as a treasurer, as a patron. We totally dispensed the rental issue. Until 1980 we paid rent. We informed the department of local government unanimously that we would not pay the rent until they issue deeds for these houses. We made this a playground through *Shramadana* (offering labor). We removed garbage, made garbage cans. We cleaned these drains. We couldn't continue at least six months. Disruptive elements emerged from within. We thought all these things were meaningless tasks. I thought, "Why do we have confrontations with people?" Since then I do not have any connections with these things. I do not visit people, they do not visit me; if we meet on the way, we smile at each other, and say *Ayubowan* [live long—a form of greeting]. (06/02/1985)

A 70 year old male, dependent on his children, presently believes in the orthodox religion. He is affiliated with the Sri Lanka Freedom Party and says:

> I do not go to temple. I stopped going to temple about 17 years back. Those days I went to Weluwana temple. The "Nayaka" said this was a private temple. Therefore, I stopped going. In those days we established a Buddhist society against this temple; we

> sponsored *bana preaching* (Buddhist sermon) for a three month period. Some of the leading national-level Buddhist monks came for *bana preaching*. Those monks did not like that this temple had been established. I do not know the reason. (06/09/1985)

A person from the indigenous professional group, one of the key members in the Weluwana temple Dayaka Sabawa (Patron Committee), presently detached from the temple, expressed his views by saying:

> We practice rituals these days. Those are myths. If we observe our religion well, whatever happens, it is according to the *Karma*. (08/03/1985)

A male from the leading business group, actively involved in politics and affiliated with the Sri Lankan Freedom Party, played a role of leadership at the area level. In his case, he described his alliance with Weluwana temple and his cutoff relationship with Gnanawimala temple:

> We maintained a relationship with the temple. The karandapitiya monk is a person from our own village. I went to karandapitiya for his father's funeral. I am not a *Dayaka* (contributing patron) but I help the temple with money. I sponsor two *bana* preachings per year. I was a *dayakaya* of Gnanawimala temple during 1954-1955. Then Gnanawimala *Nayaka thera* (incumbent) had the leadership. Once I was the *Anusasaka* (patron advisor) of Mutual Funeral Aid Society. Then I became secretary for one year and treasurer for another year. In the 1960s, I relinquished from my *dayakathvaya* and from the activities of Funeral Aid Society. I cut off my connection with the temple, The behavior of chief monk is not so good. Therefore, I have no connection with this temple. Only a few families from Gnanawimala Road go to this temple. . . . I am not going to temples. My family members are going to Weluwana temple. If we do not do sinful acts, as human beings, if we observe *pansil* (five precepts of Buddhism), why do we often go to temple and worship statues and observing *sil* (precepts)? If we light the lamp at home, I do not think these things are necessary. I do not believe in ritual practices, but listen to my family's requests. They believe in those. (03/31/1985)

These attitudes and perceptions reveal religious faith and practices in relation to the changing circumstances of the community. It is obvious in these examples that the changing faith is an outcome of individuals' interactions with religious and community activities within the political context of the area. At this point, it is interesting to place religious institutions within this community context.

BUDDHIST TEMPLES: PATRONAGE AND POLITICS

Presently there are four temples in this community of Dematagoda; one is defunct. The Galepansala is the oldest temple in this community. Once the Weluwana temple was erected, the big debate started between these two temples on the grounds of sectarian affiliations. The Galepansala belongs to the *Siam Nikaya* (sect) which is limited to people of the *Goyigama* ("farmer" caste or highest caste). The Weluwana temple belongs to the *Amarapura Nikaya* which opened the *Sanghas* (monks) to other castes in the 19th century. The incumbent of Weluwana temple is from *Salagama* caste (one of the lower castes known as cinnamon peelers).

In this caste confrontation of these two temples, Galepansala obtained external ideological patronage from Siam Nikaya. Nonetheless, this external ideological patronage was not sufficient to expand and develop the temple in this community. The Weluwana temple received more financial support from the patron family than ideology from the *Amarapura Nikaya*. The patron family offered their own land to expand the temple and did maintain temple buildings annually with their own money. The ordinary residents of the community were not in a position to make substantial contributions to maintain any temple in the community.

The Weluwana temple was established in 1923, sponsored by one patron family. In the 1930s the indigenous professional group actively participated in the activities of the temple in association with the patron family. This family was originally from Galle district in the south. The *Nayaka* at the temple was also from the south. In the 1940s *dayaka sabawa* (patron committee) was formed by the indigenous professional group, and it was continued up to 1965. In 1967 it was dissolved as a result of conflict that arose with the incumbent. The indigenous professional group that played a prominent role got away from temple activities. The Funeral Aid Society, which was under their control, was also detached from the temple and reorganized under another name.

Conflict between the incumbent and the *dayaka sabawa* in 1965 was rooted in political changes. The socialist-oriented political parties lost power, and the United National Party was able to take political office. The *Nayaka* had an alliance with this new political power, while indigenous professional groups had their alliance with the leftist-oriented politics. However, the first confrontation between ordinary residents and the incumbent began in 1969, once the Nayaka exiled the leftists from the temple garden. Then most of the residents boycotted the temple. At this point, the leading indigenous group, which was largely affiliated with the then ruling party (United National Party), replaced the position of the indigenous professional group in temple activities, in association with the patron family.

After 1969, only a small percentage of residents accepted the ways in which temples conducted their activities. In 1970 the political power was changed. Left of center politics again came into power, and they continued up to 1977. During this political regime, residents remained departed from the temple. Those who had affiliated with the temple had limited interactions with their neighborhoods. These residents, by and large, were patronized by the temple. Recommendations, advice, and assistance in their life crises are reciprocated by loyalty to the temple. The majority of these residents are southerners, and, as a result, other residents tend to think that southerners are favored by this temple. This idea has been expressed through an adage: "This temple does not permit even a beggar to stay who has not come from the southern part of the country."

The conflict caused many residents to find an alternative place for their religious activities. The indigenous professional group started to visit Kolonnawa temple (a well known temple outside this community, more similar to Weluwana temple), while other residents have chosen temples with their own preferences, in peripheral locations of the community. The indigenous professional group deliberately avoided going to *Ali Denna Pansala* (the temple with two statues of elephants) since the indigenous leading group had controlling power over that temple. The indigenous leading group also avoided visiting Weluwana and Gnanawimila temples of the community and the Kolonnawa temple of the periphery.

The political changes that took place in 1977 enabled the Weluwana temple to be attractive in the community. The ordinary residents re-established connections with the temple despite previous hostile attitudes between the *Nayaka* and the community residents. One of the important reasons for this new attraction and re-establishment of relationships was the changes in the political attitude of the residents. The proportions of left wing and right wing affiliations were changed over time. The changes over a period of ten years time are given in table 8.7.

It can be assumed, from this data, that the significant drop in left wing (both SLFP and LSSP/CP) affiliation and newly emerged no affiliation and indifferent groups provided the basis for re-establishment of connections with the temple.

Presently, both the indigenous leading group and the leading business group take interest in the activities of the temple. However, there is still no *dayaka sabawa* (patron committee) to manage the temple activities. The initial patron family has transferred some of their properties to a temple committee that has the authority to maintain the temple. In addition to this, there are a few patron families living in Colombo, who are wealthy entrepreneurs. In 1979, a well-known contractor had the paintings of the main temple buildings renovated.

The community interaction with Gnanawimala temple was more pronounced then than today. The community's view is that this temple lost its attraction due to the unrighteous behavior of the chief monk. Most of the residents think that the chief monk violated *Sangha Vinaya* (monastic discipline). Some of these violations are: (1) He has no interest in developing this temple and has allowed it to become a family temple because his father belongs to the leading business group and owns a saw mill. (2) He keeps boarders. (3) He does not want to have a *Dayaka Sabawa* (patron committee). (4) He keeps a woman and maintains a family outside Colombo City, and there is rumor that this woman is from this community. (5) He partakes of *alms* only from some selected families, and he has disappointed some families on several occasions when everything is prepared for the *alms-giving*, frequently he gets his meals from his own home, and he does not go round the community with a *pathraya* (begging bowl). (6) He does not perform traditional observances and ceremonies connected with the Sinhala New Year, such as ringing of temple bells to signify various auspicious hours and distribution of oil for the traditional oil bath.

Table 8.7

Political Affiliation During Two Periods of Time

Political Affiliation	*N*	1975 (%)	*N*	1985 (%)
United National Party (UNP)	20	50.0	35	41.0
Sri Lanka Freedom Party (SLFP)	15	37.0	14	16.0
Marxist Parties (LSSP/CP)	4	10.0	6	7.0
Tamil United Liberation Front (TULF)	1	3.0	0	—
No Affiliation	0	—	15	18.0
Indifferent	0	—	15	18.0
Total	40		85	

Note: The data on political affiliation in 1975 were taken from a study on Rural–Urban Relations (Neville 1979).

As a result of the laxity in observing *Sangha Vinaya* (monastic discipline) one of the monks of this temple has aroused some of the locals to petition to the *Sangha Saba* (a committee which has authority to examine the discipline of Buddhist monks). The petition was forwarded to a higher body, but there was no effective result from this petition. The chief monk of the temple is able to continue in the same way. Some of the Sri Lanka Freedom Party supporters claim that this temple is pro-United National Party. Nonetheless, people who are affiliated with that party found fault with the temple over its general performance. The lack of connection with residents was justified by the chief monk saying, "Close connections with residents in this area is not so good. It leads to lack of respect of each other" (02/18/1985).

Bodirajaramaya was established in the early 1980s. This temple is situated near the government *flats* (Colombo Municipal Council housing project in this location). This temple was established by a young Buddhist monk with the support of one of the community leaders from the government *flats*. Before the establishment of the temple, this monk used to visit Gnanawimala temple, and he established connections with this community leader. Political networks, prevailing social conditions, and the nature of residents' relationships with the existing temples were factors conducive to establishing the new temple.

Politically, both the head monk of the new temple and the community leader are strong UNP supporters and have helped the election campaign of the present member of Parliament from this electorate. They used these political connections to obtain a permit from the Prime Minister to put up a temple on this land. It can safely be assumed that there was a happy conjunction between this Buddhist monk's motive and the residents' aspiration for this new temple establishment.

One of the important social circumstances was that the many residents of the government *flats* for a long period of time were looked down upon by the rest of the community. There was hardly any social intercourse between these two groups. Most of the residents were reluctant to go to Gnanawimala temple, not because of the bad character of the head monk but because of the social gulf between those who visited that temple and themselves. Secondly, the numerical Buddhist dominance of this deprived social category was a contributing factor in this respect. Thirdly, there was a Hindu *kovil* (temple), in a temporary structure, on this land. Sinhala-Tamil ethnic tension in a majority-dominant community gave ideological legitimization to put up a Buddhist temple instead of a Hindu *kovil*. All of these social circumstances might have indicated the potential clientele for a new temple.

The long standing residents of this community criticize the behavior of this head monk on the ground of *Sangha Vinaya* (monastic discipline). The major criticisms that were leveled against this monk are: (1) he protects social undesirables, (2) he keeps a woman, and (3) he does no proper Buddhist missionary work. One of the long-term residents expressed his views:

> This temple has no motivation for missionary work or properly maintaining the temple, but rather wishes to occupy private land and have a temple. (03/31/1985)

Despite these criticisms, the head monk patronizes some of the poorer residents, both from the government *flats* and from surroundings, who have loyalty to the temple. In this patronizing process, he is able to play a political role for the community. His behavior is characterized by the Mandala structure of the religious galactic polity (Mines and Gourishankar 1990, 769). Also, this phenomenon has been noted as a complex relationship between the Buddhist institutions and the urban poor (Silva and Athukarala 1991, 150). The head monk of Bodirajaramaya opens up political channels for some residents who need employment. He intervenes in police matters on behalf of some of the residents who get caught for minor illegal activities such as selling narcotics, alcohol, thefts, and fighting. He is able to play this patron role since he has established connections with external power centers. Some of the recent ceremonial functions that took place in this temple were attended by the members of Parliament, the District Minister, the central figure of the Colombo race entrepreneurship (the main agent in bootlegging in Colombo), and headquarters inspectors of most of the police stations in Colombo. As a result of his network and patronage capacity, he is becoming a powerful figure in this community.

Even though these temples are community based, the community has no power over them. None of the temples has a *dayaka sabawa* (patron committee), which is the usual form of supervision, particularly in rural communities. The ideals of a healthy relationship between the temples and the community are far from being realized. The ordinary members of the community are not economically able to maintain temples. This situation is conducive to the intrusion of external political elements with a substantial package of resources for temple maintenance. As a result, the political network woven into the temple activities is perceived as a potential channel for access to the political centers by some of the residents who have limited choices. These external political elements are always in tune with internal politics. In this process, temples become either pragmatic or ideological political agents. The level of performance of the head monk is determined by various factors such as personality, his aspirations, and the quality of resources that he requires for the maintenance of the temple.

Chapter 9

Patterns of Mobility and Community Integration

The preceding Chapters 4 through 8 examined the total spectrum of the network of relationships of the community and its ideological manifestations. This chapter focuses on the impact of the network of relationships on mobility patterns and community integration.

The mobility aspirations of Dematagoda inhabitants can be broadly divided into two categories: inward and outward orientation. However, these two categories are not homogeneous. Many behavioral manifestations are identified within each category. It is necessary to examine the nature of these behavioral characteristics in terms of mobility options, strategies, and decisions. This chapter addresses these questions: What is the permanent and transitory character of individual or household behavior? What is the level of aspiration in the continuum of inward–outward orientation? What is the level of the aspiration gap? How do people in this community see their aspiration gap? How do they justify their decisions and strategies? What factors determine their decisions and strategies?

The geographical mobility pattern of this community includes variables such as ethnicity, age, duration of stay, occupation, house ownership, political affiliation, leadership type and the degree of neighborhood relationships. However, these factors have no direct positive or negative correlations to inward–outward behavior. Each factor has a different weighting for different individuals and households in determining the nature of transitory or permanent behavior. These factors provide a complex and dynamic interplay in their strategies and decision. The pattern of mobility and the structural relations of the community have reciprocal interactions. On the one hand, the patters of mobility is a reflection of the community integration; on the other hand, the pattern of mobility has significant implications on the community structure.

A Profile of Inward–Outward Orientation

The data on ethnicity and mobility orientation reveals that the majority of the Sinhala (61.7%) and the Muslims (75%) aspire to leave this community. In contrast, the majority of Tamils (55.6%) are inward oriented (table 9.1). As far as age and geographical mobility are concerned, the majority of young and middle aged people tend to be more outward oriented than the older people in this community. There are 29 respondents within the age group of 26 to 40; 28% of this group are inward oriented. Of the total 34 respondents within the middle age group, 31% are inward oriented (table 9.2).

The length of stay is not strongly correlated with the aspiration of geographical mobility of the respondents. One can generally assume that the greater number of years in one place may establish more economic and social ties to the area. As a result of these ties people may develop inward oriented sentiments. The data indicates that the majority of the respondents who have been in this location less than 20 years are outward oriented. However, the respondents who fall within the categories between 21 years and 50 years are equally divided into both categories of inward and outward orientation. It is also noted that the older people who have been staying in the community more than 30 years tend to be totally inward oriented (table 9.3).

Table 9.1

Inward–Outward Orientation by Ethnic Groups

Ethnic	*N*	Inward (%)	Outward (%)
Sinhalese	60	38.3	61.7
Tamils	9	55.6	44.4
Muslims	16	25.0	75.0
Total	85		

Table 9.2

Inward–Outward Orientation by Age Group

Age Group	*N*	Inward (%)	Outward (%)
Below 25	2	—	100.0
26-40	29	31.0	69.0
41-55	34	29.0	71.0
Over 55	20	65.0	35.0
Total	85		

Table 9.3

Inward–Outward Orientation by Duration of Stay

Duration	*N*	Inward (%)	Outward (%)
0-5	16	31.3	68.7
6-10	8	25.0	75.0
11-15	7	—	100.0
16-20	18	33.3	66.7
21-30	15	53.3	46.7
31-40	12	41.7	58.3
41-50	6	50.0	50.0
Over 50	3	100.0	—
Total	85		

The higher percentage of both upper level professionals and lower level white collar employees living in this community tend to be more outward oriented than other categories of employees. Among the blue collar workers 58% of skilled workers and 69% of unskilled workers are outward oriented. The unemployed and retired people also are outward oriented. The majority (57%) of the self-employed business category shows inward orientation. However, these data do not confirm a particular correlation between occupational categories with inward–outward orientation (table 9.4).

Despite the fact that housing is a critical factor in metropolitan life, home ownership alone is not a magnet for the residents of this community. The variety of other factors which shape the options available to the individuals, add meaning to their sense of ownership. Under such circumstances, housing becomes key for some people of the community. It is striking to note that most of the residents are aspiring to move out from this community, irrespective of the type of ownership. Seventy-eight percent of the residents in the government housing scheme, 62% from among shanty dwellers, and 72% of tenants are outward oriented. Among the residents who obtained ownership recently from the National Housing Department, only 35.7% are outward oriented (table 9.5). In order to understand this distribution pattern of housing ownership and mobility aspiration, a qualitative analysis will be presented in the second part of this chapter.

There is a correlation between per capita income and geographical mobility. The data indicates that a proportionately increasing percentage of people tend to be outward oriented from lower end up to Rs. 1000 of per capita income. Then beyond this point, the trend is reversed. The majority of higher income earners have more permanent stakes in this community. It can easily be generalized that a significant percentage of lower income categories and a high percentage of top income categories are more inward oriented than the rest of the people of this community (table 9.6).

As far as an established network is concerned political affiliation and neighborhood relationship are vital to this study. However, there is no direct relationship between surface level political affiliations and geographical mobility aspirations. The majority of respondents are outward oriented irrespective of their political affiliation, except in the case of socialist party affiliated respondents. The majority (66.7%) of

Table 9.4

Inward–Outward Orientation by Occupational Status

Occupational Status	*N*	Inward (%)	Outward (%)
White Collar	15	26.7	73.3
Blue Collar	28	35.7	64.2
Business/Service	14	57.1	42.9
Unemployed & Retired	28	35.7	64.2
Total	85		

Table 9.5

Inward–Outward Orientation by House Ownership

Types of House Ownership	*N*	Inward (%)	Outward (%)
Obtained from Housing Department	14	64.3	35.7
Tenants	11	27.3	72.7
Government Housing Scheme	19	21.1	78.9
Built on Reservation Land	2	100.0	—
Shanties and Squatter Settlers	14	35.7	64.3
Owned	17	47.1	52.9
No ownership (including relative owned)	8	12.5	87.5
Total	85		

Table 9.6

Inward–Outward Orientation by Per Capita Income

Per Capita	*N*	Inward (%)	Outward (%)
Less than 50	2	100.0	—
51 - 100	5	20.0	80.0
101 - 200	14	35.7	64.3
201 - 300	16	43.7	56.3
301 - 500	21	38.1	61.9
501 - 750	10	30.0	70.0
751 - 1000	8	12.5	87.5
1001 - 2000	6	50.0	50.0
2001 - 4000	3	66.7	33.3
Total	85		

them (socialists) are inward oriented. This is due to the fact that this community was originally considered as one of the bases of leftists. The majority of these inward oriented leftists are original inhabitants and their long-standing stay and property ownership make them as different from some other residents of this community. The no affiliation group is more or less equally distributed between two groups—inward and outward—while the majority (80%) of the indifferent group are outward oriented (table 9.7).

It is interesting to note that the majority of those who hold a leadership position in this community are inward oriented. In fact, both area leaders and community leaders have more permanent stakes than garden leaders (table 9.8).

The respondents who maintain a high neighborhood relationship tend to be inward oriented. It may also be the other way around since the neighborhood relationship is an important niche in the community network. It has already been noted in Chapter 5 that the majority of the people in this community maintain a good relationship with their neighbors irrespective of their inward and outward orientation (table 9.9). However, those who do not maintain a good relationship within the community could be categorized into three groups: (1) The majority of respondents who are unable to maintain a healthy relationship due to a variety of reasons may develop outward orientation attitudes. (2) Respondents who are unable to maintain a relationship, have no options to move out, live in isolation, and have the least power in the community. (3) Respondents who do not need to maintain a close relationship within the community, having alternatives in terms of network, but possess inward oriented attitudes due to a variety of other reasons. Therefore, it is necessary to do a close examination of these relationships with regard to inward–outward orientation.

Respondents' Explanations for Their Inward Orientation

The factors which determine inward orientation can be understood through each respondent's justification in terms of choices and constraints for their destiny in life. These individual justifications given in this study allow for some generalized categories. These categories with their numerical strength in the sample are given in the following tables.

Table 9.7

Inward–Outward Orientation by Political Affiliation

Political Affiliation	*N*	Inward (%)	Outward (%)
UNP	35	37.2	62.8
SLFP	14	28.6	71.4
LSSP/CP	6	66.7	33.3
No Affiliation	15	53.4	46.6
Indifferent	15	20.0	80.0
Total	85		

Table 9.8

Inward–Outward Orientation by Leader Type

Leader Type	*N*	Inward (%)	Outward (%)
Area Leader	8	87.5	12.5
Community Leader	8	62.5	37.5
Garden Leader	9	22.2	77.8
Membership Only	10	11.1	88.9
Non-members	50	34.0	66.0
Total	85		

Table 9.9

Inward–Outward Orientation by the Degree of Neighborhood Relationship

Neighborhood Relationship	*N*	Inward (%)	Outward (%)
Very Good	20	65.0	35.0
Good	19	26.3	73.7
Moderate	26	38.5	61.5
Limited	11	18.2	81.8
Very Limited	9	22.2	77.8
Total	85		

CLOSE PROXIMITY TO WORKING PLACE

This group consists of four respondents from the sample. Three of them are Sinhalese and the other is a Muslim. They are 12.5% of the total inward oriented group. This group has limited choices for social and geographical mobility, despite some of the environmental dissatisfactions. These people are compelled to stay in this community. For them all the other desirable ends are imaginative, not realistic goals. The following cases illustrate these characteristics.

Case No. 1 is a 54 year old male. His duration of stay in this community is 26 years. He moved into this place because of his marriage. When he moved, his wife's family were tenants in this house. Now it has been transferred to them by the Department of Housing. Presently he is self-employed by doing contracts on carpentry and masonry, within Colombo city. His average monthly income is Rs. 3200. When he first moved to this community he was heavily involved in leftist politics both inside and outside of this community, but now is totally inactive. He maintains a moderate level neighborhood relationship. He described his position in the following manner:

> I do not expect to give up this residence. We are not in a position to leave this place. But we would like to live in a quiet environment, in a detached house, a little away from Colombo. The demand for masonry and carpentry work is here in this area. In every respect we are not in a position to leave this place. (05/02/1985)

Case No. 2 is a Sinhalese female, 54 years old, who moved into this location in 1980, living in a shanty house near the Government housing scheme. Her son has no permanent job. He finds his earnings from temporary labor jobs within the city of Colombo. This family maintains a high neighborhood relationship with no political affiliation but aspires to use political channels for permanent employment and to secure their residency. She says:

> My main expectation is to get a job for my son. Otherwise he has no future. We do not have any problem living in this area. Even if we have problems here, we cannot afford any other place. I do not know whether we have to leave this house. (05/02/1985)

Case No. 3 is a 48 year old Muslim, living in a housing unit received from the government *flats*. He moved into this location in 1968. He is engaged as a collection agent in bootlegging activities of the area. His monthly income is about Rs. 1150. He maintains a moderate neighborhood relationship and is affiliated with the UNP political group of the area. He says:

> I would like to leave this place, but there is no way. No money. Even if I sell this house, it is not easy to buy a house in a proper place. That money will not be enough. This environment is very noisy. It is not clean, but we do not have any disturbances from the people of the area. (06/23/1985)

NEWLY RECEIVED OR ASPIRING OWNERSHIP

This group newly received their ownership largely from the Department of Housing or are aspiring to that ownership in the near future. There are five respondents in this category in the sample which show the inward orientation. Of these, three are Sinhalese, one Muslim, and a Tamil. Some of the people in this group have already invested or have taken steps to renovate, rebuild or extend. These respondents are somewhat satisfied with their new ownership. It is one of the achievements in their life. Thus, the sense of ownership was the main decision factor for their inward orientation. They do not see any other desirable option having considered their life constraints.

Case No. 1 is a Muslim male, 63 years old. He moved into this location in 1976. His monthly family income is about Rs. 1000. He maintains a high neighborhood relationship and no affiliation in politics. He is a bankrupt business man. He says:

> This environment is good. We are used to it. I do not like to leave this place. I do not have any problem in this area. If children want, they can leave after their marriages. We expected to renovate this house. We did not do that earlier because we were not quite sure that we were going to get this ownership. Now it is difficult to afford. We need about Rs. 50,000 to renovate this house according to our wish. My second daughter has gone abroad. When she comes back, we want to renovate this house. (06/23/1985)

Case No. 2 is a Tamil, 57 year old skilled worker. His monthly family income is Rs. 1000. He migrated into this location in 1963. He received the ownership from the Department of Housing. He says:

> I do not want to leave this place at all. We are used to this location. I want to live here the whole of my life. This is good for my death too. In 1945, my father bought a piece of land as burial ground for our family in Boralla Cemetery. My expectation is to build a good house in this place. I can get a loan and do that, but if I take a loan, it is difficult to live. I do not want to take a loan from banks, because the interest rate is high. My intention is to lay the foundation first and build up gradually. I can get a loan from the Harbor (place he is employed) to lay the foundation. (06/09/1985)

Case No. 3 is a Sinhala male, 33 years old, and an artist. His monthly income is Rs. 3700. He moved into this location four years ago. He built his house on a reservation land of the Government. He says:

> This environment is not bad. I am used to it. This land is a government land. I hope that I can get the ownership for this land. We built this house with our savings. We spent nearly Rs. 65,000 for this house. (06/20/1985)

PRIVATE OWNERSHIP OR SECURED RESIDENCY

This group is largely comprised of old age people with no particular aspirations. This group consists of both English educated, professional lower level white collar retired people and indigenous entrepreneurial type people. The following cases illustrate this situation.

Case No. 1 is a Sinhala female, 63 years old, and a retired school teacher. Her husband is an engineer. She is a long-standing resident in this community (duration of stay is 57 years). She maintains a limited neighborhood relationship with no political affiliation, and owns property in this location. She says:

> We expect to continue here. It is easy for us. All facilities are there, marketing, transport and other things. This is our property. We don't want to go anywhere. We don't have children. (05/04/1985)

Case No. 2 is a Muslim male, 70 years old. He moved into this location 40 years ago. He is retired from his government service. His monthly family income is Rs. 5300. He maintains a very limited neighborhood relationship. He is a tenant, paying his rent to the Department of Housing. His rent is relatively very low, compared to the open market price. He says:

> I can be here the rest of my life. . . . This house is enough for my family of five. I bought a little property at Gampaha in 1965. 20 perches of land. I want to sell that land and deposit that money and get interest. (06/09/1985)

Case No. 3 is a Sinhala male, 70 years old. He moved into this location 42 years back. He is a businessman within the City of Colombo. His monthly family income is Rs. 12,000. He maintains a good neighborhood relationship. He is affiliated politically with the ruling party. He built his house in this location 18 years back. He says:

> The total cost of building this house was Rs. 50,000. The present value is two hundred thousand to three hundred thousand. I am going to be here. At least one child will stay with me. (06/19/1985)

Case No. 4 is a male Muslim, 26 years old. He moved into this location in 1980. He works as a butcher in a meat shop within the city. He has plans to start his own business. His neighborhood relationship is limited because of his limited time. He says:

> We are going to continue in this location. We do not have any problem in this location. I bought this house for Rs. 95,000. I sold our jewelry and borrowed some money to buy this house. (06/09/1985)

ELDERLY DEPENDENTS WITH NO CHOICES

This category is totally dependent on their children or live on a meager pension drawn from their government service. Two such examples illustrate their conditions.

Case No. 1 is a Sinhala male, 70 years old. Has been living in this location the last 54 years. He is completely dependent on his children (his wife is politically active in this community). He lives in a house which his wife obtained ownership of recently from the Department of Housing. He says:

> I will stay in this house until the end of my life, at least whatever is given to me by my children. I have no other expectation. I do not think about children's marriage or their future. I can't do these. (06/09/1985)

Case No. 2 is a Sinhala male, 55 years old. He moved into this location 29 years back. He has retired from government service. The sole income is his meager pension. He moved into this location as a tenant. Now he has the ownership as a result of the 1973 Housing Ceiling Act. He described his difficult situation.

> My family totally depends on my pension. I am having a difficult time. I got the deed for this house from the National Housing Department. Now I do not pay rent. But I cannot do any improvement in this house. I can't put in any money. This roof is leaking. I can't afford a replacement of roof. After my retirement I have had horrible expenses and illness. I am looking for at least a part-time job. Nothing is wrong with this place. Everything is convenient. No problem in this environment. I do not have place. I don't want to move out. It is left to my children, after their education and employment. (06/22/1985)

COMMUNAL RIOTS AND MINORITY PROTECTION

The Indian origin Tamils living in Colombo are victims of the communal riots in Sri Lanka, even though the majority of them do not sympathize with the separatist movement of the northern part of the country. The Tamil people who establish good relationships with their Sinhala neighbors are reluctant to move out despite their dissatisfaction with the environment. The most likely possibility is to move into a Tamil concentrated area within the northern part of Colombo. But this is only an imaginary sanctuary, when compared to the other areas. There is no guarantee for their protection. For these people outward mobility means establishment of new relationships in a new environment. It is a time consuming and risky business under the present communal tension prevailing in the country. Therefore, the first priority of these poorer Tamils is the protection of their lives. The following cases illustrate this situation.

Case No. 1 is a Tamil male 42 years old who has lived in this location nearly 23 years in a shanty house. He is living in extreme poverty conditions. His monthly income is Rs. 150. He maintains a good neighborhood relationship. He says:

> I do not go anywhere from this *garden*. If the government sends us somewhere, giving a house, then we have to go. There is a rumor like that. There are some quarrels when people get drunk. But these quarrels are temporary things. Strangers can't come here and make troubles for the people in this *garden*. . . . The people of this *garden* (Sinhalese) protected us during the last communal troubles. (06/02/1985)

Case No. 2 is a Tamil male 34 years old, working in a private company, monthly income is Rs. 675, living in a shanty house, who maintains a very good neighborhood relationship. He has been staying in this *garden* seven years, but he was born in an adjacent location. He says:

> I do not intend to go anywhere from this *garden*. We can't live elsewhere other than this place because of the country's situation today. We do not know anybody in other places. In this place we know people since our childhood. That's why we were protected during the last communal trouble. Our parents are also living in this garden. (06/02/1985)

INWARD ORIENTATION BASED ON OWNERSHIP AND NETWORKS

The majority of this group occupy positions in the social network and are political actors and entrepreneurs. They are mainly concerned with income stability balanced with political career and/or status consciousness. The majority of them are either area leaders or community leaders. Their economic activities largely are based in the community and in the surrounding areas. Their established social, economic and political network brings meaning into their life. If they are removed from this community they will definitely lose their identity and personality.

OUTWARD ORIENTATION AND THEIR DESTINY

Residents of this community who aspire to outward mobility have a different destiny in the spatial scale. Six possible categories in this scale have been identified from no specific place in mind to their original native place. The high concentration will be in the Colombo periphery, both suburban and rural units in metropolitan region. A small percentage will remain within the city limits.

There are two groups in the scale which have no geographical location in their mind. The first group is outward oriented in general. They do not have any particular interest in a place where they should go. They simply want to move out due to a variety of other circumstances. This group contains 26.4% of the total outward oriented category. The second group (13.2%), has made no decision yet. This group is mainly characterized by the absence of a time horizon in their decisions. Nevertheless, all these destiny categories are a reflection of a realistic decision scale in terms of their choices, capabilities and the degree of strategic planning towards their desirable ends. However, within each category, the degree of specificity differs from person to person depending on their socio-economic and network circumstances.

The outward orientation is largely a reflection of upward social mobility aspirations of individuals which are constrained either by the structural characteristics of this community or by a variety of other socio-economic circumstances. It is important to note at this point the objectives of upward social mobility which have been revealed in this study: (1) permanency in residence with general family advancement, (2) escape from a congested and unhealthy environment, (3) living in a protective social environment and healthy social network, and (4) having a quiet life with free mind.

Even though the upward social mobility pivots around the ownership of a house or a permanency in residence, mere ownership does not fulfill all the spectrum of social mobility. Fifty-four point seven percent of the total outward oriented people have ownership rights in this community. Despite their ownership they desire to move out from this location and some are in the process of making their outward oriented plans. The empirical evidence reveals some specific aspirations and preferences in terms of outward oriented objectives. Six categories have been identified. Category A: Desire to have a piece of land and/or a separate house. The people in this category are relying on one or more of the following sources: (1) sell the present ownership rights in this community—if they have them, (2) future income from potential Middle East employment, or (3) expect a house from the Government. Category B: Middle-aged employed people who aspire to move out to suburban areas which have easy access to the city of Colombo in order to maintain their economic and social ties. Category C: People who desire to move out to the rural periphery of Colombo after their retirement from employment. They aspire to engage in home gardening in order to supplement their daily needs or as a leisure time activity. Some of the people in this category have a strong desire to have a free life escaping from complexities and dissatisfaction of the city life. Category D: People who aspire to go back to their native places. Category E: People who aspire to have a quiet life in the periphery of Colombo while maintaining their property connections in this location, with economic interests. Category F: Tenants with limited choices, potential continuity as tenants in another area of Colombo (including other reasons).

As far as these desires are concerned, the respondents of this community could be categorized into a continuum of aspiration gap. This gap ranges from low to high in terms of their abilities and constraints. Four categories have been identified in this continuum: (1) high gap—a dreaming state of mind, (2) significant gap—embryonic form of plans, (3) medium gap—tangible plans, working with at least one or two options, and (4) low gap—steps already taken or near completion.

The distribution of outward oriented respondents in the sample by their aspiration gaps is given in table 9.10. The total number of outward oriented respondents is 53. Of this, 39.6% fall within the Category A, 15.1% in B, 22.6% in C, 2.9% in D, 11.3% in E, and 9.4% in F. As far as aspiration gap is concerned, 20.7% of the outward oriented group is in a dreaming state of mind about their desires. The majority in this group are living in extreme poverty conditions. For some people, it is too early to take steps to materialize their desires. Eighteen point nine percent of the outward oriented people fall within the category of significant gap which have a very embryonic form of plans. The majority fall within the medium level (47.2%) and the low level gap (13.2%). The outward oriented desires and the differences of nature of gap have varying impacts and consequences upon the social network of

Table 9.10

Outward Oriented Aspiration Gaps and Plans

Aspiration Gap	A (%)	B (%)	C (%)	D (%)	E (%)	F (%)	Total (%)
High	13.2 (7)	3.7 (2)	—	—	3.7 (2)	—	20.6 (11)
Significant	13.2 (7)	3.7 (2)	2.0 (1)	—	—	—	18.9 (10)
Medium	11.3 (6)	2.0 (1)	15.0 (8)	2.0 (1)	7.5 (4)	9.4 (5)	47.2 (25)
Low	2.0 (1)	5.7 (3)	5.7 (3)	—	—	—	13.2 (7)
Total	39.6 (21)	15.1 (8)	22.6 (12)	2.0 (1)	11.3 (6)	9.4 (5)	100.0 (53)

Note: Figures in parentheses are base Ns for the adjacent percentages.

this community. A few possibilities can be assumed with regard to potential impacts upon the community structure: (1) The greater the aspiration gap, the higher will be the tendency to participate in community activities and maintain good relationship. (2) The lower the aspiration gap, the higher will be the tendency to be aloof from community activities and maintain distant relationship. (3) The greater the aspiration gap and greater the tendency to be aloof from community activities and distant relationship, the higher will be the isolation and powerlessness in the community. Some of the people in this group may substitute community relationships with external kinship relationships. (4) The lower the aspiration gap and greater the tendency to involve in community activities and maintain good relationships, the lesser will be the feeling of isolation and powerlessness in the community.

DESIRE TO HAVE LANDOWNERSHIP AND A SEPARATE HOME

Let me first focus on the Category A, aspiration and the nature of the gap. The majority of poorer people who do not have ownership tend to associate their unsystematic lifestyle and the social mobility constraints with the non-permanency of their residences. These people live in substandard housing in a shanty environment or in rented houses. There are two groups in this category: (1) people who expect a house from the government, and (2) people with little hope of getting a house from the government. Most of these people, despite their outward orientation, are compelled to maintain inward oriented attitudes with regard to the sphere of common neighborhood activities. Nevertheless they are dissatisfied with their immediate environment. All of their dissatisfactions are expressed emphasizing high density and unhygienic conditions. The two cases given below, best exemplify the mobility aspirations, constraints, and the plans and efforts that respondents are making.

Case No. 1 is a Sinhala male 34 years old, a longstanding resident in this location (nearly 30 years), an unskilled laborer employed in a private sector company, monthly income of Rs. 675, and married with four young children. He maintains a limited neighborhood relationship and high kinship connections with relatives who live outside. He is a leftist but has no political involvement in this community at all. He says:

> Now I have decided to do my expenses in a systematic way. I want to see whether I can save money, buying food stuff once a month. It is difficult to do anything systematically since we do not have permanent residency. Thus, there is no permanency in our lifestyle too. My main reason for moving out from this *garden* is that there is no place to hang our washed clothes. When we live in an overcrowded place like this, there are many diseases. My desire is to put up our own house. The problem is money. Now I have an intention to go abroad. I got my passport and went to many places, employment agencies. They ask for money. There is no one I can borrow money from. I am looking for an employment agency who sends people without charging money. (06/03/1985)

Case No. 2 is a Sinhala male 33 years old, married, and employed as a laborer in Government Railway. His wife has gone to the Middle East as a housemaid for two years. His regular monthly income is Rs. 900 (Middle East income is not included). Duration of stay in this location is ten years. He maintains good neighborhood relationships and very limited kinship relationships. He has no political affiliation in the community, but used political connections through friends and got his job. He says:

> My wife will be back in six months from abroad. When she comes we will renovate this house a little bit. I do not have money until she comes. When she will be back next time from abroad, my plan is to buy a piece of land a little away from Colombo and build a house, at least a wooden house. In this place houses are too close. It is difficult to raise a child in this environment, too many diseases. I can not be satisfied with this environment, we stay here because we do not have money. (05/28/1985)

SUBURBAN DESTINY

In Category B, there are two types of people: (1) the poorer people and (2) some professionals who stayed in this location temporarily a short period of time.

The poorer people (as in Category A) have a very far reaching goal of outward orientation. For some people the ownership of their home in this location is the major resource for their whole life. They heavily weigh the value of the present ownership in their strategic planning.

Case No. 1 is a Tamil male 44 years old, unmarried, self-employed electrician doing house wiring. He has ownership rights in the Government housing scheme. His maximum monthly income is about Rs. 2000. But his income is not fixed and often fluctuates. He maintains very good neighborhood relationships in the community. He offers for free his electrical skills for common activities in the community. He would like to move out in the long run. He is the only Tamil in the sample who expressed his willingness to move out from the Colombo city limits. (All the others are scared to move out because of communal violence.) However his plans are still in the dreaming stage. He says:

> I do not know where I will go, perhaps, I might go to a place where I could marry. Wherever I go I can have a friendly relationship. Two, three months after I go I can make friends by offering my skills. (06/05/1985)

In the short run, he has a plan to sell his ownership right and make an investment for his living. In the near future he does not want to move out from this location, even after selling this house. He describes his plan:

> I can sell this house for Rs. 60,000 to Rs. 70,000. I will sell this house and give Rs. 25,000 for my sister to buy a shanty house in the vicinity. Then I will invest the rest of the money for my own living. (06/05/1985)

Case No. 2 is a Sinhala male 50 years old, employed in the Government Administrative Service, who moved into this location five years ago. He maintains a moderate level relationship only with the people who have the same social background. He considers most of the people in this community as having lower status, and interaction with them is a difficult task. As a professional he is looking for a permanent place for his residence:

> When I chose this location, I inquired from the H.Q.I. (Headquarter Inspector) of Dematagoda Police Station. At that time one Tamil gentleman was there. He asked me why I wanted to come to this place. He said that the only places in Dematagoda suited for people like us are Abaya place and Dematagoda place. The H.Q.I. asked me, "All right, you can come to Abaya place, but don't mix with other *gardens* like Melwatta."

> I came to this location from Veyangoda because of transport problems. I had a house there. I sold it out. I bought land in Kollonnawa—50 perches. It cost me about Rs. 85,000. Now I sold it out for Rs. 75,000. That area is not suited for me, as a professional man. I bought another land in Jubili Post—12 perches. It cost me Rs. 150,000. I have drawn a plan to put up a house. The estimate is Rs. 350,000. I hope to go to that house by mid year of 1986. That area is good for me. It is more professionals out there in that area. (07/20/1985)

In contrast to Case No. 2 in this category are the long-standing professionals who have no ownership of residence in this location and tend to maintain good relationships with their neighbors despite status differences. A 39 year old Sinhala male is an example of this behavior. He is a long-standing tenant and employed as a computer programmer in the Department of Education. His wife also is employed as a clerk. His monthly income is Rs. 3500. He is planning to move out to Kandana as he owns a piece of land from his mother's inherited property. He says:

> My expectation is to build a house in my Kandana land. I am going to get a bank loan. I have already applied for a loan by mortgaging that land. My brothers and sisters are also living in that area. (06/20/1985)

RURAL PERIPHERY

The majority of respondents in this category are near retirement from their work. They usually are faced with two problems: (1) financial constraints and (2) inability to take immediate steps to move out until the children's education is completed. Some of the residents in this category face a paradoxical situation. Both the main reason for moving out and the main constraints of moving out are associated with the betterment of children. They perceive this environment as unhealthy for the development of children and at the same time, this is a convenient place for children's schooling. They are not in a position to move out until the children's education is completed. The only exception to these are the people who have already completed these obligations with a sound financial background. One such example illustrates this exception in this study.

Case No. 1 is a Sinhala male 57 year old businessman, a watch repairer who migrated from Kalutara district and has stayed in this location for 26 years. He owns his residence, and he has additional property in other parts of the country. He maintains very limited neighborhood connections and high kinship connections. He has no political affiliation. He has already taken very clear tangible steps to move out from this location. He expressed his views:

> I bought land away from Colombo. I expect to sell this house for Rs. 500,000 to Rs. 600,000 and buy a house for Rs. 300,000 seven to eight miles away from Colombo. I will deposit the rest of the Rs. 200,000 in a bank and live on the interest. I have done enough of this job. I am getting old and I can't work anymore. This environment is now densely populated. When we came to this land this was not densely populated like now. For all these reasons I expect to take the above decision as soon as possible. (06/30/1985)

ASPIRATION GAP AND TANGIBLE PLANS

Case No. 1 is a Sinhala male, born in an adjacent location to this community, 29 years old, married, and employed as a security guard in the Department of Education. In addition to his formal employment he has two other income sources: (1) He runs a small cafeteria in a public school, and (2) he has five small houses rented out in the same *garden* where he lives. His monthly income is ranging from Rs. 2500 to Rs. 3000. He plays a role of *garden* leader, and he was politically involved in order to maintain infrastructural facilities in this *garden*. Presently he is dissatisfied with that political involvement and has adopted a different view. He maintains good relationships with his neighbors and still is interested in community activities. He maintains good relationships with his relatives and his spouse's relatives who both live in adjacent locations and in the same *garden*. He has very entrepreneurial plans. He intends to move out to the rural periphery of Colombo, after establishing his economic interests. He presents his entrepreneurial options for his small piece of land in this location: (1) He wants to establish a bathing well for the city dwellers. His estimated income is Rs. 500 per day. (2) He also wants to build a two-story building: a bakery and small houses upon the bakery and run a boarding house. His estimated income from the bakery is Rs. 100 per day and Rs. 2500 per month from the boarding house. Presently he earns only Rs. 800 from renting out these small houses. He describes his outward orientation.

> I have a desire to be away from this society. This place is congested. After I lay the foundation for my economic activities in this place, I would like to buy land in a peaceful environment and live freely, in a place like Gampaha with rural environment. I will embark on that journey after I establish the economic foundation and ownership in this location. (06/23/1985)

Case No. 2 is a female 51 years old and widow. Her duration of stay is 29 years and she is dependent on children, but she owns this house and some other property in this location. The monthly family income is Rs. 6000. Her husband was killed in this location over a dispute of land. She maintains good neighborhood relationships but has no political affiliation. General family advancement and comfortable life is her main aspiration. She describes her outward orientation and her plans as follows:

> This is very dense, because of that we have to stay inside the house. I do not like these row houses. We would like to lease out this house and rent a house in a good place. We do not like to sell this house, because of the high value of houses in this area. It is better to have a house in the city, but it is better to reside in a quiet environment too. (07/08/1985)

LIVE IN THE PERIPHERY AND PROPERTY TIES TO PRESENT LOCATION

There are two types of tenants in this category: (1) People who have been in this community a short period of time and accept the fact that their residency is temporary in this location. (2) Long-standing tenants who are reluctant to accept the reality of their position of limited choices.

Case No. 1 is a Sinhala male, 38 years old, migrated from down south, Matara district, and employed at the Ceylon Transport Board. His duration of stay in this community is three years. He has very limited neighborhood relationships, has high external kinship relationships, is politically UNP but dissatisfied with the government as he could not get a promotion, and failed to obtain a house from the government. He describes his dissatisfaction as a tenant without having ownership of residence.

> My father worked in the Survey Department. For the whole of our life we have been living in rented houses. My father did not have his own house. That's why we go place to place like *Gypsies*. We lived for seven years in Kelaniya then went to Ragama. Then came here. We have been here now three years. We go place to place because of housing. When landlords ask for the house, we find another place; I asked for a house from the government, at least in a housing scheme, but they did not give me one. They said that priority should be given to shanty dwellers, but I know the government has given houses to non-shanty dwellers too. But they did not give me one. That's why I hate this government. . . . We do not have close relationships with these neighbors. There is a community development organization in this area, but I am not involved in that. We are here temporarily. Community development organizations are good for the people who have ownership of a house in this community. We might stay two to three years in this location. Why should we be involved in those only for this brief period? (05/26/1985)

The second type of tenants (those who reside in houses which are not subjected to the Housing Ceiling Act of the National Housing Department) have realized that there is no option for their outward mobility. However, they are rather reluctant to accept this reality due to their economic constraints and the incompleteness of the implementation of the Housing Ceiling Act. Under such circumstances, these residents tend to find a reason to confront their landlords. Some residents in this category have already started paying Government estimated rents directly to the Department of National Housing, disregarding their initial agreements of paying market rates directly to the landlord. These people, without giving up this far reaching goal, embark on all the other possible options to achieve the objective of permanent residence. In such an example, a 38 year old Sinhala male, unmarried, shares the present rented house with his brother and considers marriage as one option to this problem. He says:

> I have to get married to a woman who has a house. Otherwise I have to ask my brother to find a house elsewhere and leave this place, then I can stay here. However, according to the time in which we live, it is difficult to live with an expectation; things are dependent on changing circumstances. (05/13/1985)

GEOGRAPHICAL MOBILITY AND ITS IMPLICATIONS

It is possible to draw some policy implications from the empirical evidence of inward–outward aspirations of this community. (1) The degree of inward–outward orientation shapes the attitudes and nature of neighborhood relationships. It has an effect on community development activities, the degree of participation, conflicts, etc. It has a greater impact on politics of the community. (2) The government housing ownership right is considered as a major resource, beyond residential purpose. Some people use it as a means of resolving their economic crisis. This has a spillover effect and increases shanty dwellings around these government housing schemes or on any government reservations. (3) Most of the government housing schemes are not satisfactory solutions for better human habitations. It largely serves the purpose of a transitory phase of life. (4) There is a demand for financial institutions (for those who want to move out immediately but need financial help to buy lands and building houses). (5) Resource flow out from urban areas to the metropolitan periphery. (6) The outward mobility of shanty dwellers has no effect on reducing high density. They just transfer their residential rights to new migrants. (7) The inflow–outflow content may alter the demographic composition of the community. (8) The government's inability to cope with the demand for housing creates opportunities for bureaucratic corruption, patronage politics, nepotism, and favoritism in the process of distribution of scarce resources. This situation has a tendency to develop hostile attitudes toward political and governmental machinery. Thus, an environment for disruptive sabotage elements with regard to municipal and central government programs develops. (9) Unhealthy landlord–tenant relationships develop.

Chapter 10

Conclusion

South Asian social structure is rooted in the context of historical caste, kinship, lineage, ethnic and religious differences. This cultural heterogeneous heritage tends to be rural, urban and regional in scope. Urbanization and modernization do not always contradict these social and cultural heritages. Thus the traditional and modern elements are not mutually exclusive in social patterns of South Asia. However, the emerging urban community structures do not constitute a uniform pattern in the Indian subcontinent.

This study of Dematagoda does not reveal all the complex and intricate elements of wide variations of urban communities in South Asia. Nonetheless, the underlying structural mechanism of Dematagoda in Colombo provides a strong skeleton upon which we can build conceptual models of emerging patterns of urban communities. The analysis of the dynamics of urban institutional systems comprising economic livelihood, kinship, neighborhood, religion, and factional politics sheds a great deal of light on the total network of relationships and the distribution of power.

What are the policy implications of the community structure of Dematagoda? In other words, how do traditional patronage politics confront, harmonize or blend with modern democratic ideals? What are the political and institutional imperatives that could be utilized for policy planning and implementation? What inferences can we draw as alternative forms of community structures and relevant policy options?

EMERGING PATTERNS OF COMMUNITY STRUCTURES

Four types of urban community structures appear to emerge from this study: (1) strategic integration, (2) polarized communities, (3) fragmented structures, and (4) individualized community structures. table 10.1 presents a summation of characteristics in terms of economic livelihood, politics, kinship, neighborhood, and mobility patterns.

STRATEGIC INTEGRATION

The strategic integration is characterized by absence of tensions and ideological confrontation on the political front. This is an outcome of the interrelationship between external political trends and the internal structural conditions. The urban communities which were split into major groups on an ideological basis began to be changed, forcing them to make alliances. The process of transition from factionalism to political alliances provides an alternative for the people who lose power to uphold their status in the community. The economically marginal groups which had been associating with these previous power centers tend to shift their faith quickly to the more popular political groups. The limited choices in the socio-economic opportunity structures of communities in major cities of South Asia make the marginal groups form these new alliances. Nonetheless, the communities with strategic integration contain hidden factionalism within the context of popular politics. This hidden confrontation reflects the attitudes of the people who are aloof from community activities and socially marginal groups. There are three possible outcomes which can be identified as a result of this confrontation: (l) A segment of a socially marginal group, low caste and ethnic minorities, is absorbed into the system of patronage as clients who can play a subservient role in the community. The mutual solidarity and reciprocity submerges the tension between dominant and

Table 10.1

Major Characteristics of Urban Community Structures in South Asia

Types of Communities	Economic Livelihood	Politics	Kinship	Neighborhood	Mobility
Strategic Integration	Economic opportunities and political structure are interwoven	Political alliances and patronage politics	Both external kinship ties and affective kin relationship	High and moderate level relationship	Significant degree of inward orientation and aspiration gap
Polarized	Competitive politics dominate livelihood	Sharp cleavages High degree of factionalism with the system of patronage	External kinship ties	Selective relationship on the basis of political and ascriptive cleavages	Outward mobility among those who do not take part in cleavages
Fragmented	Group competition with opportunistic approaches	Quasi-social groups Temporary nature of political factionalism	High degree of affective kinship within social groups	Based on group consciousness	High degree of inward orientation (limited choices)
Individualize	Economic independence	Political neutrality	Exclusively external kin ties	Friendship on selective basis	High degree of stability

dominated categories. (2) Another segment of the population having sound economic position lives in an isolated manner. It does not confront, by any means, the system. (3) The last category who are aloof from community activities show the direction of outward mobility making room for newcomers. The process of recruitment of newcomers into the community is closely monitored through the social network and the patronage system, diluting the free market characteristics.

Patronage politics is a prominent character of the communities with strategic integration. The strength of the relationship between the needy and the political representatives at various levels in the process of local politics is an important phenomenon in patronage politics. The strength of this relationship is determined by three factors: (1) contribution to political campaigns (e.g., money, labor, loyalty) made by the needy or the political agent who speaks on behalf of the needy, (2) the relationship between the MP of the area and the minister of the respective functional jurisdictions, and (3) the degree of flexibility of governmental and ministerial policies and regulations. In this context of patronage network, factional politics and power changes will have an adverse impact on people's livelihood in the community. This unfavorable circumstance causes residents of these communities to tend to adopt strategies and make alterations in their political relationships. Despite their previous political identities, they make continuous efforts to get access to the present political channels. In this process, friendship, local identity, kinship, and neighborhood belongingness form the *modus operandi,* rather than ideological commitment.

In addition to these *modus operandi,* reciprocity and social legitimation have been developed in communities with strategic integration. Thus political support in electoral campaigns is reciprocated with tangible benefits. The scarce resources such as employment, housing and infrastructural facilities are distributed in this manner. The contractual form is hidden in this reciprocal arrangement and it has direct or indirect impact on governmental decision-making at local and national levels in the sphere of resource allocation. Nonetheless, the frequent violation of this norm is apparent. Malpractices, such as corruption and nepotism, creep into the system and sometimes make for tension, unhappiness and disappointment within the community. Furthermore, this tension is reflected within the sphere of neighborhood relationships and the relationship between residents and governmental service organizations, such as municipal councils, housing agencies and utilities boards.

Political agents assume informal arbitrator roles in such situations, patronizing supporters and distributing party-directed benefits. They engage in organizing, contribution and mobilizing political support allegiance to the parties and politicians. Political agents as mediators have attributes of both clients and patrons. The main objective of these mediators is to stabilize their income sources, which require external political support, and to enjoy status in the community. Hence they engage in continuously seeking political patronage from national politicians while they develop clientele from the community.

The patronizing capacity of political agents is determined by their resources and networks as well as party-directed benefits. Personality attributes and skills of these agents and their directions in life also are factors which determine the nature of the role of political agents. Most of the mediating actors possess entrepreneurial, professional or religious attributes. This phenomenon is somewhat similar to the South Indian Galactic Polity and its Mandala structure (Mines and Gourishankar 1990, 49: 761-784). They have power over both clients and their patrons. This behavior is largely characterized by political manipulation, reciprocity, networking and enormous tensions at all levels, such as household, neighborhood, community. In general, three possible patterns could be traced, at the community level, with regard to the behavior of political actors. They are: (1) the political scene is dominated by the power holders while losers are inactive, (2) opponents may make alliances with the dominant group, and (3) sharp cleavages and conflicts are not resolved. In the case of strategic integration the tendency is to change from sharp cleavages either to acceptance of political dominancy of power holders or to the pattern of making alliances. This does not necessarily mean a linear progression of integration among political actors. The cohesion is characterized by indifferent attitudes and passive behavior, or by making alliances with dominant groups. These types of political adaptation appeal to all parties. This strategy is a result of conditions of both internal and external socio-economic and political trends: the degree of political stability at the national level, and the numerical composition of social categories at the community level. These are decisive factors which determine the nature of political adaptation. Thus the variations in community political structures are by-products of the nature of macro–micro interlocking of certain conditions.

The externally introduced political hierarchy is operational either at nominal levels or is now disappearing. This has weakened the politics of an ideological kind in the face of strong patron-client ties and social networks. The social relationship of strategic integration is characterized by a high density network with a significant number of political agents (fig. 10.1). This high density network has a potential to break through the ascriptive elements of the system. The political agents play a mediating role between power centers and the community. Networking is an essential task for them to play this patronage role, and by doing that they enjoy self-esteem and status. Cross-over politics and cross-channeling of benefits are also a byproduct of this patron–client relationship. The people who cross over very often play a subservient role in the political structure of the community while expecting potentially equal status with current power brokers. The act of crossing-over legitimates the positions of political power brokers in the community.

Today, this important political adaptation takes the form of transition from an ideological to pragmatic politics. This process of transition is very conducive to receiving the concept of community development and its associated institutional structures which have been newly introduced under the umbrella of urban development policies. Cross-sectional representations, in terms of ethnic, income and political differences, characterizes the form of community development organizations within the environment of this strategic integration.

Neighborhood and kinship. Neighborhood relationships are a significant phenomenon in the social network of strategic integration. The majority of communities tend to maintain either a high or moderate level of connections. The intimate neighborhood relationship is very frequently referred to as *friendship*. In certain cases, the high degree of intimacy changes into bonds of affinity. The interaction primarily pivots around normal life crises such as sickness, death, emergency situations, and ritual ceremonial functions. However, the intensity and the type of reciprocity in neighborhood relation may vary from one family to another and depends on the nature of the crisis.

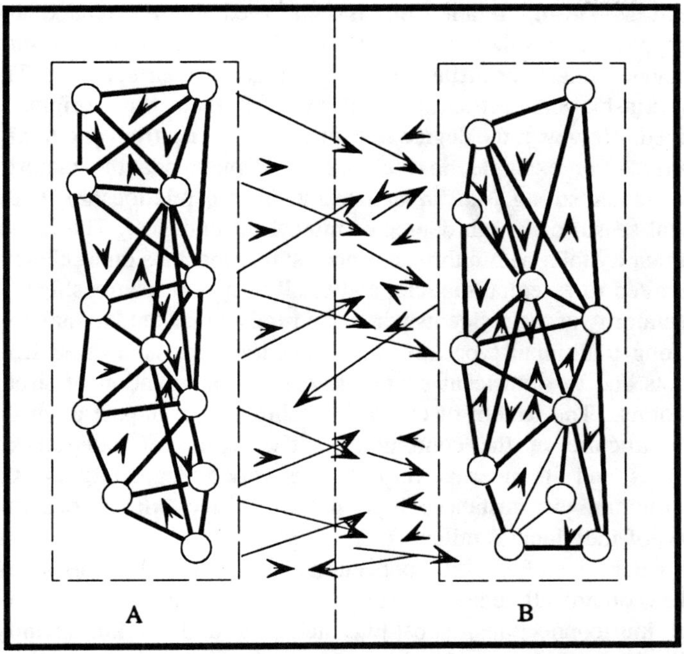

Fig. 10.1. Community of Strategic Integration

Community Boundary

Political Boundaries

A B Two Major Political Groups

Political Actors (All Levels)

Interactions Among Political Actors Within the Same Party

Cross Chanelled Patronage System Between Two Major Political Divisions

High Degree of Social Interaction (Both Vertical and Horizontal)

As far as kinship relationship is concerned, both extended and nuclear types are prevalent in these communities. The extended family units include inmates or affines of householders or their spouses. The external kinship connection, particularly with their rural origin, is maintained. However, the degree of connections varies from one family to another. For example, in the case of Dematagoda the majority maintain either strong *Nedakama* (strong kinship relationship in the traditional sense) or a high degree of mutual dependence. The rest of the community falls within three categories: relationships on a selective basis, limited to essential matters, and totally severed relationships.

The majority of the residents who have rural origins tend to maintain very strong traditional type kinship connections unless severed from their roots due to significant economic reasons or violation of strong social norms. The pattern of external kinship has an impact upon the internal structure of the community. The nature of external kin connections and its internal impacts are varied depending on the socio-economic circumstances and the social network options and decisions of individual families.

Four categories of kinship connections have emerged in this study. First, the economically marginal categories of the communities, with no external kin connections, substitute neighborhood as kin affinity. Secondly, the residents who have few neighborhood connections, substitute external kin connections; some members of this category either provide a necessary network for their kinsmen who want to migrate or provide some financial support for their rural relatives. Thirdly, residents maintaining both kinship and neighborhood connections equally. Members of this third category generally have sound economic position, property-based kin connections, and relatively high status in the community. For them external kin connection is one of the sources of status. The kinship network of this third category played an important role with regard to in-migration from rural areas. In the cases of Dematagoda, the leading business group provides, in the first place, employment opportunities for these new migrants. The fourth category is the isolated and powerless in the community. They have extremely limited kinship and neighborhood relationships. In most cases, the extreme level of poverty and geographical distance prevent kinship connections. In summary, the relative importance of neighborhood and kinship depends on the options available to a household in the total network of the community.

POLARIZED COMMUNITIES

Dematagoda was a polarized community with political factionalism, though it has been changing direction towards strategic integration. Three variations can be conceptualized under the polarized community structure: (1) political factionalism, (2) ascriptive polarization (ethnic, caste, kinship clans) with external political factionalism, and (3) communities with strong ascriptive polarization.

Political factionalism. Polarized community structures, with strong political ideologies, are characterized by dual hierarchial relationships. More formalized social network with a dual patronage system appear to emerge (fig. 10.2). Power and wealth are concentrated at the apex of this hierarchy. The economic strength and political organizational positions of the community provide the skeleton for vertical relationships. The ascriptive elements are largely submerged in these types of communities. Therefore, the members of these communities seek alternatives to ascriptive elements. These alternatives are ideological weapons. As presented in the analysis, this ideological confrontation is directly associated with the two bases of resources: legitimate and illegitimate source of income, and factional politics. The legitimacy of income sources and the normative aspects, based on democratic ideals, with regard to the operation of urban institutions are emphasized and take the form of ideological stances, as opposed to the illegitimacy.

The Dematagoda community structure, particularly during the 1960s and 1970s, was polarized by legitimacy and the normative content of the urban institutions. Despite different status groups (ranking) in terms of migrational history, ethnicity, local identities, and the numerical strength of each group, a sharp distinction was prevalent in the community on the basis of political ideologies. The community had been divided into two major groups: right wing and left wing. Local identities, such as Southerners and original inhabitants, were reflected at the apex of the hierarchy since it had economic polarization. The lower strata had cross-sectional status group affiliation irrespective of local consciousness.

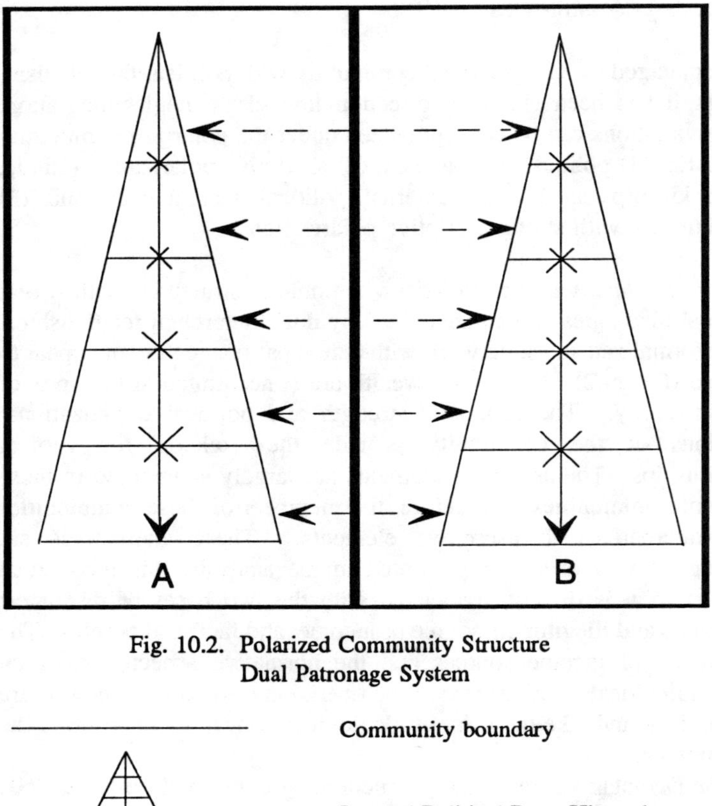

Fig. 10.2. Polarized Community Structure
Dual Patronage System

Community boundary

Internal Political Party Hierarchy

Political Separation

A B Two Major Political Groups

Conflicts Between Political Factions

The apex of the community hierarchy in the case of Dematagoda consists of three major groups: (1) the indigenous leading group, (2) the indigenous land owning professional group, and (3) the leading business group. The first group is affiliated with right-wing politics (United National Party). The second group is affiliated with left-wing (Marxist parties—LSSP/CP) and the leading business group is affiliated with the left-wing of moderate political group (SLFP). The latter two groups were more often political alliances than opponents.

As described earlier, the power structure has been completely reversed shifting from the indigenous land owning–professional group to the indigenous leading group. This was due to two major reasons: (1) the political changes occurring at the national level, and (2) the changing character of demographic composition as a result of in-migration. These changes did not alter the polarized relationship of the community.

The degree of political polarization is determined and maintained by the numerical strength of marginal categories which need economic and social support from the patronage network. The degree of basic needs (employment opportunities, social security and improvement of housing conditions), dependency, and the patrons' capacity to provide these needs are determining factors for patron–client politics. The patrons' capacity is determined by the quality of their linkages to the national and regional level politics. Thus the patrons' capacity of internal political mobilization and the quality of external linkages reinforce each other. Political polarization is maintained with the balanced power of dominant groups.

Ascriptive polarization with political factionalism. The ascriptive elements of community structures and external political factionalism are a magnet to each other. On the one hand, this form of ascriptive elements invites political factionalism in order to wield power over the opponent group. On the other hand, factional politics infiltrates into community structures exploiting internal ascriptive elements for their own power battle at the macro level. This political infiltration is determined by the nature of population dynamics which is characterized by the ascriptive composition of the region.

Richard G. Fox (1969) has presented community polarization on the basis of inter-caste and lineage disputes, communalism with religious hostility, associating it with political factionalism in the north Indian market town of Tezibazar (1969). According to Fox's study the intensity and quality of Hindu-Muslim conflict is comparable to caste antagonism. In Tezibazar town the most anti-Muslim of status categories are the Beniyas and the Brahmins who retain the spirit of Hinduism in social habits and ideals.

During the early period of this century this conflict did not take a communal form. In the 1920s, inter-caste and lineage disputes spread into the political field. One of the Umar lineages involved in this conflict consisted of the Umar Zamindars who opposed their Muslim counterparts. On either political side, lineages and castes in opposition to one or the other gathered with little concern for community. The Umar lineage which opposed the Umar Zamindar lineage sided with the Muslim land owners. Muslims, on a caste and lineage basis or an individual basis who disliked the Muslim Zamindars, joined ranks with the Umar Beniya Zamindars. Neither of these two groups was organized communally. Muslim leadership was not based on ideological utilization of such a unity. Religious alignment had not yet crystallized into a politically significant form.

Gradually, the formal political machinery came increasingly under Beniya control, particularly that of Umar Zamindars. At the same time, inter-caste and lineage levels had increasing ramifications in the political sphere. This progression was accompanied by the rising influence of the big merchants. However, during World War II the British administration subsidized the Muslim's power claims as a counter force to Hindu independence and sentiments.

With independence in 1947 communal politics became more important than caste or lineages. In Tezibazar town, however, caste and lineage conflicts continued to play major roles in determining electoral allegiance and enmities. Whether it is communal or caste lineage, the political realities of population became meaningful with the broadening of the electorate.

Since independence, organized Muslim communal apparatus emerged to meet the challenge of a Hindu majority. This was mainly due to three factors. First was the creation of an entire structure of government, from the national level down through state and district, town and village strata. Second were the economic changes brought on by the Second World War. These replaced the old Beniya Zamindar class with the big Beniya Merchants. This was an economic threat to the Muslims since they were the second largest trading community in

Tazibazar town. Third were the National government's efforts to make changes in the Muslim personal law. This created countrywide agitation among Muslims and it was conducive for local conflicts. All these factors intensified the antagonisms between these two groups because the local level apparatus linked smoothly with the regional level communal voting bodies which are based on sentiments.

Communities with Strong Ascriptive Polarization. The most prominent ascriptive elements in marginal residential communities are caste, ethnicity and lineage. The poor quality housing and caste segregation in a geographical entity are attributes of social isolation from surrounding areas. On the basis of these ascriptive attributes, the externally-imposed negative stigma is very strong.

In the case of Sri Lanka, some suburban communities have been created to relocate the squatters of regional urban centers who occupied various parts within the city limits (Gamini 1983). These residents are dependent on employment opportunities of the city. These people are originally from rural areas and have strong connections with their home towns. Unlike the shanty communities within the metropolitan city limits, the suburban resettlements of regional centers have official recognition because of the ownership of land. The social isolation from external environments, and internal social distinction in terms of locality of origin, ethnicity or caste, are common to these communities. The ascriptive polarization is maintained through internal physical segregation and it reflects in every sphere of community life.

The leadership is largely in the hands of the dominant social group irrespective of the political spectrum of the ascriptive elements. This internal social distinction is strong enough to maintain polarized social relations within the community. Therefore, the dominant group usually enjoys more privileges in using infrastructural facilities of the community.

Each ascriptive group maintains a high degree of cohesiveness and it reflects through the sense of caste or ethnic and locality bound neighborliness within each group. These lower socio-economic status groups also maintain high kinship connections with their home towns.

This type of internal–external connection has a great impact upon social contours of the urban setting. Ascriptive communities have a greater tendency to promote in-migration from rural areas. A study of marginal community in Bangalore City has revealed a pattern of in-migration based on the ascriptive elements.

> Migration of individuals or families followed a pattern based on spontaneous strategy along the social slope—caste, kinship, language and religion—through information flows channeled through social links. Kinship network played an important role in the recruitment of migrants to jobs and the choice of locality for residence. Caste and kinship loyalties are strong among all migrants. They are stronger among the lower castes. (Prakasa 1983, 234)

Factional politics is also common in the Indian market communities in association with communal and caste lineage attributes. Rodney W. Jones, in his book *Urban Politics in India*, has discussed this type of community factionalism. According to this study, in Indore City "each market had a quasi-autonomous governing body dominated by the locally powerful groups, each market clique looked upon the existence of the other market as an economic threat" (Rodney 1974, 331).

In such situations, the powerful seek external political, legislative, and other institutional supports to restrict the operation of their competitors. For example, the Madhya Predesh Agricultural Produce Market Act was passed to restrict the number of other markets in each city, hoping to abolish the opponent group in the market place. The existence of opponent groups is dependent on their strength to refuse to go out of business. The existence of opponent groups gradually became accepted as an exception to the legislative rule. This example is a good illustration of urban community polarization with business and political cleavages within the same political party:

> The arena of agricultural produce market competition is particularly interesting because of how it reveals the summation of area and ascriptive community cleavages with business and political cleavages within the local congress party. It further illustrates vertical linkages between allied local and state level political leaders and how government influence is brought to bear in the form of discriminatory legislation and in the local purchasing practices of

> bureaucratic agencies. The arena of agricultural markets is also significant as a political base for certain business cum political entrepreneurs seeking wider scope for their political influence. (Rodney 1974, 333)

As far as most of the market towns of Sri Lanka are concerned, ascriptive polarization is disappearing (Neville 1979, Gamini 1979). Factionalism was the common feature in district centers and most of the market towns in the central province and the north central province of Sri Lanka until the mid 1970s. Factionalism was based on either ethnic strife (Sinhala, Tamil, and Muslim) or local identities (up country Sinhalese and low country Sinhalese). The economic competition provided the basis for political cum business entrepreneurship.

The low-country dominance in local business and its social assimilation into the local condition gradually integrates them into the local politics. Thus entrepreneurial or political factionalism began to be reduced. The religious homogeneity among Sinhalese provided the ideological basis for this integration. The social integration further led indigenous people to start businesses in the district town. As a result, instead of competition, oligopolistic entrepreneurship has been developed and the functional significance of the district center provides the basis for unity of the community.

Up country–low country integration was strengthened in the context of communal tension in the country. The Sinhala-Tamil communal business factionalism is no longer valid. Communal riots displaced the Jaffna Tamils from their business while Muslim traders maintained harmonious and more balanced entrepreneurship in these market towns. However, the political subordination of Muslim traders is quite obvious unless the numerical strength in the region is substantial. The displacement of Jaffna Tamils is not the result of ad hoc mob attacks which took place in communal riots. It is closely associated with the political and economic complexities of the civilians. It has been noted that "the South Asian rioters are 'purposive' as to the destruction of property" (Tambiah 1990, 751).

Kinship-neighborhood matrix. The political or ascriptive polarization provides the basis for neighborhood relationships. Neighborhood clusters are usually divided into opponent camps on the basis of two types of polarization: (1) small disputes between households, and (2) larger political conflicts. Small disputes between households, over the issues of sharing common infrastructural facilities, may turn into larger neighborhood conflicts. Hence, the social exchange and day to day interaction are completely based on this polarization. In the case of political factionalism and ascriptive polarization with political factionalism, high tension can be seen during election time.

Unlike strategic integration, neighborhood relationships have a more wider collective meaning than individual reciprocity. The unequal status and social distance in each neighborhood cluster are submerged by the neighborhood unity as they engage in political confrontation with other neighborhood clusters.

The neighborhood relationship is more important than kinship, but all the external kinship connections may provide a strength for neighborhood unity. The recruitment of rural migrants to urban community is strongly monitored through a three dimensional framework of neighborhood, kinship and politics. Unlike in strategic integration, there is a limited scope for personal variations in polarized communities. In the case of political polarization, even the patrons have to be congruent with the political rules. Otherwise, the political opponents tend to criticize every single act of the power holders and try to exploit all opportunities to mobilize people against the system. The political ideologies are strong in these communities and the patron–client system is buttressed by respective ideologies. Party membership and loyalty to the party are strong attributes which can be used for personal benefits within the system. In conclusion, neighborhood and kinship connections are encircled with a political boundary.

FRAGMENTED COMMUNITIES

Fragmentation is a very common phenomenon in shanty communities. A rapidly growing urban population in South Asia is largely concentrated in these settlements along canal banks, alleyways and on marginal lands in larger cities. These communities subsist without amenities, such as water and toilets. They are improvised houses made of materials such as packing cases, wattle and daub, or tin sheets. The majority of families in these communities live without having regular or visible income. The scarcity of resources makes for tension among the residents of these communities.

The fragmented communities are characterized by quasi social groups emerging from neighborhoods. Locality feelings and length of stay are the basis for this neighborhood consciousness. The intense rivalry between neighborhoods and temporary alliances are frequent phenomena in their social relations in fragmented communities (fig. 10.3). These conflicts and alliances are occurring over the issues of infrastructural facilities, income sources, distribution of governmental and non governmental benefits and the nature of interactions with external agencies. One of the community development efforts in Colombo City, sponsored by the United States Save the Children Federation, defined the type of social relationship of these groups as:

> The fissiparous collection of individuals grouped in gardens, owing allegiance to an assortment of dubious social groups, preying on one another as and when necessary, and preying on the larger society. (Asia/Pacific Regional Team and Sri Lanka Field Office Team 1982, 7)

Despite those quasi social groups, the reality of *geographical contiguity* makes for social distinction from the larger society. The residents of shanty settlements are experiencing a social isolation from the mainstream life of the city. Hence, the community's frame of reference is based on this social isolation in terms of the existing situation inside the geographical entity pertaining to police brutality, lack of amenities, unemployment and physical isolation from the larger urban society. This community frame of reference is, further, enhanced by the enviable living condition among the surrounding affluent neighborhoods. The needs of shanty settlements reflect this contrast in living conditions. The following statement best exemplifies this situation:

> The degree of alienation was reflected in the cynicism that shanty residents displayed on matters such as authority, development, politics, social responsibility, etc. Moreover, the physical needs appeared to be as much symbols of social needs as they were basic needs. For instance, speaking of the lack of an access road into the shanty, residents complained bitterly that they could never bring a friend or colleague, nor have a decent funeral. It was evident that the more basic need was integration into the mainstream of society. (Asia/Pacific Regional Team and Sri Lanka Field Office 1982, 8)

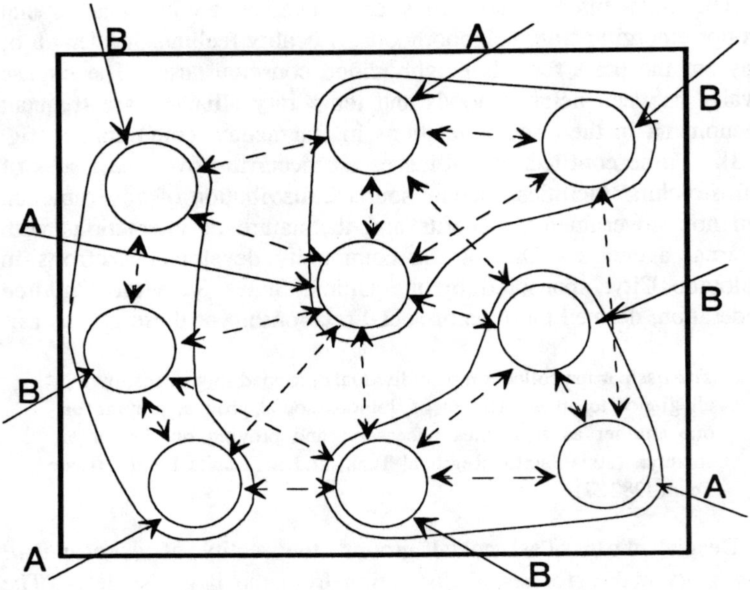

Fig. 10.3. Fragmented Community Structure

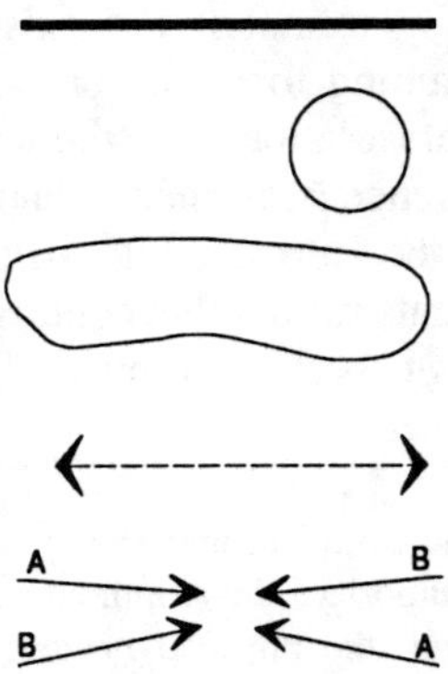

Community Boundary

Quasi-social Groups in Neighborhood Clusters.

Alliances Among Quasi-social Groups.

Conflict Between Quasi-social Groups.

Temporary Approaches by Two Major Political Parties.

Despite the fact of this physical and social isolation, these communities are connected to the mainstream politics on an ad hoc basis, particularly during election times. The external power brokers from different political parties usually approach these quasi social groups and quasi-leaders to win the community support for election campaigns. Most frequently, the individuals and groups are used for political thuggerism in larger society. In this context these people could be identified as *Lumpen Proletariat* as neo-Marxists did. This situation is not conducive to community-based patronage politics, which is common in integrated social structures. The cleavage politics tends to associate different neighborhoods in terms of ethnic, old–new distinctions, etc. Political cleavages usually come to the forefront during the period of national or regional political campaigns and tend to disappear or be submerged by other local factions at other times. The local factions and conflicts are increased by the lack of internal facilities, while internal consensus is promoted by external threats or the higher standard of living of the outside communities. This temporary consensus does not provide a solid foundation to introduce democratic measures for community development, but it has potential attributes.

Some of these problems and characteristics have been noted by one of the community development programs sponsored by the Urban Development Authority of Sri Lanka (Gamini 1983). For example, one of the oldest shanty communities of Colombo City exhibits four major quadrants in which political factionalism cuts across the two social divisions (fig. 10.4).

OLD RESIDENTS PRO-GOVERNMENT	NEW RESIDENTS PRO-GOVERNMENT
OLD RESIDENTS ANTI-GOVERNMENT	NEW RESIDENTS ANTI-GOVERNMENT

Fig. 10.4. Political Factionalism and Social Divisions

As a result of the initiative and the numerical strength of the old residents, this community is usually able to absorb outside resources into their community, but the internal organizations and institutional systems are not strong enough to allocate their resources in a healthy manner. This situation is conducive to group competition, and it produces irrational measures for the distribution of resources in the community. The leadership fails to maintain unity and to organize the community towards achieving their objectives.

The internal disunity tends to disappear temporarily when these communities are engaged in direct confrontation with non-affluent surroundings. This is more possible once shanty settlements are established within old, poor quality, residential areas. The internal rivalries, which are common due to lack of facilities, are not permitted and are subjected to informal sanctions. The quasi-leadership usually keep their eye on such incidents. The high degree of community cohesiveness is strengthened as a result of external stigmatization, including being labeled by words such as *Palapth, Maddukku,* and *Koriyawa.* These labels carry the Western theoretical connotation of *subculture* and *culture of poverty.* The majority of the residents of these communities, unlike in the strategic type, are urban-born people, with possible rural ancestry. Some of these families have experienced a high degree of internal geographical mobility within city limits. The majority tend to continue within the shanty area, and hence marriages are confined to the people of the community. Kinship ties are at a high level. Their economic standards are very low. Therefore they have no outward mobility. All these factors contribute to the physical and social isolation of these communities from the larger society.

However, it is unrealistic to conclude that these communities do reflect a sub-cultural homogeneity within the social setting of South Asian cities. The cultural metaphor has to be understood within the context of the social structure of these communities. The empirical evidence contradicts the *culture of poverty* argument developed in the Western world. It is noted in the study of Watta-dwellers that the social life in any of these communities cannot be described in negative terms such as marginality, rootlessness, and anomie (Silva and Athukorala 1991, 130). It is possible to identify varying degrees of upward aspirations of the people in these shanty communities. They are engaged in a struggle for day-to-day living, dreaming of upward social mobility within the accepted normative framework of the society. Thus any type of externally imposed stigma is highly destructive. This group cannot be placed within a moral vacuum. Some people in these communities have a contradictory state of mind emanating from a conflict between morality and the struggle for living. Under such circumstances the basic needs aspiration is not merely for an achievement of material comfort. It is also both a moral and political imperative. Therefore, it is possible to argue that these communities are potential breeding grounds for the development of democratic institutional mechanisms which are required for community development.

INDIVIDUALIZED COMMUNITIES

The anatomy of the individualized community structures can be drawn from Dematagoda, even though it is marginally reflected in the system. This type of community has a broad-based equal power structure as it does not have an internal resource base. The members of these communities draw their income from external professional and business activities. Both the absence of an internal resource base and the possession of individual infrastructural facilities provide the basis for individualization within a demarcated residential territory.

Political factionalism has no meaning in their residential jurisdiction. Though the political identity is anonymous, life is heavily governed by politics of the larger society. Thus political self identity is the reality in these communities (fig. 10.5).

The internal network of relationship is largely confined to one or two neighborhood friendships. This friendship has no tangible reciprocity as in other forms of neighborhoods. The purpose of this type of friendship is to share common experiences in their professional and business activities, and to have entertainment.

The appearance of their life is more modern while integrating certain indigenous values into the meaning of their life. For example, the surface life style is materialistic in the Western sense, while having modified versions of kinship, religious cultural values governing their own behavior. The external social interactions are significant in those areas of life events. As elaborated in this study, all the types of relationship in the continuum of kinship can be identified in individualized communities. The external social network also encompasses political, religious, professional and business territories.

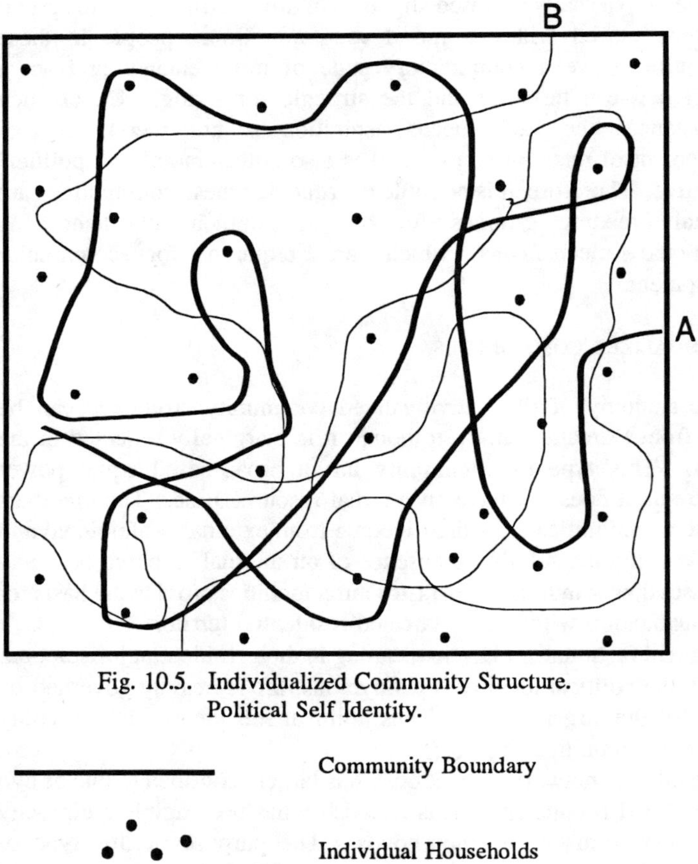

Fig. 10.5. Individualized Community Structure.
Political Self Identity.

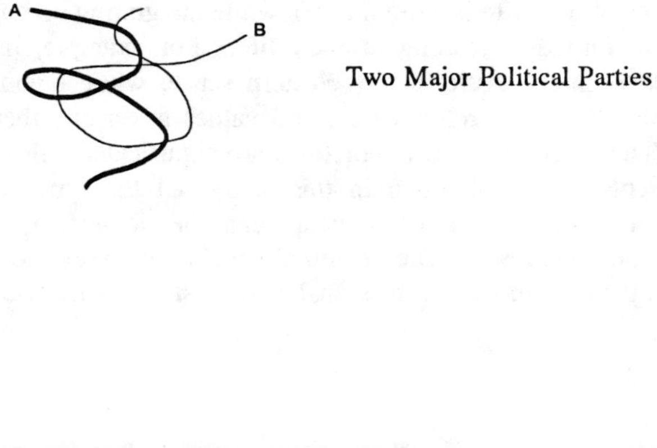

In conclusion, members of these communities are integrated into the larger society, having more individualized attributes within their own residential area. However, the sense of community is a form of *status category*.

Policy Implications

The policy implications can be theoretically understood by using analytical categories developed by Theodore Lowi (1964) and by Robert H. Salisbury (1958). There are four major categories of public policies: distribution, regulation, redistribution, and self-regulatory policies.

Distributive policies deal with direct benefits to specific individuals and groups. Conflict occurs over the distribution of shares, because of the scarcity of urban resources handled by municipal councils or by national governments of these countries. Distributive policies in these urban communities consist of basic infrastructural services related to housing, education, health and ordinary patronage.

Re-distributive policies are concerned with transferring benefits from advantaged groups to people in disadvantaged categories. For example, the Housing Ceiling Act of 1972 was passed in Sri Lanka to redistribute extra houses of landlords among tenants. These policies have great impact on community structures. In the case of Dematagoda, the conflict between potential winners and losers goes back to the mid-1950s. They engaged in intense conflict over the policy-making process, taking sides along political lines. Soon after the dramatic political shift from the right wing to the left wing, landlords of Dematagoda anticipated the upcoming re-distributive measures and made attempts to sell their houses to outsiders, evicting tenants in the process. For example, one attempt to auction houses in 1964 was prevented by the tenants. Tenants took the matter up with the then Prime Minister. As a result they got the assurance that the government would acquire the houses to ensure that the tenants would not be evicted.

Regulatory policies consist of general rules drawn for specific cases within a broader guideline. These policies constrain the behavior of particular groups and open or close opportunities for acquiring benefits in the future. This is more possible if regulatory policies will not have a negative impact on the political process. Regulatory policies are employed by governmental agencies for communities with strong ascriptive polarization, without having political divisions. For example, the Urban Development Authority in Sri Lanka once imposed constraints on newly relocated suburban communities, asking them to form representative committees, giving up their caste loyalties (Gamini 1983). As long as they did not come up with representative committees, the external benefits were not channeled into these communities.

Self-regulatory policies are more or less similar to the regulatory policies. Despite externally imposed constraints upon groups, they perceive these rules differently with increasing potential benefits. Self-regulatory policies involve more democratic principles such as delegation of authority to functional groups in the interpretation of regulatory standards. For example, fragmented communities make integrated demands but their decisional structure is characterized by disunity. Thus self-regulatory policies promote unity avoiding the conflict.

The community development project in Kirulapana Shanty Community, sponsored by the United States Save the Children Federation, has proven application of self-regulatory policies is improving results. The potential shift from fragmentation to integration has been proven through democratic representation, enthusiasm, growing responsibility and initiative of the community committee. Vertical linkages between the shanty and outside institutions have been developing. The social isolation is disappearing.

The policy categories presented by Lowi and Salisbury have direct impact on the power structures of urban communities, and self-regulatory policies are more in conformity with pluralist structures of decentralized power. The results of these policies are compromises among contending power groups. However, these policy categories are not empirically confined to one or another community type presented in this chapter (table 10.2). The actual policies usually consist of a mixture which is based on different structural conditions of communities.

It is my contention, in this study, that each community system reveals different mechanics at the conceptual level. Figure 10.6 illustrates these concepts. This means the interplay between resources, power, network of relationships and the system of ideology has different forms of operational system in different types of communities. The change can be initiated from any point of this system, but the existing form of vibration has to be identified.

Table 10.2

Community Types, Demand and Decisional Patterns and Policy Mixture

Types of Communities	Political Structure	Demand Pattern	Decisional pattern	Policy Mixture
Strategic Integration	Political alliances between dual hierarchy	Both integrated and fragmented demand	Integrated	Redistributive and regulatory
Polarized	Sharp cleavages and dual hierarchy	Fragmented demand patterns	Fragmented Contending groups	Distributive and regulatory
Fragmented	Power contention	Compatibility of demands Integrated	Disunity	Distributive and self-regulatory
Individualized	Absence of political structure Neutrality	Diversity	Absence of decisional patterns	Distributive

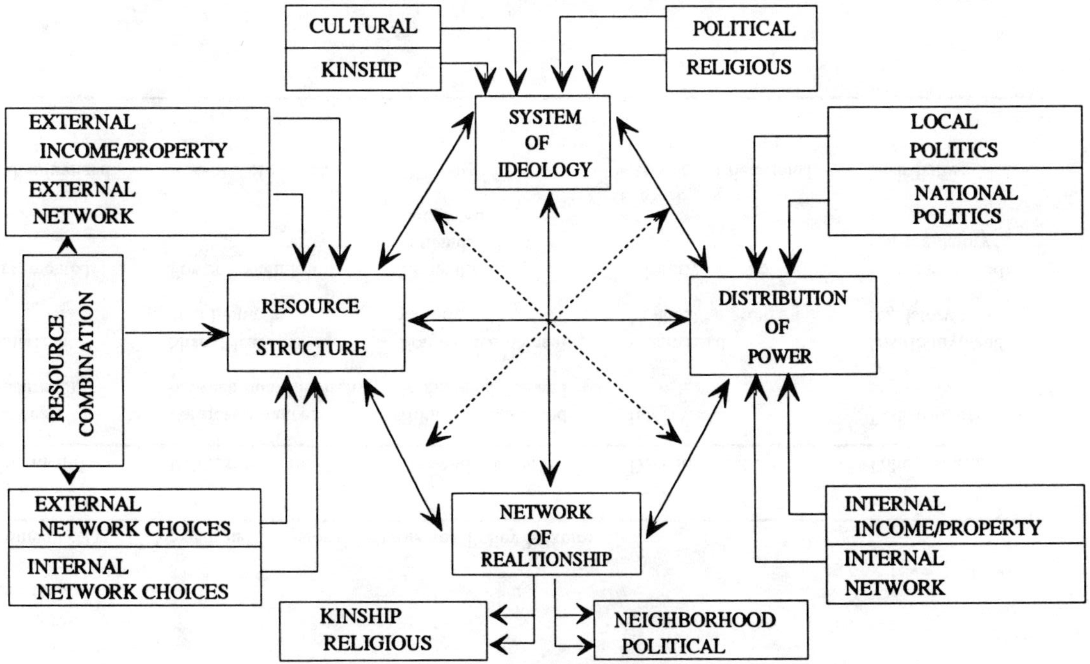

Fig. 10.6. The Form of Vibration of A Social System

FURTHER RESEARCH

A close examination of urban community structures is of vital importance to estimate the strengths and weaknesses of each system. All the spectrum and operational characteristics of demand and decisional patterns have to be understood in the context of distribution of power, prior to any policy action. Also, the distribution of power has to be examined in the context of the micro–macro framework of South Asian countries. The macro changes (economic, political at various national and regional levels) and the micro changes have reciprocal connections and tension.

It is beyond the scope of this modest academic endeavor to explore in-depth the macro–micro reciprocity and tension arising out of dynamic interactions of different groups in the urban context. In this regard, there is a wealth of data that remains to be uncovered through sustained efforts of a community of scholars who specialize in social research in the Indian subcontinent.

Appendix 1

Preliminary Data List of the Community

1. The history of the community
2. The ownership and use of land
3. Occupational structure and income distribution pattern
4. Individual wealth within or outside the unit
5. The nature of the infrastructure services and their conditions and changes
6. The level of education
7. Kinship connections
8. The character of neighborhood
9. Religious interactions
10. Class, status and ethnicity
11. Factions and leaders
12. Local level institutions
13. Municipal administration and politics
14. Entertainment
15. Geographical mobility
16. Burning issues in the area

Appendix 2

Intensive Stage Data List
(Data Collected From Each Household)

1. General Data
   The composition of each household with background characteristics--age, sex, education, relationship to household head.
2. Economic Activities
   Occupation, income, wealth, moveable, immovable, internal and external.
   Investment pattern.
   Nature of house type.
   Special attributes related to their occupation and income, special skills, education, etc.
3. Expenditure
   Broad pattern of expenditure.
4. Family and Kinship Network
   The background characteristics of their relatives and the nature of the connections.
5. Class, Status and Ethnicity
   Perceptions on these.
6. Neighborhood
   Observation of neighborhood behavior should be the major part of the fieldworker's role.
   Uncover the nature of reciprocity with neighbors.
   Neighborhood disputes, if any.
7. Interactions With Religious Organizations (temples, churches)
   What is the commitment to and participation in orthodox religious activities?
   Explore ideology and emphasis.

8. Civic and Political Activities

   With what leaders do they link up? If any factions, explore the details.

   History of participation in particular civic and political activities.

   Reactions to and versions of recent episodes.

   Reactions to municipal and national level governmental programs and policies.

9. Aspirations

   What is the direction of mobility which the household is pursuing either jointly or individually?

   How is the position expressed?

   What obstacles do they encounter?

   What options they have in mind if the most desired one doesn't work.

Appendix 3

Basic Survey Format

1. Household number
2. Names of the household members
3. Sex
4. Marital status
5. Ethnicity
6. Religion
7. Relationship to household head
8. Age
9. Education
10. Number of school-aged children who are dropouts
11. Name of the school
12. Occupation
13. Nature of occupation (whether permanent or temporary)
14. The sector of employment
15. Income from main occupation
16. Nature of income (daily/weekly/monthly)
17. Other income sources
18. Income from other sources
19. Place of origin (respondent, mother and father)
20. Duration of migration in Colombo/in location
21. Nature of house (permanent, semi permanent, improvised)
22. Number of rooms
23. Lighting
24. Water facilities
25. Latrine facilities
26. House ownership
27. If purchases, the year and the amount
28. Life style (investigator's observation)
29. Number of kinship family units in the location
30. Previous residence before coming to this location
31. Investigator's general observations and comments

Appendix 4

Field Work - Data Base (Sample Size)

Method of Data Collection	Sample Total *N*	Sample Size (%)
Base Line Survey	724	100
Key Informants	8	—
In-Depth Interviews	85	12
Observation and Discussions	Selected	Selected

Note: Data collected from October, 1984 to July, 1985.

Appendix 5

In-Depth Interviews Code

B1 Background: age, family size, family type

B2 Education: level of education, perceptions about own level of education, problems, episodes

B3 Place of origin: self, mother, father

B4 Life history: major decisions, experiences, mobility, problems

B5 Parents' occupations

B6 Migration: geographic mobility, reasons for migration, duration in present location, problems, difficulties

'7 Occupational mobility (respondent and other members): type, sector permanency, horizontal/ vertical mobility, stability, level of influence, occupational choices, involvement in occupationally related organizations and activities such as trade unions, welfare, 'creational, etc., occupational aspirations, occupational effects respondent behavior

ne: occupational income, other sources, pattern of income, and problems

'/land ownership, tenancy and land aspirations within and e community, the location, issues, problems

conditions/problems/access to housing in the facilities, issues, conflicts, etc.

sehold goods, food habits, consumption level, rations

ions/level

'aspirations

ebt, credit

related to his own marriage and others): y considerations, wedding functions,

's origin

business role, sharing work, ther, kinsmen influence on this

B19 Brothers and sisters: both sides, where do they live, their marital status, employment
B20 Position in the family circle: self (family) in relation to other relatives, comparison, reference points
B21 Kinsmen locations: except own/spouse, brothers and sisters
B22 Kinship connections: attitudes, perceptions, conflicts, visiting patterns, rationalizations, etc.
B23 Parents/children relationship
B24 Connections with native place: property relations, kinship relations, ritual connections, episodes, perceptions
B25 Neighborhood relationship: nature of relationship, degree of reciprocity, norms, values, attitudes about neighbors, special connections with some neighbors, conflicts. How neighbors perceive the respondent's family and/or family position in the neighborhood
B26 Racial differences/connections in the neighborhood: connections, attitudes, perceptions, conflicts, reference to national issues and its effects on self, neighborhood, community
B27 Caste differences in the neighborhood
B28 Attitude about environment: in general, regarding relationships, facilities, conditions
B29 Mobility aspiration: inward–outward, preferred location, rationalizations, efforts made so far, problems, choices, etc.
B30 Religious beliefs, practices, ritual beliefs: (including festival customs, practices, temple affiliations, attitudes about temples, ritual services
B31 Attitude about community and political leadership, political dynamics
B32 Political affiliation: involvement, party identification (within the community), connection with political leaders, influence, decisions, political conflicts, interests and aspirations
B33 Community politics (general)
B34 Community participation (previously): issues, nature of involvement, level of influence from others, role, perceptions, problems encountered with respondent and his immediate family members

B35 Community participation (presently): issues, nature of involvement, level of influence from others, role, perceptions, problems encountered with respondent and his immediate family members

L1 Attitude about community organizations/presence/absence attitudes, functions, level of operation

L2 Community general information: facts, changes, history, political or otherwise, conflicts, general customs/ practices, conception of community reference points - "Gama", "Pita"

L3 Community conflicts: with or without his involvement, degree of conflicts/harmony, garden level/community level

L4 Community functions: with or without his involvement

L5 Individual network: community level, outside the community, friendships, household functions and his network

L6 Political involvement outside the community: political activities engaged in, process, decisions, what effects, ideological changes

L7 Family planning: attitudes, control, practices, perceptions, rationalizations

L8 Children's education/employment/marriage problems, efforts, attitudes, aspirations

L9 Health services: accessibilities, perceptions, issues, health problems

L10 Administrative services: accessibility, perceptions, issues

L11 Entertainment

L12 Self: role in the community/outside, perceptions about himself, how others perceive his role, influence, support

L13 Philosophy of life: moral position, norms, obligations, values about life, human relations, issues related to his own moral position

L14 General aspirations

L15 National issues: attitude about national issues, major concerns, political ideology, perceptions, attitude about government activities, functions, hypothetical reference to the neighborhood and community, impact on domestic life

Appendix 6

Master Sheet
Transformation of Qualitative Data Into Quantitative Data

1. Interview No. (number)
2. Name of the neighborhood/garden no.
3. Name of the respondent
4. Ethnicity
5. Religion
6. Sex
7. Age
8. Marital status
9. Occupation
10. Degree of occupational mobility
11. Birth place
12. Reasons for migration to Colombo and to the location
13. Duration of stay in the location
14. Monthly household income
15. Socio-economic group
16. Kinship relationship
17. Neighborhood relationship
18. Degree of kinsmen concentration in different locations (same garden, other gardens, periphery of Colombo, other parts of Colombo, other districts)
19. Political party affiliation
20. Land ownership
21. Property connection with relatives
22. House ownership/if bought, price of the house
23. Kinship connection with native place
24. Investment and savings
25. Value of household goods
26. Leadership type
27. Geographical mobility aspiration
28. Migration (degree of push factors)
29. Access to the community/housing
30. Religion/nature of practice
31. Per capita income

Bibliography

Abu-Lughod, Janet L., and Richard Hay, Jr. *Third World Urbanization.* Chicago: Maaroufa Press, 1977.

Acharya, Sarthi. "The Informal Sector in Developing Countries—A Macro Viewpoint." *Journal of Contemporary Asia* 13, no. 4 (1983): 436–445.

Ahmed, Saghir. *Class and Power in a Punjabi Village.* New York and London: Monthly Review Press, 1977.

Al-Haj, Majid. "The Changing Arab Kinship Structure: The Effect of Modernization in an Urban Community." *Economic Development and Cultural Change* 36, no. 2 (1988): 237–238.

Ames, M. M. "Religion, Politics and Economic Development in Ceylon: An Interpretation of the Weber Thesis." In *Symposium on New Approaches to the Study of Religion.* Edited by M. E. Spiro. Seattle, WA: Symposium on New Approaches to the Study of Religion, 1963.

Apter, D. E. "Political Religion in the New Nations." In *Old Societies and New States.* Edited by C. Geertz. London: Collier Macmillan, 1963.

Asia/Pacific Regional Team and Sri Lanka Field Office Team. *Adaptation of Save the Children's Community Based Integrated Rural Development Approach to Urban Community Context in Sri Lanka. A Self-Evaluation Statement.* Medford, Massachusetts and Colombo, Sri Lanka: 1982.

Bailey, Anne M., and Joseph R. Liobera. *The Asiatic Mode of Production.* London: Routledge and Kegan Paul, 1981.

Banton, Michael. "Anthropological Perspectives in Sociology." *The British Journal of Sociology* 15 (1988): 95–110.

Barrett, A. Lee. "Testing the Decline of Community Thesis: Neighborhood Organizations in Seattle: 1929 and 1979." *American Journal of Sociology* 89 (1984): 1161–1188.

Basham, Richard. *Urban Anthropology: The Cross-Cultural Study of Complex Societies.* Sydney: Mayfield Publishing Company, 1978.

Beteille, Andre. *Caste, Class, and Power: Changing Patterns of Stratification in a Tanjore Village.* Berkeley: University of California Press, 1965.

Blau, Peter M. *Approaches to the Study of Social Structure*. London: Collier Macmillan Publishers, 1974.

______. "Structural Sociology and Network Analysis, An Overview." *Social Structure and Network Analysis*. Edited by Peter V. Marsden and Nan Lin. Beverly Hills: Sage Publications, 1982.

Boeke, J. H. "Dualism in Colonial Societies." In *Sociology of South East Asia: Readings on Social Change and Development*. Edited by Hans-Dieter Evers. Oxford: Oxford University Press, 1980.

Bonifat'Yeva, L. T. "Some Characteristics of the Urban Network in the Countries of South and Southeast Asia." *Soviet Geography* 7 (1966): 60–70.

Bourne, L.S., R. Sinclair, and K. Dziewonski. *Urbanization and Settlement Systems: International Perspectives*. Oxford: Oxford University Press, 1984.

Brookfield, H. *Interdependent Development*. London: Methuen, 1975.

Bulmer, Martin, and Donald P. Warwick. *Social Research in Developing Countries: Surveys and Censuses in the Third World*. Singapore: John Wiley and Sons Ltd., 1983.

Burt, Ronald S. "Power in a Social Topology." *Social Science Research* 6 (1977): 1-83.

Burt, Ronald S., and Michael J. Miner. *Applied Network Analysis, A Methodological Introduction*. London: Sage Publications, 1983.

Caplan, Patricia A. *Priests and Cobblers: A Study of Social Change in a Hindu Village in Western Nepal*. Toronto: Chanler Publishing Company, 1972.

Center for Society and Religion. "Housing and Amenities." In *The City of Colombo: A Theological Search*. *Quest* 62 (1980): 13.

Cheema, Shabbir G. *Institutional Dimensions of Regional Development*. Nagoya, Japan: UNCRD, 1981.

Choldin, Harvey M. "Urban Cooperatives at Comilla, Pakistan: A Case Study of Local Level Development." *Economic Development and Cultural Change* 16, no. 2 (1968): 189–218.

Christenson, James A. "Gemeinschaft and Gesellschaft: Testing the Spatial and Communal Hypotheses." *Social Forces* 63 (1984): 160–168.

Clark, David. *Basic Communities: Towards an Alternative Society*. London: SPCK, 1977.

Conway, Dennis, and Nanda Shrestha. "Urban Growth and Urbanization in Least-Developed Countries: The Experience of Nepal, 1952 to 1971." *Asian Profile* 8, no. 5 (1980): 477–486.

Cook, Karen S. "Network Structures from an Exchange Perspective." *Social Structure and Network Analysis*. Edited by Peter V. Marsden and Nan Lin. Beverly Hills: Sage Publications, 1982.

Curson, P. H., and T. G. Bester. "Urbanism as a Way of Life: Reality or Myth?" *International Journal of Contemporary Sociology* 9, no. 1 (1972): 15–26.

Davis, Kingsely. "Asia Cities: Problems and Options." *Population and Development Review* 1 (1965): 71–86.

______. *The Population of India and Pakistan*. Princeton: University Press, 1951.

______. "Urbanization in India: Past and Future." In *India's Urban Future*. Edited by R. Turner. Berkeley: University of California Press, 1962: 3–26.

De Mel, Henry J. "The Impact of the City of Colombo on Its Suburbs: A Case Study of Kolonnawa." Thesis submitted to the Dept. of Town and Country Planning, University of Sri Lanka, 1982.

Dumoulin, H. *Buddhism in the Modern World*. New York: Macmillan, 1976.

Eames, Dewin, and Judith Granich Goode. *Anthropology of the City: An Introduction to Urban Anthropology*. New Jersey: Prentice-Hall, 1977.

Eisenstadt, S. N. "Reflections on a Theory of Modernization." In *Nations by Design*. Edited by Arnold Rivkin. New York: Anchor Books, 1969.

______, and Louis Roniger. "Patron-Client Relations as a Model of Structuring Social Exchange." *International Quarterly* 22, no. 1 (1980): 42–77.

Elliott, Brian. "Mannuel Castells and the New Urban Sociology." Review Article, *British Journal of Sociology* 31, no. 1 (1980): 151–158.

El Shakhs, S. "Development, Primacy, and Systems of Cities." *Journal of Developing Areas* 7 (1972): 30–31.

Engelmann, Hugo O. "Internation Analysis and Community Typology." *International Journal of Contemporary Sociology* 14, no. 1 and 2 (1977): 1–10.

Epstein, A. L. *Urbanization and Kinship, The Domestic Domain on the Copperbelt of Zambia 1950 to 1956.* School of African and Asian Studies, University of Sussex. London: Academic Press, 1981.

Erickson, B. H. "Networks, Ideologies, and Belief Systems." In *Social Structure and Network Analysis.* Edited by P. V. Marsden and N. Lin. Beverly Hills, CA: Sage, 1982.

Evers, Hans-Dieter. "Urban Expansion and Landownership in Under-Developed Societies." *Urban Affairs Quarterly* 11, no. 1 (1975): 117–129.

Field, John O., and Nimali Kannangara. *Save the Children's Program of Community Development in Kirillapona Shanty, Sri Lanka, An Evaluation.* Medford, Massachusetts and Colombo, Sri Lanka: 1981.

Fisher, Charles A. *South-East Asia: A Social Economic and Political Geography.* London: 1964.

Fox, Richard G. *From Zamindar to Ballot Box: Community Change in a North Indian Market Town.* New York: Cornell University Press, 1969.

Frank, A. G. *Latin America: Underdevelopment or Revolution?* New York: Monthly Review Press, 1969.

Fraser, John. "Viewpoint Community, the Private and the Individual." *The Sociological Review* 35, no. 4 (1987): 795–817.

Freitag, Sandria B. *Collective Action and Community: Public Arenas and the Emergence of Communalism in North India.* Berkeley: University of California Press, 1989.

Gamini de Alwis. "An Approach to Community Development in Low Income Settlements." Unpublished Master's Thesis. Colombo, Sri Lanka: University of Sri Jayawardanepura, 1984.

______. "Rural Urban Relations in the Kegalle District of the Intermediate Wet Zone—A Study of the District Capital, Kegalle." In *Study on Rural-Urban Relations in Sri Lanka.* Nagoya, Japan: UNCRD (1979): 349–403.

Gardezi, Hassan N. "Contemporary Sociology in Pakistan." *International Journal of Contemporary Sociology* 8, nos. 3 and 4 (1971): 132–141.

Geertz, C. *Peddlers and Princes.* Chicago: University of Chicago Press, 1963.

Gist, N. P. *Urban Society.* New York: Thomes Y. Growell Company, 1974.

Glaser, Barney G., and Anselm L. Straus. *The Discovery of Grounded Theory Strategies for Qualitative Research.* Chicago: Aldine Publishing Company, 1967.

Gombrich, R. *Precept and Practice: Traditional Buddhism in the Rural Highlands of Ceylon.* Oxford: Oxford University Press, 1971.

Gunatilleke, Godfrey, Neelan Tiruchelvan, and Radhika Coomaraswamy. *Ethical Dilemmas of Development in Asia.* Toronto: Lexington Books, D.C. Heath and Company, 1983.

Gunatilleke, S. "The Formation of Culture in Sri Lanka, Legneds, Information and a New Interpretation of Archaeological Findings." In *The Racial Problem and Social Change in Sri Lanka.* Edited by the Society of Sociologists. Colombo: Karunaratne and Sons, 1984.

Gutkind, Peter C. W. *Urban Anthropology.* U.S.A.: Harper and Row Publishers, 1974.

Hajda, Jan. "A Reconceptualization of the Social System." *International Journal of Contemporary Sociology* 9, no. 1 (1972): 1–14.

Hauser, P. M. *Urbanization in Asia and the Far East.* Calcutta: UNESCO, 1957.

Heinecke, R. L. "New Capitals of Asia." *Geographical Review* 48 (1958): 435–436.

Higgot, Richard, and Richard Robinson. *Southeast Asia: Essays in the Political Economy of Structural Change.* Routledge and Kegan Paul, Malbourne and Henley, 1985.

Hoselitz, B. G. "Generative and Parasitic Cities." *Economic Development and Cultural Change* 3 (1955): 278–294.

International Labour Office, Employment, Income and Equality. *A Strategy for Increasing Productive Employment in Kenya.* Geneva: ILO, 1972.

Irving, Henry W. "Social Networks in the Modern City." *Social Forces* 55 (1866): 867–880.

Jaksic, Miomir. "The Theory of Modes of Production and Changes in International Economic Relations." *Journal of Contemporary Asia* 15, no. 3 (1985): 361–373.

Jay, E. J. "The Concepts of Field and Network in Anthropological Research." *Man* LXIV (1964): 177–178.

Jones, Rodney W. *Urban Politics in India Area, Power, and Policy in a Penetrated System.* Delhi, Bombay, Bangalore, Kanpur: Vikas Publishing House, PVT Ltd., 1974.

Kahn, A. H., and Eddy Lee. *Poverty in Rural Asia.* Bankok: ILO-ARTEP, 1984.

Kelein, Ira. "Urban Development and Death: Bombay City, 1870-1914." *Asian Studies* 26, no. 4 (1986): 725–754.

Keyfitz, N. "Political-Economic Aspects of Urbanization in South and Southeast Asia." In *The Study of Urbanization.* Edited by Hauser and Schnore. New York: Wiley, 1964.

King, Anthony D. *Colonial Urban Development: Culture, Social Power and Environment.* Routledge and Kegan Paul, London, Henley and Boston, 1976.

Knox, Robert. "An Historical Relation." *The Ceylon Historical Journal* VI (1956 to 1957) nos. 1–4 (1958).

Lakha, Salim. "Character of Wage Labour in Early Industrial Ahmedabad." *Journal of Contemporary Asia* 15, no. 4 (1985).

Lansing, and E. Mueller. *The Geographical Mobility of Labor.* Ann Arbor: Survey Research, University of Michigan, 1967.

Laquian, Aprodicio A. "The Asian City and the Political Process." In *The City as a Centre of Change in Asia.* Edited by D. J. Dwyer. Hong Kong University Press (1972): 44.

Leach. E.R. "Pulleyar and the Lord Buddha." *Psychoanalysis and the Psychoanalysis Review* 49 (1962): 80-102.

Lefeber, Louis, and Mrinal Datta-Chaudhuri. *Regional Development Experiences and Prospects in South and Southeast Asia.* The Hague: UNRISD, 1971.

London, Bruce. *Metropolis and Nation in Thailand: The Political Economy of Urban Development.* Boulder: Westview Press, 1980.

Louis, Witrh. "Urbanism as a Way of Life." *American Journal of Sociology* XLIV (1938): 3–24.

Lowi, Theodore. "American Business, Public Policy, Case Studies, and Political Theory." *World Politics* 16 (1964): 677–715.

Malalgoda, K. *Buddhism in Sinhalese Society 1750-1900. A Study of Religious Revival and Change.* Berkeley: University of California Press, 1976.

Mangalam, J. J. *Human Migration: A Guide to Migration Literature in English 1955–1962.* Lexington: University of Kentucky Press, 1968.

Marga Institute. "National Dialogues for Development, Kirillapone Shanty Community." *Marga Document RES/63.* Colombo: 1980.

______. "The Informal Sector of Colombo City, Sri Lanka. A Study Prepared for the International Labor Office Within the Framework of the World Employment Program." Vol. 7, *Marga Research Studies*. Marga: 1978.

______. "Rural-Urban Relations in Sri Lanka, A Case Study." *UNCRD Country Monograph*. Nagoya, Japan: United Nations Centre for Regional Development, 1979.

Marsden, Peter V. "Brokerage Behavior in Restricted Exchange Networks." In *Social Structure and Network Analysis*. Edited by Peter V. Marsden and Nan Lin. Beverly Hills: Sage Publications, 1982.

Mayer, Adrian. "Quasi-Groups in the Study of Complex Societies." In *The Social Anthropology of Complex Societies*. Edited by M. Bunton. 1966.

McBride, William Leon. *Social Theory at a Crossroads*. Pittsburgh: Duquesne University Press, 1980.

McGee, T. G. *The Southeast Asian City: A Social Geography of the Primate Cities of Southeast Asia*. New York: Frederick A. Praeger, 1967.

______. *The Urbanization Process in Third World: Explorations in Search of a Theory*. London: G. Bell and Sons, 1971.

McNamara, Robert S. "The Population Problem: Time Bomb or Myth?" *Asian and Pacific Quarterly of Cultural and Social Affairs* XVII, no. 1 (1985): 1–24.

Mehta, S. K. "Some Demographic and Economic Correlates of Primate Cities: A Case for Reevaluation." In *The City in Newly Developing Countries*. Edited by G. Breese. Englewood Cliffs: Prentice Hall, 1977.

Mines, Mattison, and Vijayalakshmi Gourishankar. "Leadership and Individuality in South Asia: The Case of the South Indian Big-Man." *The Journal of Asian Studies* 49, no. 4 (1990): 761–786.

Ministry of Local Government, Housing and Construction, Sri Lanka. *Upgrading Steps, A Manual for the Shelter Improvement Program for Urban Low Income Groups*. Sri Lanka: 1984.

Mitchell, J. Clyde. *Social Networks in Urban Situations. Analyses of Personal Relationships in Central African Towns*. Manchester: University Press, 1969.

Mitra, Phani. "Planning the Tide of Urbanization." *Asian Review* 5, no. 1 (1971): 5–9.

Mohan, Raj P. "Contemporary Sociology in India." *International Journal of Contemporary Sociology* 8, nos. 3 and 4 (1971): 37–45.

Mookherjee, Debnath. "A Note on Urbanization Trends of a Developing Nation—India." *Asian Profile* 5, no. 2 (1977): 161–163.

Moore, Wilbert E. *Social Change*. Englewood Cliffs: Prentice Hall, 1963.

Motwani, X. "The Impact of Modern Technology on the Social Structures of South Asia." In *UNESCO, Social Change and Economic Development*. 1980: 99–109.

Mukherjee, Radhakamal. "Ways of Dwelling in Communities of India." *Asia* 40 (1940): 287–290.

Naseem, S. M. *Underdevelopment, Poverty and Inequality in Pakistan*. Lahore: Vanguard Publications, 1981.

Neville S. Arachchige Don. *Assessment of the Slum and Shanty Improvement Projects of the U.S. Save the Children Fund and the Norwegian Redd Barna*. Colombo: UNDP and UDA, 1981.

______. "Effectiveness of Village Level Organizations in Sri Lanka." Unpublished Master's Thesis. Colombo, Sri Lanka: University of Sri Jayawardanepura, 1984.

______. "The Emerging Patterns of Urban Community Structures and Their Policy Implications in South Asia with Special Reference to Sri Lanka." Unpublished Ph.D. Dissertation. University of Wisconsin-Milwaukee, 1990.

______. "New Parameters for a Study of Micro-Level Processes in Relation to National Planning." In *Methodological Issues in Village Studies, Doc. M/660*. Colombo: Marga Institute, Sri Lanka Centre for Development Studies, 1982.

______. "Religion and Politics: Behavioral Adaptations in an Urban Community of Sri Lanka." *Research in the Social Scientific Study of Religion* 4 (1992): 129-157.

______. "Rural-Urban Relations in the Dry Zone, A Case Study of a Lower Order Center and a Village in the Periphery." In *Study on Rural-Urban Relations in Sri Lanka*. Nagoya, Japan: UNCRD, 1979.

______. "Study of a Metropolitan Community in Close Proximity to the Rural Hinderland." In *Rural-Urban Relations in Sri Lanka*. Nagoya, Japan: United Nations, Centre for Regional Development, 1979.

Obeyesekere, G. "The Great Tradition and the Little in the Perspective of Sinhalese Buddhism." *Journal of Asian Studies* 22 (1963): 139-153.

______. "Religious Symbolism and Political Change in Ceylon." In *The Two Wheels of Dhamma: Essays on the Theravada Tradition in India and Ceylon*. Edited by G. Obeyesekere, F. Reynolds, and B. L. Smith. Chamsbersburg, PA: American Academy of Religion, 1972.

O'Connor, Richard A. "A Theory of Indigenous Southeast Asian Urbanism." In *Research Notes and Discussion Paper No. 38*. Institute of Southeast Asian Studies: 1983.

Otsuka, Keijiro et al. "Community and Market in Contract Choice: The Jeepney in the Philippines." *Economic Development and Cultural Change* 34 (1985).

Poplin, Dennis. *A Survey of Theories and Methods of Research*. New York, London: Macmillan Publishing/Collier Macmillan Publishers, 1979.

Prakasa, Rao, V.L.S. *Urbanization in India: Spatial Dimensions*. New Delhi: Concept Publishing Company, 1983.

Pye, Lucien. "The Political Implications of Urbanization and the Development Process." *Social Problems of Development and Urbanization*. United States Conference on the Application of Science and Technology for the Benefits of the Less Developed Areas, Washington 7 (1963): 84.

Qadeer, M. A. "Do Cities Modernize the Developing Countries? An Examination of the South Asian Experience." *Comparative Studies in Society and History* (1974): 266–267.

______. *Urban Development in the Third World*. Internal Dynamics of Lahore. Pakistan, New York: CBC Educational and Professional Publishing, A Division of CBC, 1983.

Ratnam, K. J. "Policy Towards Social Sciences in Asia and Oceania." *Report on the Meeting of Experts*. Bankok: UNESCO, 1978.

______. *Social Sciences: In Response to Policy Needs, Four Case Studies from Asia*. Ramashy Roy, India; Taufic Abudulla, Indonesia; Zukaria Haji Ahamad, Malaysia; S. P. F. Senaratne, Sri Lanka. Bangkok: UNESCO Regional Office of Education in Asia and Oceania, 1980.

Raza, Moonis et al. *Spatial Organization and Urbanization in India: A Case Study of Underdevelopment, Rural Area Development Perspectives and Approaches*. Edited by R. P. Misra and K. V. Sundaram. Sterling, 1979.

Ross, Robert J., and Telkamp Gerard. *Colonial Cities*. Boston: Martinus Nijhoff Publishers, 1985.

Rowe, Alan R. "Social Change and Urbanization: Toward a Paradigm of Social Organization." *International Journal of Contemporary Sociology* II, no. 4 (1974): 177–196.

Salisbury, Robert H. "The Analysis of Public Policy: A Search for Theories and Roles." In *Political Science and Public Policy*. Edited by Austin Ranney. Chicago: Markham, 1968.

Senaratne, S. P. F. *An Approach to Social Research.* Dacca: Bangaladesh Institute of Development Studies, 1977.

______. *A Program of Micro-Level Studies in Rural Sri Lanka.* Colombo: Marga Institute, 1975.

______. "Socio-Economic Data Requirements." *Needs for Data About People, Institutions, and Factors and Income Distribution.* Conference on Data Requirements for the Rural Development Planning in the Asian Tropics. Organized by Resource Economics and Agribusiness. Australia: UPM and Development Studies Center, ANU.

______. "Why Village Studies." In *Perspectives on Rural Change in Sri Lanka, Studies of Selected Locations, Doc.: INT/11(2).* Colombo: Marga Institute, 1976.

Sharan, A. K. "Sociology of Knowledge." Lecture at the University of Wisconsin, Milwaukee, 1986.

Shaw, R. Paul. "Migration Theory and Fact: A Review and Bibliography of Current Literature." *Bibliography Series Number Five*. Philadelphia: Regional Science Research Institute, 1975.

Silva, Kalinga Tudor, and Karunatissa Athukorala. "The Watta-Dwellers: A Sociological Study of Selected Urban Low-Income Communities in Sri Lanka." Lanham, New York, London: University Press of America, 1991.

Singh, Andrea Menefee, and Souza. *The Urban Poor: Slum and Pavement Dwellers in the Major Cities of India*. Manohar: 1980.

Singh, Yogendra. "The Role of Social Sciences in India: A Sociology of Knowledge." *Sociological Bulletin* 22, no. 1 (1973).

Sovani, N. V. "The Analysis of Over-Urbanization." *Economic Development and Cultural Change* 12 (1964): 113–122.

Srinivas, M. N., and Andre Beteille. "Networks in Indian Social Structure." *Man* LXIV (1964): 165–168.

______. *The Cohesive Role of Sanskritization and Other Essays.* Oxford: Oxford University Press, 1989.

______. *The Remembered Village*. Berkeley, Los Angeles, London: University of California Press, 1976.

Stepanek, Joseph G. *Bangladesh—Equitable Growth?* Paris: Pergamon Press, 1979.

Stifel, Laurence D., Ralph K. Davidson, and James S. Coleman. *Social Sciences and Public Policy in the Developing World*. Lexington, Massachusetts: Lexington Books, D. C. Heath and Company, 1980.

Stolper, W. "Spatial Order and the Economic Growth of Cities: A Comment on Eric Lampard's Paper." *Economic Development and Cultural Change* 3 (1955): 141.

Susskind, Edwin C., and Donald C. Klein. *Community Research: Methods, Paradigms, and Applications*. New York: Praeger Publishers, 1985.

Suttles, Gerald D. *The Social Construction of Communities*. Chicago and London: The University of Chicago Press, 1972.

Tambia, Stanley J. *Buddhism Betrayed: Religion, Politics, and Violence in Sri Lanka*. Chicago and London: University of Chicago Press, 1992.

______. "Presidential Address: Reflections on Communal Violence in South Asia." *The Journal of Asian Studies* 49, no. 4 (1990): 741–760.

______. *Sri Lanka: Ethnic Fratricide and the Dismantling of Democracy*. Chicago: University of Chicago Press, 1986.

Taylor, R. C. *The Implications of Migration from the Durham Coal Fields: An Anthropological Study*. Unpublished Ph.D. Dissertation. University of Durham, 1966.

______. "Migration and Motivation: A Study of Determinants and Types." In *Migration*. Edited by J. A. Jackson. Cambridge: Cambridge University Press, 1969.

Teilhet-Waldorf, Saral, and William H. Waldorf. "Earnings of Self-employed in an Informal Sector: A Case Study of Bangkok." *Economic Development and Cultural Change* 31, no. 3 (1983): 587–607.

Thomlinson, Ralph. *Urban Structure: The Social and Spatial Character of Cities*. New York: Random House, 1969.

United Nations. *Economic and Social Commission for Asia and the Pacific, Migration, Urbanization and Development in Sri Lanka*. New York: United Nations, 1980.

Uppal, Jogindar S. *Economic Development in South Asia.* New York: St. Martin's Press, 1977.

Uzzell, Douglas. "Conceptual Fallacies in the Rural-Urban Dichotomy." *Urban Anthropology* 8 (1979): 333–350.

Uzzell, Douglas J., Ronald Provenchev. *Urban Anthropology.* Dubuque, Iowa: WM.C. Brown Company Publishers, 1976.

Vapnarasky, C. "On Rank-Size Distributions of Cities. An Ecological Approach." *Economic Development and Cultural Change* 17 (1969): 584–595.

Weber, M. *Religion of India.* Glencoe, IL: Free Press, 1958.

Weiner, Myron. "Social Science Research and Public Policy in India." In *Social Sciences and Public Policy in the Developing World.* Edited by Laurence D. Stifel, Ralph K. Davidson, and James S. Coleman. Lexington, Massachusetts: Lexington Books, D. C. Heath and Company, 1980.

Wriggins, H. W. *Ceylon: Dilemmas of a New Nation.* Princeton, NJ: Princeton University Press, 1960.

Yalman, N. "The Structure of Sinhalese Healing Rituals." *Journal of Asian Studies* 23 (1964): 115-150.

Author Index

Subject Index

About the Author

Neville S. Arachchige Don received his B.A. and M.A. degrees in Public Administration from Sri Lanka and has a Ph.D. in sociology from the University of Wisconsin-Milwaukee. He has also earned a degree in urban development planning from the Katubedda University of Sri Lanka, designed by the United Nations.

He has an extensive research background both in rural and urban development. These policy oriented studies were sponsored by various international agencies including the United Nations. He has published, in various forms, his research studies on comparative organizational systems, informal sector economy, village development, rural–urban relations, regional development, religion and politics, Third World development, and research methods. He has participated in and contributed to numerous international conferences held in Sri Lanka, Japan, Italy, France, and the United States,

He has previously worked at the Marga Institute, Sri Lanka Center for Development Studies, as a social science researcher and at the University of Sri Jayawardanepura, the University of Colombo, and the University of Wisconsin-Platteville, U.S.A. as a lecturer. He has also worked as a consultant at the Sri Lanka Institute of Development Administration.

At the Cambridge Community College Campus of Anoka-Ramsey in Cambridge, Minnesota, he is a professor of sociology and a member of the Honors Council.

Neville's research interests focus on grass root issues. He is editor of the *International Journal of Contemporary Studies* and director and founder of the International Research Foundation for Development.

His emphasis is on grass root empowerment and the formation of a collective voice for global policy making.

